THE CLARINET

THE CLARINET

Some Notes upon its History and Construction by

F. GEOFFREY RENDALL

THIRD EDITION

Revised and with some additional material by

PHILIP BATE

LONDON   ERNEST BENN LIMITED

NEW YORK   W. W. NORTON & COMPANY INC.

First published by Williams and Norgate Limited 1954

Ernest Benn Limited
Bouverie House, Fleet Street, London, EC4A 2DL

and W. W. Norton & Company
55 Fifth Avenue, New York 10003

Second revised edition 1957
Second impression 1963
Third edition 1971

Printed in Great Britain

ISBN 0510–36701–1

TO
M.K.R.

Preface to the Third Edition

THE LATE Geoffrey Rendall's book on the Clarinet – the 'founder member' of the Instruments of the Orchestra Series – first appeared in 1954, and has been reissued several times. Though never intended as a treatise, it has enjoyed the continued approval of scholars, both for its readable style and for the amount of information it embodies in a relatively small compass.

During the last fifteen years, however, the science of Organology has made great advances; student interest in the history and development of musical instruments has extended to a remarkable degree; and a great deal of new and important, if not fundamental, work has been done by instrument-makers, especially in connection with the Boehm System in Germany. Moreover, Acoustics today is undergoing a major revision, in the course of which many of the characteristic features of woodwinds, acquired empirically over the years, and hitherto explained by Classical Physics, are now being investigated quantitatively by modern research techniques. These matters can now be expressed in terms of absolute mathematics, and we find that some of the assumptions of Classical Acoustics require rethinking. In preparing the original edition of this work Rendall made only a limited excursion into the acoustic field, confining himself to the strictly practical player's viewpoint, and for this he found the textbook physics of his time sufficient. (See Bibliography.)

Taking these factors into account, the publishers have given much thought as to how the value of a new edition of the book might be enhanced for the present-day reader. Rendall had a remarkable gift for viewing his subject 'in the round', and he saw the activities of the player, the composer, and the instrument-maker as complimentary throughout the history of the clarinet. This resulted in an account which he described as both 'digressive and discursive', yet loaded with information. To such a work it is neither easy nor elegant simply to tack on additional chapters; nor is there much of the original that one would wish to alter or omit – always bearing in mind that some of the opinions expressed

were extremely personal. There are very few points about the behaviour
of the clarinet that Rendall did not observe and note.

After much thought, therefore, it has been decided to amplify some
of the descriptive matter and supplement it with additional text-figures,
cross-references, and some acoustical comment, mainly in the form of
footnotes. Rendall omitted reference to certain experimental or out-of-
the-ordinary instruments from considerations of space, though some are
of great interest. A few of them are now discussed.

In common with the great majority of orchestral players, Rendall had
no great opinion of bi-tonal or 'combination' clarinets, though he
admired the fine craftsmanship often found in them. In spite, however,
of the general failure of such clarinets in professional circles, inventors
and instrument-makers have persevered with the idea; and early in the
present century the concern of some modern composers with microtone scales created an interest in woodwinds designed to be instantly
transposable through a smaller interval than the semitone, thus increasing the number of notes available within the octave. This being so, it has
been thought useful to extract Rendall's observations on the subject from
the main text, and to present them with some additional material in a
new chapter at the end of the book. Finally, some additions have been
made to the Bibliography, though this must still be regarded as selective.

Most unfortunately Rendall did not live to see the actual publication
of his book, and at the request of the late Mrs Rendall the present
writer accepted the task of seeing it through the press. I regard being
asked to prepare this new edition as both a compliment and a heavy
responsibility, and I have undertaken it as tribute to an old and valued
friend. I believe that had he not died comparatively early, Rendall
would himself have done this work. At the time he wrote he was undoubtedly the leading authority on the clarinet in this country, probably
in the world. I hope my contribution may help to bring to yet wider
readership the work of a remarkable and much loved man.

In preparing the following pages I have had most valuable advice and
assistance from Dr A. H. Benade, and Messrs James Howarth, Alan
Hacker, and John Steward, as well as from some of the gentlemen
whose names appear in the original acknowledgement list. To all of
them I tender my most sincere thanks.

                                                            P.B.

Preface to the First Edition

IT IS the best part of half a century since the first history of the clarinet was written, Wilhelm Altenburg's *Die Klarinette*. This well-informed little book, written by an enthusiast when the clarinet was far less favoured than it is today, has been supplemented by three short Italian works of which the most important is Agostino Gabucci's *Origine e storia del Clarinetto*. There is no history available to English readers, a delightful paper by a distinguished amateur, the late Oscar Street, excepted. In view of the increasing popularity of the instrument in England and America a short history in the mother tongue has long been wanted. This work is designed to meet the need. It is not a treatise. This remains to be written, when an author who is at once a player, a musician, an acoustician, a mechanic, and historian can find the necessary leisure to write it. The present book is rather a collection of notes upon the history and construction of the instrument gathered over a number of years from printed sources and from conversations with makers and players. It is of purpose digressive and discursive. In compiling even a short history of the clarinet the writer is faced with several formidable difficulties. One, and not the least, is the size of the family. We are dealing not with one instrument but with many. Here subdivision would seem a necessity. After discussing materials and mechanism which are applicable to all members of the family whether great or small, I have proceeded to the history of the familiar orchestral instruments. Later chapters deal with the higher- and lower-pitched members. Each chapter is intended to be complete in itself and is provided with its separate history. Another difficulty, hardly less formidable, is to select from the many the most interesting and important models to discuss. No instrument, not even the flute, has been built with such a wide variety of fingerings. The choice is bewildering. I have had perforce to select the few which are available for examination in public or private collections in this country or which are described in some detail in catalogues. I shall be glad to hear of others. Acoustics have been handled entirely from the practical, the player's, standpoint.

Mathematics and theory have been avoided. For the curious in these matters references have been provided in the Bibliography. In the historical sections the physical and musical histories of the instrument have been considered together and both are mingled with short notices of famous players of the past. For obvious reasons living players are not discussed; the reader must fill this lacuna himself. And here it has seemed better to consider many players rather than to give extended notices to a few.

A word about the Appendix. Here will be found a List of Makers, a List of Music, and a Bibliography. They are selective. The List of Makers could easily have been doubled; I have chosen names which the collector is most likely to encounter. In assigning dates I have been much assisted by Mr Lyndesay G. Langwill's exhaustive *List of Wind and Brass Instrument-Makers*. In compiling the List of Music I have attempted a judicious mixture of the old, the middling, and the new. Some old works have been inserted for their historical interest, others have been omitted because they have long been unobtainable. Only a few transcriptions have been noted. This list again could be trebled or quadrupled. In making it I acknowledge gratefully the help of Mr Frederick Thurston and of the late Mr Geoffrey Sturt and the unfailing courtesy of Messrs Chester, of Messrs Schott, and of the United Music Publishers. The line-drawings in the text I owe to the kindness and skill of Mr Philip Bate.

Many other friends have lightened my labour with their counsel and with the loan of notes, of photographs, of instruments, and not least with their encouragement. I am in particular much indebted to: Mr A. C. Baines, Mr A. Carse, Mr R. B. Chatwin, Mr G. H. Child, Mr T. K. Dibley, Mijnheer M. Flothuis, Mr K. Haas, the Rev. N. Bonavia Hunt, Mr B. Izen, Mijnheer W. Jansen, Mr W. Lear, Mr E. MacGavin, Mr B. Manton-Myatt, and Mr R. Morley-Pegge. Nor must I forget the kindness of Dr Lautenschlager, Direktor of the Landesbibliothek, Karlsruhe, in furnishing me with details of J. M. Molter's concertos. The secretarial work of Miss Vera Ledger and Miss Rosemary Norris has been invaluable.

For permission to reproduce photographs of instruments in the collections under their charge, I am much beholden to the authorities of two museums – to Dr René Lyr, Conservateur of the Musée Instrumental of the Conservatoire Royal of Brussels, and to Dr Kurt Heckscher, Kustos of the Museum für Hamburgische Geschichte. In addition two well-known firms – Messrs Boosey & Hawkes of London and Messrs Heckel of Biebrich am Rhein – have greatly assisted me with photographs and with leave to reproduce them.

A final word. In writing this little book I have had two purposes in mind – not only to interest the reader but to stimulate him to further inquiry. If I succeed in either I shall have good reason to be satisfied with my endeavour.

F.G.R.

Contents

Collections, Catalogues, etc.

COLLECTIONS of musical instruments will be indicated by the names of the cities in which they are situated. Catalogues will be known by the name of the author. The principal public collections referred to are:

BERLIN. Sammlung der Staatlichen Hochschule. *Catalogue:* Sachs, C. Beschreibender Katalog, 1922.

BRUSSELS. Musée instrumental du Conservatoire Royal. *Catalogue:* Mahillon, V.-C. Catalogue 'descriptif et analytique'. 5 vols., 1893–1922.

HAMBURG. Museum für Hamburgische Geschichte. *Catalogue:* Schröder, H. Verzeichnis, 1930.

MUNICH. Baierisches Nationalmuseum. *Catalogue:* Bierdimpfl, K. A. 1883.

NEW YORK. Crosby Brown Collection. The Metropolitan Museum of Art. *Catalogue:* 1902.

PARIS. Musée du Conservatoire National. *Catalogue:* Chouquet, G. Catalogue raisonné, 1884. Suppléments, 1894, 1899, 1903.

STOCKHOLM. Musikhistoriska Museet. *Catalogue:* Svanberg, J. 1902.

Other collections known by the Collector's name are:

CARSE. Adam Carse Collection of Musical Wind Instruments. Horniman Museum, Forest Hill, London. *Catalogue:* L.C.C. 1951.

HEYER. Musikhistorisches Museum von Wilhelm Heyer in Cöln. *Catalogue:* Kinsky, G. Kleiner Katalog, 1913.

MASON. Leslie Lindsey Mason Collection. Museum of Fine Arts, Boston, Mass. 'Ancient European Musical Instruments, etc.' Bessaraboff, N. 1941.

SCHEURLEER. D. F. Scheurleer Collection. Gemeente-Museum, The Hague. *Catalogue:* Balfoort, D. J. 1935.

STEARNS. The [Frederick] Stearns Collection, University of Michigan, Ann Arbor. *Catalogue:* Stanley, A. A. 2nd edition, 1921.

Other catalogues are:

SNOECK. Catalogue de la collection d'instruments de musique anciens ou curieux formée par C. C. Snoeck. 1894.

DAY, C. R. The Royal Military Exhibition, London, 1890. Descriptive Catalogue, 1891.

SAX, ADOLPHE. Catalogue du Musée instrumental de M. Adolphe Sax. Paris, 1877.

Abbreviations

A.M.Z.   Allgemeine Musikalische Zeitung

G.S.J.   Galpin Society Journal

I.M.G.   Internationale Musikgesellschaft

J.A.S.A.   Journal of the Acoustical Society of America

M.G.G.   Musik in Geschichte und Gegenwart

P.M.A.   Proceedings of the Musical Association (since August 1944, the Royal Musical Association)

THE TONALITY OR PITCH of a clarinet is indicated by a Capital, e.g. clarinet in A or A clarinet. To save innumerable musical examples the following method of staff notation has been adopted:

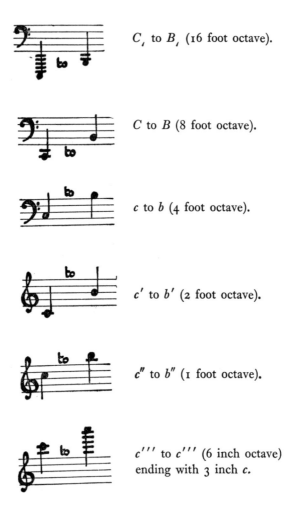

$C_{,}$ to $B_{,}$ (16 foot octave).

C to B (8 foot octave).

c to b (4 foot octave).

c' to b' (2 foot octave).

c'' to b'' (1 foot octave).

c''' to c''' (6 inch octave) ending with 3 inch c.

List of Illustrations

PLATE I   Early Clarinets.
  a.   *German.* (High A) 2 keys. Munich 19.
  b.   *Klenig.* (C) 2 keys. Stockholm 141.
  c.   *Scherer.* (D) 2 keys, large bore, ivory. R.C.M.
  d.   *Lindner.* (A) 3 keys. Brussels 913.
  e.   *J. Denner.* (C) 2 keys. Brussels 912.
  f.   *Willems.* (A) 4 keys. Brussels 919.
  g.   *Scherer.* (D) 3 keys. Brussels 924.

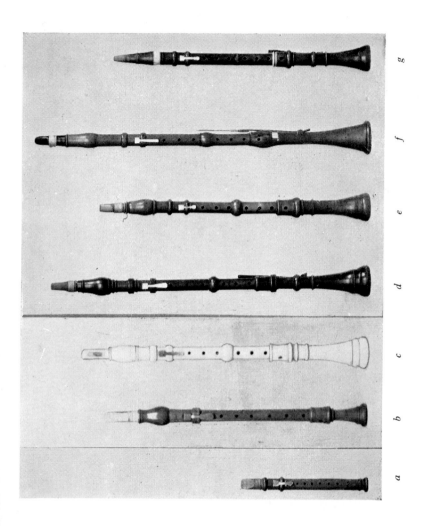

PLATE 2   Early English Clarinets from the Bate Collection, University
of Oxford.

a. *Anon.* 4 keys. 1760?
b. *Payne, London.* 5 keys. *c.* 1795.
c. *Key, London.* 13 silver keys. 1834.
d. *Blackman, London.* 8 keys. *c.* 1825.
e. *J. Wood, London. c.* 1830.

Some of the keys of the instrument (*e*) are mounted on pillars.
The design for L. little finger was patented by George Wood in
1819.

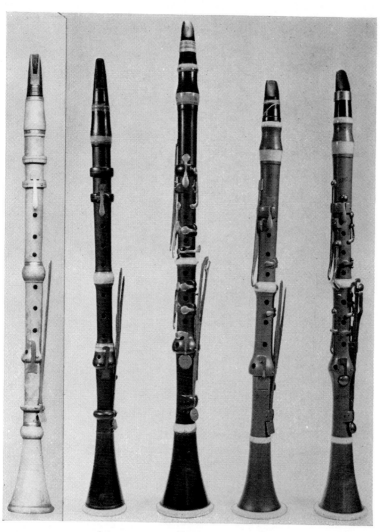

PLATE 3 Clarinets of Well-known Players.

a. *Key, London.* Basset-horn. *c.* 1825. Rendall Collection.

b. *Key, London.* (A) clarinet, 13 keys, with later additions and enlarged bore. *c.* 1820. Boosey & Hawkes Collection.

c. *Fieldhouse, London.* (A) clarinet with Boehm improvements. *c.* 1855. Rendall Collection.

d. *E. Albert, Brussels.* (A) clarinet, 16 keys. *c.* 1865. Rendall Collection. The above were property of Henry Lazarus.

e. *Fieldhouse, London.* (B♭) clarinet in ebonite, 13-key system with vent-keys. 1862. Formerly owned by Julian Egerton.

f. *German.* (B♮) clarinet, 13-key system, with ivory barrel and metal mouthpiece. *c.* 1825. Formerly owned by the Duke of Sondershausen, the pupil of J. S. Hermstedt.

g. *Vinatieri, Turin.* (B♮) clarinet, 16 keys and 4 rings. *c.* 1860. Formerly property of Ferdinando Busoni. Berlin No. 1442.

h. *Pask, London.* Basset-horn, Boehm model. *c.* 1865. Formerly property of H. Lazarus. Boosey & Hawkes Collection.

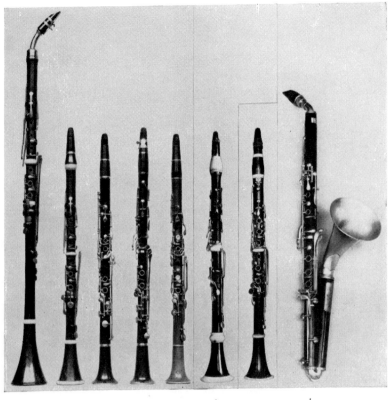

a   b   c   d   e   f   g   h

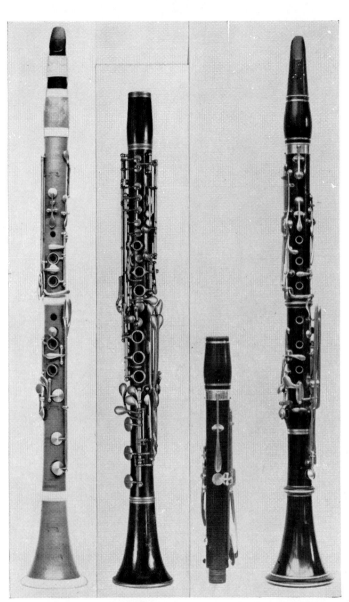

a   *b*   *c*

PLATE 5   Modern Clarinets.
  a. *Boosey & Hawkes, London.* (B♮) Clinton-Boehm.
  b. *Mahillon, Brussels.* (B♭) Pupeschi system, Barret action with long tenon, and additional lever for f. Low *e flat*, *c.* 1900. Rendall Collection.
  c. *Loosey & Hawkes.* (B♭) Full Boehm.
  d. *Marigaux, Paris.* (B♭) Plain Boehm.
  e. *Oehler, Berlin.* (B♭) Oehler system.

PLATE 6 Basset-horns from the Museum für Hamburgische Geschichte.

- *a.* *A. & M. Mayrhofer, Passau. c.* 1770.
- *b.* *Kirst, Potsdam. c.* 1790.
- *c.* *Griessling & Schlott, Berlin. c.* 1820.
- *d.* *Grundmann, Dresden.* 1799.
- *e.* *Grundmann, Dresden.* 1787.
- *f.* *Zencker, Adorf* (?). *c.* 1820.
- *g.* *Strobach, Carlsbad. c.* 1815.

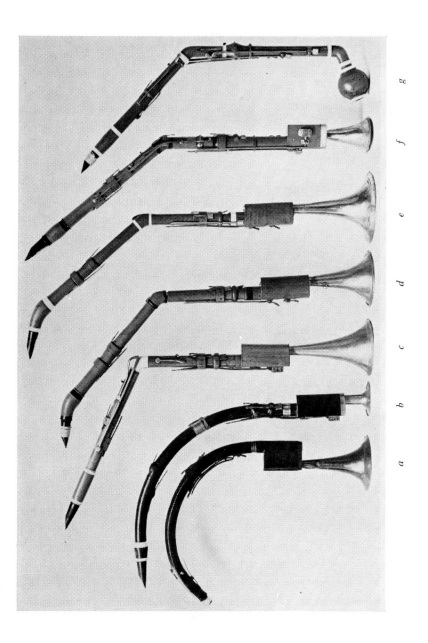

a b c d e f g

a   *b*   *c*

a   *b*   *c*   *d*

Preliminaries. Nomenclature
The family of clarinets

THE CLARINET may be defined as a woodwind instrument of partially cylindrical bore sounded with a single beating reed and made in many pitches and dimensions.

The name is plainly a diminutive of *clarino*, the Italian for trumpet, and particularly for the higher register of this instrument, much used in the 17th and 18th centuries, and much in vogue when the clarinet was invented. To J. G. Walther, writing in his *Musicalisches Lexicon* of 1732, 'it sounded from far off not unlike a trumpet'.

The first occurrence of the word *clarinetto* has yet to be determined. It is of course the standard Italian name from which other languages derived their names for the instrument. An early variant, at least as early as 1720, is *clarone*, subsequently used for any clarinet of deep pitch, and now appropriated as an alternative and familiar name for the bass clarinet. It may be noticed in passing that *clarinetto* is frequently abbreviated to *clarino* by modern Italian writers and is also commonly used to denote a clarinettist.

In French the word *clarinette* occurs at least as early as 1716, in which year Estienne Roger, the music publisher of Amsterdam, was advertising 'airs à deux clarinettes'. This spelling has remained fairly constant, though J.-B. Laborde in his *Essai sur la musique* (1780) describes Valentin Roeser, with whom we shall deal later, as *maître de clarinet*. But not in German. In 1730 J. G. Doppelmayr, writing of J. C. Denner, to whom the invention of the clarinet is attributed, in his *Historische Nachricht von den Nürnbergischen Mathematicis und Künstlern*, uses the word *Clarinette*, but J. G. Walther in 1732, and Zedler in his *Universal Lexicon* of 1733, give their preference to *Clarinetto*. Thereafter there is great diversity of spelling; *Clarinette, Klarinette, Clarinet, Clarinett*, are all found in the 18th and in the first half of the 19th centuries, and *Clarinet* as late as 1900. It is only within the last fifty or sixty years that the gender has been determined as feminine and the spelling as *Klarinette*.

The English name has been from the beginning *Clarinet*. It occurs at least as early as 1733 as the name of a popular song in the ballad opera *Achilles*. The spelling with an *o* inserted was favoured by the poets, by Cowper in 1784; and the resulting 'clarionet' is also preferred by Keats and by Sidney Lanier, American poet and flautist. This grandiose form lingered on into the early years of the present century, but has now, it is to be hoped, vanished for ever. For the curious in these matters it may be observed that the longer form is found in use as a surname in 1559–60, when one Marmaduke Clarionett was named as an escheator for the City of York.[1]

The family of clarinets is a large one, ranging from the high A flat, a little more than 14 inches in length, to the contrabass which measures all but 9 feet. The compass is in theory the same for all, from written *e* to *c''''*, three octaves and a sixth in all. The compass is occasionally

Fig. 1   Compass of the clarinet

extended to *e flat* in the case of the B flat, to *c* in the case of the bass and contrabass. It will be seen that the members of the orchestral family can between them cover rather more than six octaves. The lowest note of the extended contrabass just comes within the 32-foot octave while the highest note of the sopranino E flat is a minor third above 3-inch C. The active members number at least a dozen, a number which can be doubled if all recorded members are added. A table is added for convenience at the end of this chapter, in which obsolete or obsolescent members are printed in italics. From this it will be seen that the clarinet has been built from the beginning as a transposing instrument in many different pitches and dimensions. This matter will be dealt with in a later chapter. Here it may be said that, speaking quite generally, the method of construction and the mechanism are the same for all. Divergences and differences are found chiefly in the lower-pitched instruments where the greater length of body calls for modifications in construction. These will be noticed as they occur. The clarinets most commonly encountered are those pitched in B flat and A, the *vade mecum* of the soloist and of the orchestral and chamber musician.

In the chapters which follow note- and finger-holes and keys will generally be identified by the notes which they sound in the fundamental register. This is not the usual practice, which is to identify the notes by their twelfths. This seemingly illogical practice can be traced back well into the 18th century, and may have been occasioned by the preference shown by the earlier composers for the *clarinet* register. It is not until the 18th century was well advanced that the *chalumeau* notes are used at all frequently. An alternative practice, rather common in makers' catalogues, is to give both fundamental and twelfth; thus the note emitted by the second finger-hole of the upper joint would be shown as *e'/b''*. This seems waste of printer's ink and wherever possible will be avoided. To the method of nomenclature proposed above there will be a few exceptions. Certain well-known improvements in mechanism such as the 'Forked B flat, the F sharp/G sharp shake or articulated G sharp, the Vented F, the patent C sharp key' have always been known by these terms. To rename them a twelfth lower would be sheer pedantry.

Finger-holes will be numbered from the top, the mouthpiece, down. Thus the hole covered by the third finger of the left hand will be known as the third finger-hole. L. and R. will be used as abbreviations for the left and right hands. It is perhaps hardly necessary to observe that for more than 200 years, that is as soon as the clarinet assumed more than two keys, the upper joint was fingered by the left hand, the lower by the right hand. There are of course exceptions to every rule, and very occasionally clarinets, even of elaborate construction, are found with the keys reversed. The players for whom such instruments are made are known to the French makers as 'gauchers'.

And finally to save continual and confusing transposition the instrument will be regarded for purpose of reference as pitched in C. This is, indeed, the general practice of the player, who always refers to the written, not the sounded, note. Thus in testing, for instance, an A clarinet he may find the 'low' *e* a little sharp, or 'top' *c'''* a little flat. The notes actually sounded would of course be *c sharp* and *a'' natural*.

The Family of Clarinets

Octave	1.	*Clarinet in C.*
	2.	*Clarinet in B flat.*
	3.	Clarinet in A flat.
	4.	*Clarinet in G.*
Sopranino	1.	Clarinet in F.
	2.	*Clarinet in E.*

	3.	Clarinet in E flat.
	4.	Clarinet in D.
Soprano	1.	Clarinet in C.
	2.	*Clarinet in B natural.*
	3.	Clarinet in B flat.
	4.	Clarinet in A.
Alto	1.	*Clarinette d'amour in A flat.*
	2.	*Clarinette d'amour in G.*
	3.	*Clarinet in G.*
Tenor	1.	Clarinet in F.
	2.	*Basset-horn in G.*
	3.	Basset-horn in F.
	4.	Clarinet in E flat.
Baritone and Bass	1.	*Bass Clarinet in C.*
	2.	Bass Clarinet in B flat.
	3.	Bass Clarinet in A.
	1.	Contrabasset-horn in G.
	2.	Contrabasset-horn in F.
	3.	Contrabasset-horn in E flat.
	4.	*Contrabass Clarinet in C.*
	5.	Contrabass Clarinet in B flat.

NOTE

[1] 10th Report, Deputy Keeper of Public Records, App. II, p. 46.

CHAPTER 2

Components of the Clarinet
Materials: wood, metal, ebonite

As a preliminary to discussing the practical acoustics and history of
the clarinet it may be advisable in this and the following chapters to
study the components and general construction of the modern instrument in some detail. It consists as a rule of five parts – mouthpiece with
reed, barrel or tuning socket, upper or left-hand joint, lower or right-
hand joint, and bell. It will be unnecessary to discuss the physical
characteristics of the Mouthpiece at any length, since it will no doubt
be familiar to readers. Its present size seems to have become fairly
standardised by the middle of the 19th century; mouthpieces approxi-
mating very nearly to modern design and dimensions are shown in
H.-E. Klosé's *Méthode*, *c.* 1843. Fig. 2 shows a series of mouthpieces
drawn to a scale of two-thirds actual size. From this it will be seen that
the mouthpiece and reed of the earliest clarinets were almost of modern
dimensions. Later they were much diminished in size, a necessary
measure as long as the clarinet was blown with the reed against the
upper lip. It need hardly be said that the bore of the mouthpiece must be
identical with that of the instrument, not a hair's breadth more or less.
Mouthpieces are very seldom interchangeable. Very occasionally some
defect of intonation may be remedied by using a mouthpiece of larger
or smaller bore; but this is a matter for an expert tuner. Some remarks
upon this subject will be made in Chapter 5.

Mouthpieces have been made of many materials, of wood to begin
with, of ivory, of metal, of glass, of ebonite, and of plastics. Modern
practice favours ebonite, cut from the rod or moulded in a die. Glass
was used quite early in the last century, suggested no doubt by Laurent's
and Breton's glass flutes, and found some favour with those in search of
an immutable lay or facing. This material was strongly recommended
by Klosé as an alternative to *ébène* or African blackwood. It has long
been popular with Italian players. It has recently made another bid for
popularity, and gained some measure of success. There are, however,
some disadvantages in the use of this material. It is naturally brittle,
especially in the tenon, and difficult to relay – a glassworker is not

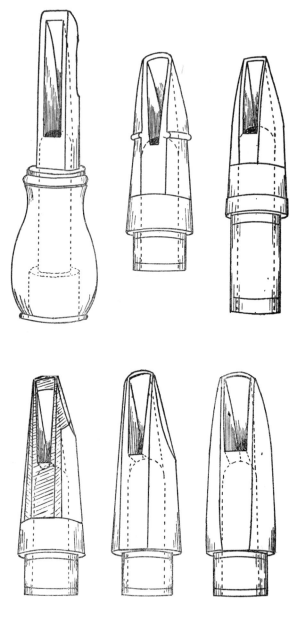

Fig. 2   Mouthpieces

always a competent relayer – and, further, moisture is apt to cling to the bore. Ebonite has none of these faults; it is less easily broken, and is sufficiently stable for all practical purposes. This material was first used for the tubes of musical instruments in 1851, and mouthpieces made of it were procurable a few years later. They are mentioned in Romero's tutor, which may be dated *c.* 1860. For the last sixty years and more the use of this material has been almost universal. Some German players are still faithful to wood, often blackwood, no doubt thinking that a more beautiful tone may be obtained from it, and are content to tolerate its many disadvantages. The principal of these is warping of the lay or facing, a fault which may be obviated to some extent by lining the lay or table with metal. These inlays do, however, have some tendency to leak after a time. In the writer's opinion [F.G.R.] the only suitable wood for the purpose is hard, well-seasoned cocus – *Brya ebenus*. Generally speaking, German mouthpieces are slenderer and thinner than those of other nations.

Metal, too, has been employed. J. S. Hermstedt (1778–1846), the virtuoso for whom Spohr wrote his concertos, played upon a gold mouthpiece with a silver lay. Aluminium has been tried, but metal generally has found little favour with serious players. It is cold and clammy in the mouth, and is considered to produce a harsh metallic tone. Theoretically the mouthpiece should be of the same material as the tube, but in practice the difference in tone engendered by a wood or ebonite mouthpiece is not discernible by the average ear. In selecting a mouthpiece the player will naturally choose one best adapted to the conformation of his lips and jaw. Some will be best suited by a broader, others by a narrower, tip. It cannot, however, be too strongly stressed that the bore and size of tone-chamber must be chosen by the maker. This is *not* a matter for individual selection. Formerly the best makers numbered each joint of their product, including the mouthpiece, with

---

Top *l.* to *r.*
  Klenig, in one piece with barrel, *c.* 1710.
  Continental pattern – stepped lay with retaining
  ring for cord, *c.* 1800.
  English pattern with long tenon for tuning.
Bottom *l.* to *r.*
  Modern German with metal inlay.
  Older French and Belgian (Albert).
  Modern French.

a serial number. This was evidence that the instrument had been tuned with that particular mouthpiece. This practice has been generally discontinued and mouthpieces are now made to standard dimensions. There is no objection to this provided that a careful watch is kept on tools and gauges and material of perfect uniformity can be guaranteed.

It has been said that the general design of the mouthpiece has been static for the best part of a century. Is there room for further experiment and improvement in the search for greater beauty of tone? If it is agreed that shape and material are in general satisfactory, further experiments might be made with the shape and size of the opening from the table into the tone-chamber. This is suggested by the researches of organ-builders. The voicers of reed-pipes have found that the size and form of the opening in the shallot, upon which the brass tongue is superimposed, are of the greatest importance in determining the harmonic constituents of the tone, in strengthening or diminishing the particular partials they consider desirable. A modification of the accepted oblong, so long in vogue, might not be without effect.

Another powerful determinant of tone-quality and of its harmonic content is found in the depth and width of the narrow passage which leads from the interior of the mouthpiece to the opening in the facing upon which the reed is placed. It makes no small difference whether the walls which define this passage are upright or sloping. An experienced maker will be well versed in these secrets.

The reed was at first attached to the table by means of waxed thread or a silken cord, rings being turned upon the mouthpiece to assist the process. The practice still obtains to a great extent in Germany. It is stated to give greater flexibility and added sonority to the lower notes. The present metal ligature was introduced by Iwan Müller in the first decade of the last century. Small modifications have been made from time to time, but it still remains much as its inventor left it. It is only necessary to say that it must fit or be adapted to the mouthpiece, and that on no account must it cut the reed at any point. If the player prefers a wooden mouthpiece he will be well advised to secure his reed with a silken cord. A metal ligature is only too apt to cut the wood or to pull it out of shape. In any case, whether wood or ebonite is used, the screws of the ligature should be slackened off after playing.

The BARREL or SOCKET is often considered the least important part of the clarinet, a totally incorrect view in the writer's opinion. If it is necessary to have one at all, which is open to question, let it be made properly. The walls, thin at the top, should thicken gradually towards their junction with the upper joint. Thus the vibration generated by reed and mouthpiece may be nourished and communicated without any diminution to the main body of the instrument. Thick walls of heavy wood, with tightly fitted wide tips of thick metal, have a constricting effect upon the whole instrument and may be damaging to the freedom of the tone. The tips may well be half the customary width and thickness and still serve their purpose of preventing or limiting cracks in the wood. Another prevalent fault of design is the shortness of the tenon

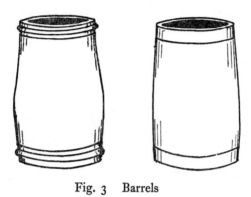

Fig. 3   Barrels

. Continental   r. English and Belgian

over which the barrel slides. Pull the socket ever so slightly, and there is a feeling of insecurity and a possibility of leakage. There are in addition two further disadvantages in the use of a barrel: possible distortion of the upper bore caused by undue pressure just where it is of prime importance that it should be exact to a hair's breadth; and the lacuna left in the bore when the barrel is pulled out. Various forms of tuning-socket have been devised to eliminate this gap. Most of them depend for their working on sliding tubes of metal, one in the bore of the upper joint, the other attached to the socket itself. But the use of metal at this point is highly undesirable, if only for the reason that the breath of the player is immediately condensed by the coldness of the metal.[1] The only satisfactory solution would appear to be to dispense with the barrel entirely. Many clarinets were built by Buffet and other French makers in this way.[2] After all, extension of the socket affects mainly the adjacent notes; it has little or no effect upon those at the bottom of the instrument (unless a flexible embouchure be cultivated [P.B.]). What adjustment of pitch is possible may be effected by pulling out the mouthpiece, which may well have a longer tenon than usual for

this purpose. There is a further advantage in this method of construction. There is less fear of cracks developing in the upper joint. As every
maker knows to his cost, sockets are a fruitful source of cracking.
Moisture will find its way inevitably to the end grain of the upper joint.
Tightly constricted by the barrel, the joint cannot expand and, unless
relieved by removing or loosening the socket, will often crack along the
upper holes.

The BODY of the instrument is in modern practice normally made in
two pieces. In early clarinets upper and lower joints were frequently
made in one. The division of the tube which seems to have come in
before the middle of the 18th century was probably not due primarily to
a desire for portability, but to allow the introduction of joints of varying
lengths to vary the pitch. These extra or supplementary joints – *pièces
de rechange* – will be discussed more fully in a later chapter. There is
much to be said for a body made in one piece. Several advantages are
obvious. It ensures wood of uniform weight, grain, and texture, all very
important considerations, and ensures further, in the case of complicated mechanism, securer mounting for the keys. It eliminates, furthermore, a tenon and socket joint, which is always a potential source of
leakage. A less obvious, but inestimable, advantage is that it makes
possible the correct placing and sizing of the *c′ sharp* hole. In clarinets
of normal construction the central division comes just where this hole
should be. The usual practice is to site the hole just half an inch too
high for correct intonation and to reduce it in size to lessen the inevitable
sharpness. The result is a muffled note of bad quality. One-piece
instruments are less frequent than they were seventy years ago. It is
unnecessary to describe the joints by which the members are united at
any length. To secure an absolutely air-tight connection cork lining is to
be preferred to waxed thread or yarn as a covering for the tenon.
Whether metal tips to tenons and linings to sockets should be fitted is a
matter of individual preference. The best makers no longer fit them as
normal practice, possibly less from motives of economy than from the
knowledge that such fittings will inevitably loosen in a dry atmosphere.

The BELL, like the socket, has not always received the attention it
merits. It is an essential part of the instrument's acoustical system, not
merely an amplifier for the two or three notes at the bottom of the tube,
or an ornamental addition. Some stages in its progress to its modern
form are shown in the illustrations of early clarinets. Experiments have
shown that it is of importance acoustically – a matter which will be
touched upon later. If this be granted, the exact form of the flare is
plainly a matter for careful calculation. Considerable attention has

recently been given to this subject and many of the most modern instruments are now made with a simple conical bell. In the meantime walls of some thickness may be recommended, thinned down towards the rim. This imparts greater solidity and roundness to the bell-notes which are only too often deficient in these qualities. Weight may well be saved by omission of the ornamental ring at the bottom. Whether shrunk on, pressed on, or merely pinned, it is an entirely useless appendage, which invariably comes loose with time or temporary disuse, and fails in its retaining duties. A clarinet without it is still a clarinet. The bells of basset-horns and bass clarinets are considered more particularly in the chapters devoted to these instruments.

The materials of which the body is made may now be examined. Firstly wood. Here several factors have to be considered. The wood must be durable, not prone to shrinking or swelling or warping, must work cleanly under the tool, must be resonant, not too heavy, and a bad conductor of heat. Beauty of appearance is the last consideration. Throughout the 18th century and well into the middle of the 19th, boxwood (*Buxus sempervirens*) was considered the ideal material. It is reasonably hard, light, very resonant, is easily turned and drilled, but has one fatal disadvantage – great susceptibility to atmospheric change. It is, in the words of a famous old maker, Cornelius Ward, 'more suited for a hygrometer than for a musical instrument'. The better qualities come from Italy and Spain, the best, the mottled Abassian boxwood, from the shores of the Black Sea. The English variety, while tougher, has a fatal propensity to warping. Cracks are seldom found in old boxwood clarinets. Careful seasoning may account in part for this immunity, but some of it may be due to the care the maker took in pinning or screwing his joints before he allowed them to leave his workshop. This practice, dead for a century or so, might be worthy of revival in the case of wooden instruments made for dry climates. It consists in screwing steel or brass wire through the danger zones, where cracks are likely to occur. There are two or three such places in the upper joint, not more than one or two in the lower. Old clarinets were occasionally made of other, softer, woods than boxwood, such as plum and pear, and occasionally maple. The latter, a favourite wood for bassoons, is used not infrequently by German makers for basset-horns and bass clarinets. It is quite unsuitable for the soprano instruments, which are in frequent use, in not possessing the necessary resistance to moisture.

Cocuswood (*Brya ebenus*) was long a popular material with English players and makers. It has every good property. It is very hard, resonant, easily worked, durable, and its high resinous content makes it very resistant to moisture and atmospheric changes. The best qualities come from Jamaica – it was long exported as dunnage in sugar ships – but is now very scarce. The Cuban wood is but little inferior and is rather more plentiful. The Alberts of Brussels and Buffet of Paris made many beautiful instruments in this material. Cocus is heavier than box, and a little lighter than the next wood to be considered. This is African blackwood (*Dalbergia melanoxylon*), the wood of a small scrubby tree which grows freely in all parts of tropical Africa. The genus comprises more than a hundred species, and the wood has many names. Some of them are Black cocus, Mozambique ebony, Grenadillo, East African ebony. It has more 'life' than true ebony, is far less brittle and far less prone to cracking. This is the *ébène* of the French makers. It has every good quality required by the maker. It is kind to tools, and takes a high polish from them, works smoothly, is resistant to atmosphere and moisture, is very durable. It has only one disadvantage – weight. It is heavier than cocus, as has been said, and half as heavy again as box.[3]

The seasoning and preparation of the wood is of great importance. On the care expended in this process will depend largely the accuracy of the bore and the life of the instrument. The traditional method is to submit the logs, some 3 or 4 feet in length,[4] to a longish period of seasoning in the open air. They are then sawn across to provide billets of convenient length for joints and split lengthwise with an axe. This method is less economical than that of sawing and gives a smaller percentage of joints per log. But since the axe must follow the grain it may be assumed that the billets thus produced will be straight-grained, and therefore less liable to cracking. The joints are next trimmed with an axe, roughly turned and bored, and submitted to a further period of seasoning, reduced to finished size, and finally immersed in a tank of linseed oil for several months. They are then allowed to dry out on racks, a lengthy process which should never be accelerated. It need hardly be said that these laborious methods have been largely abbreviated by modern makers. There is, however, no doubt whatever that natural seasoning is to be preferred to artificial drying in the kiln and splitting to sawing. It is pure waste of time to provide an instrument with a bore and tone-holes of mathematical exactness if this accuracy is soon to be distorted by warping and twisting of the wood. Makers leave the exterior finish to the choice of the player. It has no discernible effect upon the tone whether the wood is left in its natural state or varnished. Cocuswood when freshly varnished presents a beautiful appearance, but the polish soon disintegrates under the action of the fingers and of oil from the mechanism, and it is doubtful whether patchy varnish looks as well upon a clarinet as upon a Stradivarius violin. Boxwood may be varnished a golden yellow, or stained down to a rich dark brown with acid. It may also be sand-burnt, a process formerly much used by marquetry-makers in which pieces of wood are laid on a corrugated bed of sand in an iron tray over a flame. Contact with the ridges in the hot sand produces patterns of darker mottling which are much admired. Left in its natural state it soon assumes a dirty and unsightly appearance.

Hard woods suitable for instrument-making are not only costly but wasteful, owing to the cracks, shakes, and other flaws which are found in the interior of the logs. In the interests of economy experiments have been made with *laminated* wood. In theory this should be an ideal material; in practice the results have been disappointing. The tone of clarinets of this material is dull and noticeably weaker than that resulting from natural wood.

Ivory has never enjoyed much popularity. A few early 18th-century clarinets were made of it, notably by Scherer.[5] The only later instruments of this material known to the writer are a pair made about 1875 for the virtuoso Heinrich Gräff by G. Berthold of Speyer. It is a costly material, prone to cracking, and far from immutable, and, though it works easily, does not keep its shape nearly so well as seasoned wood. Its tonal qualities, too, are bleak and disappointing. It has been occasionally used for mouthpieces.

Two other materials remain to be considered, ebonite and metal. Ebonite, a compound of india-rubber, lead, and sulphur, was used for clarinets in the early 1860s. Since then it has enjoyed intermittent spells of popularity. It has many great advantages and not a few faults. It is, of course, immutable. It preserves the dimensions of the bore with absolute precision; it provides excellent seatings for key-pads; it cannot crack and is completely impervious to moisture. On the other hand it is very fragile and liable to discoloration. It works smoothly and sharply, but is particularly unkind to tools. Instruments made of it are flexible and easy-blowing, but somehow seem to lack the carrying power and expressiveness of wood. The tone can be taken just so far and no further. It lacks life and is no longer popular with professional musicians. It is of course invaluable for use in hot climates. Yet, curiously enough, William Golbourne, when manager to Boosey and Hawkes Military Department shortly before the Second World War, wrote in *Woodwind Yearbook*: 'Ebonite is prone to warping and wear from dust.' Admittedly his article concerned military instruments in the most extreme climatic conditions, but it does contain the warning that no material, except possibly metal, can be relied on to be absolutely immutable.

In addition certain artificial resins known generically as 'Perspex', and reinforced nylon materials marketed as 'Sonorite' and 'Resonite', have recently been tried out with some success. Acoustically good, they are said to be somewhat unstable as to pitch after prolonged use.

Metal has been used in clarinet construction for many years. In 1817, Halary produced a *clarinette-métallique* in brass.[6] One of his *clarinettes-alto* figures in the Sax auction sale of 1877. Brass and German silver clarinets found favour with the military, being employed to some extent in Austrian and Russian bands in the 1840s and '50s. They were no doubt well adapted to the rough and tumble of military use, and a number of specimens survive by Sulz and Schemmel, both of Vienna, Wünnenberg of Cologne, Meyer of Hanover, and by Key, Pask, Distin, and Rudall, Rose and Carte of London; the latter two almost certainly imports of Sax manufacture. The last fifty years have seen an attempted revival. There are two designs, the skeleton and the double-tube model. The former consists of a thin body, preferably seamless, to which key-mounts and short tubes to provide tone- and finger-holes are soldered. The double-tube pattern is more elaborate in construction. It comprises an inner and outer body through which the tone-holes are conducted in tubes. It has more or less the thickness and feel of a wooden clarinet. The metals employed may be brass, German silver, or silver. What has been said of ebonite may be said of metal. It has the very great virtue of preserving indefinitely the correct proportions of the bore and tone-holes and, contrary to expectation, is lighter than wood. On the other hand it has the slight deadness of ebonite, and two further disadvantages: it is extremely difficult to enlarge or reduce the size of the tone-holes for fine tuning once the instrument has left the maker's hands; it is, in addition, a good conductor of heat. The tube gets hot or cold in a moment, so the performer has to be constantly on his guard against playing out of tune. The double-walled model was designed to mitigate this evil. In fact Mr W. S. Haynes of Boston stressed the 'thermos feature' of his sterling-silver clarinet. The player breathed into the inner chamber between the walls on taking up the instrument, and a constant temperature, it was claimed, may be maintained throughout performance. Another disadvantage of metal clarinets is that the key-mounts are often fixed to the body by soft solder only, by no means a secure attachment. Metal clarinets are shown in the catalogues of many makers, but have never attracted more than passing attention from the serious musician. The foregoing remarks apply to clarinets of soprano pitch; for those of bigger dimensions metal has enjoyed some success. Sax chose brass for his *clarinette-basse recourbée* 130 years ago, and about 1931 M. Houvenaghel of Messrs Leblanc of Paris and Heckel of Biebrich were preferring metal to wood for their contrabasset-horns and contrabass-clarinets. The reasons for their choice are, no doubt, the superior lightness and permanence of the material. The wood of a clarinet, however well seasoned, however old, always maintains a certain amount of 'life', a natural tendency to swell or contract with the weather. This movement, slight though it may be, is fatal to long rod-keys and complicated mechanism.

NOTES

[1] Hermstedt had an ivory socket with silver mounts and a system of sliding tubes between the various joints of his instrument.

Not all players today share the objection to metal telescopic joints in wooden instruments. In the 1920s Besson and Co. of London were producing their 'Rolio' tuning-socket which enjoyed considerable success. In this the telescopic tubes were confined to the barrel alone, which was made in two halves, one screwing into the other. This gave a positive adjustment to the overall length of the piece which, nevertheless, could be treated as a simple barrel. No metal penetrated the bore of the upper joint.

An instrument embodying Smythe's patent fingering-system of 1867, in the Bate Collection, shows an interesting variation on the idea. Here the upper joint is metal-lined almost as far as the speaker-key. The barrel carries a very long inner tube – presumably in the interest of security – and a fine adjustment of some 6 mm. in extension only is obtainable by means of a knurled ring which screws over the outside of the upper joint. The piece has to be returned by hand as the ring is reversed.

It is not unknown for clarinettists using the simple barrel to provide themselves with a series of wooden rings of graduated thickness to fill the gap in the bore created by 'pulling out', a practice well known among 19th-century flautists.

[2] An English boxwood example by Monzani and Co., London, best known as flute-makers, and somewhat earlier than Buffet, shows this feature in extreme degree. As in Monzani's flutes the upper joint swells greatly at the top and the mouthpiece plugs directly into this, as did his flute head-joints. Unfortunately, the instrument, which dates between 1808 and 1817, is in other respects a poor thing. (Bate Collection.)

[3] It weighs about 85–90 lb. per cubic foot against the 60 lb. of box-wood and 70 lb. of cocus.

[4] It was long a generally accepted picturesque tradition that the length of the logs was conditioned by the method of transport from the interior. The wood, too heavy to be floated down by water, was stated to have been borne on the heads or shoulders of natives to the coast. The writer [F.G.R.] is now informed that the length of logs is conditioned not by

methods of transport but by the size of the tree from which they are cut.

[5] It is not known when this maker worked save for one reference which centres around 1764. See Langwill's *Index of Musical Wind-Instrument Makers*, 2nd edn., privately issued, 1962. An ivory D clarinet of his manufacture is shortly described in Chapter 7 and illustrated in Plate 1. An unmarked example with seven silver-plated brass keys in the Bate Collection appears to date from about 1840.

[6] *Rapports faits à l'Institut de France*, 1817.

CHAPTER 3

The mechanism: open and closed keys
Methods of construction and mounting
Pads and springs

'IT MAY BE ADMITTED unreservedly,' to use Rockstro's words,[1] 'that machinery of any kind on a wind instrument is an unfortunate necessity.' It *is* a necessity, since without it many note-holes would be out of reach of the fingers, and semitones could only be obtained by cross-fingering, a far from desirable method, but the only method known for the first hundred years of the clarinet's history. And if mechanism is vital to the flute and oboe, it is far more so to the clarinet, since its acoustical system demands an extension both at the top and bottom of its fundamental scale. Without keywork its compass would be reduced by two-thirds. The simplest clarinet needs twenty tone-holes to furnish an accurate chromatic scale. Of these seven are covered by the fingers, thirteen by keys; and such an instrument would be inadequate to the needs of an orchestral player faced with the difficulties of a modern score. For the last century or so the soloist or orchestral musician has demanded a far more complex instrument, pierced with at least twenty-four holes, and provided with a minimum of seventeen keys. Both numbers are not seldom exceeded.

It is not proposed at this stage to discuss systems of fingering; these will be reserved to a later chapter, but something may be said of the physical characteristics of keywork, of the materials of which keys are made, and of the various methods of manufacture. The essential parts of a key are the cup, the shank, and the touchpiece. This nomenclature will be used throughout this work. Keys may be 'closed' or 'open'; in the case of the clarinet the former are in the majority. Closed keys are so sprung as to seal the tone-hole until the finger raises the cup by pressure upon the touchpiece. They are simple levers of the first order. The open key is sprung in the reverse way. The cup stands poised above the hole until pressure of the finger overcomes the power of the spring and forces the cup down upon its seating. As soon as pressure is released the cup springs back to its former position. While modern clarinets may have as many as five open keys, the earliest had but one, a short key pivoted above the lowest hole just before the bell. It was closed by a long shank fitted to the left side of the R.H. joint and terminating in a round-headed pin, which engaged in a slot in the short key. This type of long-shanked key, known in French as *clef à bascule*, survives in modern clarinets of the older type. In more modern types it has been replaced by a shorter shank for L. little finger connected with 'rod' or 'rod-key' mechanism. Closely associated with this form of keywork are 'ring-keys' or, more shortly, 'rings'. The corresponding French terms are *tringle* and

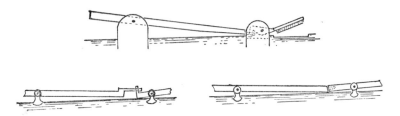

Fig. 4   Low *e* key (*clef à bascule*) of early and Müller
clarinets in knob and pillar mountings

anneaux mobiles or *anneaux*. In its simplest form a rod of thick-gauge wire is carried longitudinally down the joint and is free to revolve on pivot-screws. Touchpieces and cups are attached at right angles to it. The action is quick and positive, given perfect mounting, and is devoid of whip. The touchpiece may be replaced by a ring carefully fitted round a finger-hole. For this purpose the finger-hole is bored through a circular boss of wood raised above the surface of the joint by the thickness of the ring, and the descending finger automatically closes two or more holes in one action. The open key so closed may be at any distance from the ring; for the motion may be carried from joint to joint by means of interlocking lugs or 'clutches' (Fr. *correspondance*). The simplest form of this mechanism is seen in the *Brille* or 'spectacles' fitted to the R.H. joint of old-type clarinets, where to vent *b natural* an open key just below the fourth hole is closed automatically by R. 2 or 3. This replaces to great advantage the old closed key, which before the introduction of rings was necessarily manipulated by R. little finger and formed a great obstacle to fluent execution. A rather more elaborate use of the rod-mechanism is applied to Boehm-type clarinets. Here in addition to the 'spectacles' on the R.H. joint any of the rings under the right-hand fingers are free to close by means of a clutch an open key just

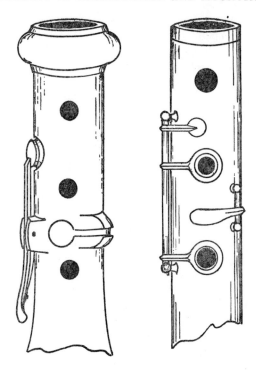

Fig. 5

l. Closed *b natural* and *b flat* keys on lower joint, *c.* 1810–40.
r. Ring-keys, introduced *c.* 1840.

under the first finger-hole on the upper joint. This is the so-called 'long' *e′ flat/b″ flat* fingering. The mechanism just described was applied to the clarinet at least as early as 1840 by Sax. He no doubt borrowed it from Boehm's first flute of 1832. The idea of the 'ring-key' was even earlier, the Rev. Frederick Nolan of Colchester having applied a ring touchpiece to a common lever-key in 1808.

Rod-keys may of course be more elaborate. Touchpieces and cups may be brazed not to solid pivoted rods, but to tubular sleeves of hinge-wire mounted upon a steel axle. More than one sleeve, each with an independent needle-spring, may be mounted on one axle, and one may be connected with another across an intervening key by means of a solid or divided clutch. Perfect adjustment between the members of a divided clutch is maintained by linings of cork or felt, or by adjusting screws. The axle may be fixed to supports at its extremities, or may be mounted between point-screws and thus made itself into a moving part. In this way two or even three different actions may be obtained from one rod. This type of mechanism, commonly applied to the flute, is only found in the most complicated clarinets, of which the Romero system may be cited as an outstanding example. This ingenious mechanism would seem to have been developed by Auguste Buffet[2] in the late 1830s.

For the simple keys of early clarinets, say from 1700 to 1830, only two metals were available, brass and silver, and of the two brass was more commonly employed. In the keywork of the modern instrument brass has been replaced by German silver. Coin or sterling silver makes only a rare appearance and that in instruments of the highest class. The manufacture of German silver was developed about 1820 by two workmen of Lyons, Maillot and Chorier. From them is derived the French name for the metal, *maillechort* or *melchior*. It is an alloy of copper, zinc, and nickel, 60–70 per cent of the first to 15–20 per cent of the last-named, and may have been suggested by the Chinese *Paktong* or 'white copper'.[3] In its purest form, when the nickel content is large, it is very white and little prone to tarnishing. It is, moreover, tough and hard, and lends itself well to forging and brazing. It takes and maintains a very high polish and is easily plated. It is in fact an admirable metal for its purpose. It came into use for key-making in the 1830s. Brass was reserved for instruments of a cheaper class and has not been used for them for more than fifty years.

The five or six keys of the primitive clarinet, one of which is illustrated in Fig. 6, called for little skill in manufacture. They were made as a rule in one piece from sheet brass, or filed up from castings. With the advance to more complicated mechanism and to more graceful design in the '20s and '30s of the 19th century, more skill and more elaborate methods were required. About this time hand-forging was developed and brought to great perfection in Paris and Brussels. The method is,

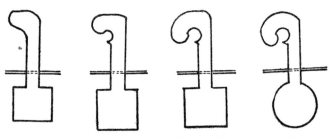

Fig. 6   The *a flat* key on the lower joint, *c.* 1760–1825

very shortly, to anneal a piece of stout forging-wire, to beat it on an anvil with a few strokes from a short-handled heavy hammer, to re-anneal and beat it again, repeating the process till the work is roughed to shape. A file succeeds the hammer and the finished pieces are firmly united with silver solder. The key, being literally wrought, is of great tensile strength, rigid, and virtually unbreakable. Such makers as Buffet, Triébert, and Bié of Paris, Mahillon and the Alberts of Brussels, excelled in the individuality and neatness of their workmanship.

This slow and laborious method of working, this literal *labor limae*, is too exacting for the present age and, if not already dead, will soon be discarded. Some German makers still offer hand-made keywork as standard on their finest models or as an extra to order on others, but the additional expense is very considerable – some 30–40 per cent on the cost price. The day of the hand-made or custom-built clarinet is passing, has perhaps already passed; and the manufacturer concentrates on one or two models, instead of the many, with which his catalogue was once adorned. For example, the illustration reproduced here comes from the celebrated Heckel catalogue of *c.* 1935. The way is clear for repetition work and economical methods. Two are now in common use for key-making – drop-forging and casting. The former has long been in favour with the highly specialised French *clétiers*, which perhaps explains why one French clarinet looks much the same as another. In this process an annealed blank of German silver is forced into a hardened steel die by a blow from a heavy descending weight or by hydraulic pressure. If the die is accurately cut, as it usually is, little subsequent filing is necessary. The heavy initial cost of the die is offset by the great cheapness and uniformity of the product. The key thus produced has not perhaps quite the stiffness and rigidity of the hand-forged product, but is good enough for all general purposes. It is certainly vastly superior to the casting, if it lacks the beauty and individuality of the hand-forging. Both hand- and drop-forged keys have a further very decided advantage over castings: they can be filed down and made thinner than castings without risk of breakage. This is an important point in the case of the smaller clarinets in which keys and holes lie close together.

There are several methods of casting keywork. Two will be considered. The cheapest and least satisfactory is sand-casting. A master key is pressed into prepared sand, and into the hollow thus produced molten metal is poured. The casting which results, though it may be bent to some extent, has no tensile strength whatever and may be both porous and pitted. To give it a workmanlike appearance some filing and

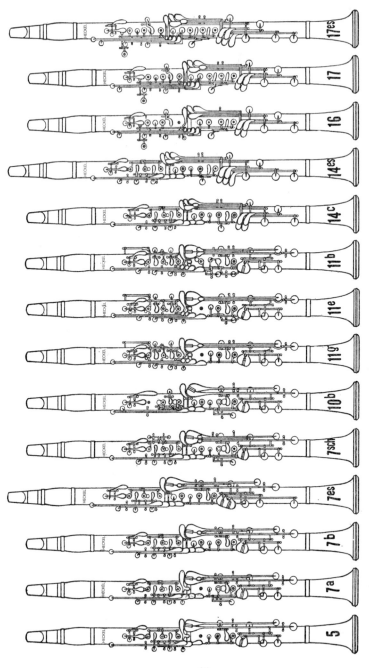

Fig. 7 Clarinets from the Heckel catalogue of *c.* 1935

trimming will be necessary. A far more satisfactory method is die-casting. In this process the metal is forced under pressure into partition-ed steel dies. This removes the possibility of blow-holes and pitting. It produces, moreover, clean and accurately dimensioned castings; further, the subsequent labour of filing and soldering together of small parts is eliminated, since even complicated keywork may be cast as a whole. There are, however, disadvantages. It is necessary to use alloys of low melting-point; the structure of the metal is crystalline, not fibrous, and, most objectionable of all, the barrels or sleeves of the keys, cast in one with the shanks, are subject to rapid wear. Cast keys have an undistinguished look and, being made of inferior metal with a large zinc content, do not take the high polish of forged mechanism. Nor do they take kindly to plating. (This point has had much attention since this book first appeared and the best cast keys now plate quite satisfactorily.)

A German silver key, highly polished with tripoli and rouge, is good enough for most players. It may, however, be silver-plated to enhance its appearance. Chromium, rhodium, and nickel have also been applied. Chromium, handsome though it be, renders keys almost too slippery for comfort and security.

Of far greater importance to the player than the shape of the key is the mounting. The most elegant key is useless unless the mounting allows it to perform its function efficiently. For at least 120 years, from 1700 to 1820, the keys of the clarinet were mounted in 'knobs'. A thick ring of wood was left on the joint where it was desired to mount a key, a channel was cut through it just wide enough to take the key shank, and a small hole was drilled through wood and shank to receive a short axle-pin of brass, steel, or silver wire. The superfluous wood was some-times, but not always, removed. In later instruments two keys might be mounted in one ring of wood. A clumsy method, perhaps, and unsightly, but more efficient in practice than theory would suggest. Hard woods wear slowly, and pins are easier to replace, when lost, than screws. When wobble inevitably developed the channel was widened, a slip of wood was inserted or, better, a cheek of brass or silver. This was a later improvement. Rather later than the knob is the 'saddle'. This consisted of two thin walls of metal soldered to a bottom plate which was sunk into the joint and secured by screws. Small saddles could be bent up from a single piece of sheet, or sawn or filed from a small block of metal. It was necessary to replace the wire pin with a brass or steel screw, which would call for lubrication. This was a neater job than the wooden block, especially when the shank of the key was reduced to fit closely between the cheeks; it was secure and allowed no lateral play. In

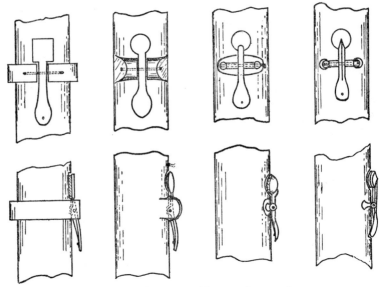

Fig. 8　Development of keys and mountings
Left to right:
    Sheet metal, square flap, in turned ring; wire pivot
    Sheet metal, round flap in 'knob'; wire pivot
    Salt-spoon cup; pillars on foot-plate; wire pivot
    Modern cup; screwed-in pillars; pivot-screw

passing, it may be noted that knobs and saddles are frequently found
together in early 19th-century clarinets. The presence of a key mounted
in a saddle on a clarinet fitted with knobs does not necessarily denote a
later addition – a mistake sometimes found in catalogues; a saddle was
often used, where it was impossible to leave a knob.

The last development was the pillar. This mounting originated in the
first decade of the last century and was of French origin. Pillars appear
on Laurent's glass flutes as early as 1806, and in England, where knob
and saddle were slow to give way to them, they were long known as
'French pillars'. As first made they were screwed and soldered to neat
oval plates which were let into the wood of the joint and firmly planted
with screws. Rather later, by 1840 or so, in the interest of economy, the
foot-plate was dispensed with and the pillars were screwed directly into
the wood. Now on no account must the hole to take the pillar be drilled
through to the bore, so plainly the length of the screwed portion of the
pillar will be short and, however well calculated the pitch of the thread,

the mounting will be far from secure. The tendency of the pillar to become loose is increased when it carries a needle-spring, when it carries more than one key, or when the hand of the player grasps the mechanism tightly to mount or dismount his instrument. It is no exaggeration to say that on most clarinets after a few years of use two or three pillars will be found to be loose, and more in countries where the atmosphere is particularly dry. The loose pillar is a bugbear to the player. It causes the mechanism to bind and may well be the cause of a 'fluffed' passage, and that through no fault of the player. The remedy is obvious. To mount all the pillars on metal straps, secured to the joint with screws – this has long been the flute-maker's practice – or at least to anchor all pillars that carry more strain than others. A pillar can only unscrew itself in one direction; one small set-screw or pin through the base of the pillar will secure it. Is this too much to ask of the makers? It is gratifying to notice that not a few of them are at last alive to this cause of vexation and are fitting the more important pillars with lugs fixed to the body with a screw. Some makers are using this very necessary and elementary precaution as a selling point.

The introduction of pillars necessitated a change in the design of the key. This was the addition of a barrel or sleeve to fit between the bosses or cheeks of the pillars. This is, or should be, made of hard-drawn, seamless, hinge-wire, let into the shank of the key and firmly united to it with silver solder. A slender steel screw passes through the barrel and

Fig. 9   Pillar and point-screw, anchored by set-screw alone
(*left*), and set-screw and lug (*right*)

screws into the further pillar. To eliminate wear, exact fitting is of paramount importance; so, too, the accurate squaring-off, and polishing of the working surfaces.

Not every key is so mounted. The long rod-keys which are now so largely used demand different treatment. These are in general made of stiff wire and pivoted at the ends on point-screws. In theory, hinge-wire rotating on a long steel screw would offer great security; in practice, this makes for more friction and heavier working, unless perfect and permanent alignment can be guaranteed. Properly designed and fitted the point-screw is entirely satisfactory. It must be of correct design and proportions, not too long or short, with a slow taper, and the hole in the rod into which it fits must be accurately centred, bored with perfect precision, and provided with an oil-sink. All these are elementary points perhaps, but they are vital to the player, and do not always receive the attention they demand.[4] Screws are frequently made of soft steel. This is an unworthy economy. Little expense is entailed in hardening and tempering a screw-head, or in providing it with an accurately cut saw-kerf. Many of the screws found in the older hand-made clarinets are works of art; it is only in the last few decades that deterioration has set in. Many of the older German makers were faithful to wire pins long after the introduction of pillars. They are still to be found in many high-class German bassoons, and are certainly preferable to badly fitted screws.

Allusion has been made to the vexation caused to the player by loose pillars and badly contrived screws; there remains the general problem of wear in the mechanism. This occurs mainly in the barrels of the keys, where these are in constant friction against the inner cheeks of the pillar. It occurs today just as frequently in the higher grade as in the cheaper instruments and is a very serious annoyance to the player. It causes lack of precision and responsiveness in the mechanism and in bad cases an intolerable rattle and clatter of keywork, quite clearly audible in a solo. The wear is far more rapid, as has been said, with a solid casting than with a forging fitted with a drawn barrel, and more rapid with German than with pure or coin silver. Some of the older makers recognised this and fitted many of their keys with silver barrels. A purely mechanical problem is involved. The barrel must inevitably be annealed or softened by the intense heat of brazing and at present too little trouble is taken to restore the hardness by burnishing. As a rule the shorter the barrel, the quicker the wear. So longer barrels provide a partial solution; another is the use of dissimilar metals at points of friction. But plainly the matter demands far more attention than it has so far received. No horologist would allow himself to be so easily baffled. It may be noted in this connection, as a matter for sober reflection for both maker and player, that the balance staff of a watch makes 420,000 partial revolutions in the course of twenty-four hours. In the case of a finely-made watch, selling for little more or possibly less than a clarinet, no appreciable wear will be found in the working parts after fifty or one hundred years of wear.

A word or two about pads and key-coverings. The primitive key, we have seen, was cut or cast in one piece. The square or rounded end which covered the tone-hole, often known as the *flap* in early clarinets, was covered with nothing more than a piece of thick soft leather. The proper functioning of the key was aided by working a flat surface in the portion of the tube adjoining the tone-hole, but nothing in the nature of a raised or recessed seating was attempted. Altogether a primitive contrivance, and only fairly efficient in practice. A step forward was taken when the tone-hole was slightly countersunk and a projecting metal tube was inserted to provide an annular seating for the flat leather. This added greatly to the efficiency of the key and is found in frequent use in the first decades of the last century. It was especially popular with the English makers, Key and Bilton of London, who gave but a tardy welcome to the next development, the stuffed pad. This was one of the inventions claimed by Iwan Müller (1786–1854), the virtuoso clarinettist, who will figure later in this work. Known in their primitive form as 'elastic plugs', these were round cushions of kid-leather stuffed with fine wool. Their introduction made two demands on the maker: firstly, an improved key to hold them, since they could not be cemented neatly or securely to a flat-piece of metal; secondly, an improved seating round the tone-hole. The first demand was met by soldering a hollow cup to the key-shank, the second by so countersinking the hole as to leave a raised rim of wood for the pad to rest upon. This is shown in Fig. 10. The profiled seating is perfectly satisfactory when close-grained hard-woods are used for the joint and a sharp fly-cutter for the drilling. It is less satisfactory in the case of softer and more porous woods such as maple and rosewood; when these are employed recourse must again be had to metal tubes or to inset ebonite bushes to provide a firm seating for the pad. The built-up key with cup and barrel came in with the pillar-mounting round about 1820. This salt-spoon type of key, efficient but somewhat clumsy and unsightly, lasted for some forty or fifty years. It was then improved, in appearance at any rate, by the substitution of a flat for a rounded cup. This was made possible by the introduction of a thinner, flatter pad, in effect the modern pad. This consists of a circle of felt, backed by a thin piece of card, and covered with one or two layers of gold-beater's skin or similar animal tissue. Kid may also be used for a covering, but, owing perhaps to the impossibility of water-proofing leather satisfactorily, it is used less frequently than tissue. Pads have been made wholly of cork or of rubber, but have not proved entirely reliable.[5]

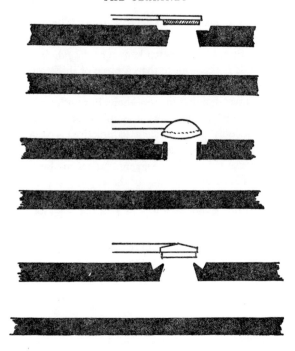

Fig. 10 Seatings in section
Plain flat on body; plain leather on flap
Inset metal tube; stuffed pad
Modern recessed and profiled seating; flat
modern pad

A small but indispensable component of the key must not be overlooked. This is the spring which is fitted to keep a key closed or open.
To discharge this function quickly and decisively it must be of well-
calculated strength, neither too strong nor too weak. Formerly springs
were made of brass and riveted to the shank of the key, an unsuitable
material most unsuitably attached. They were sluggish in action, subject to fatigue, and far from easy to replace when broken. Tempered
steel has long proved an admirable substitute. Forged-steel springs,
fitted to Laurent's glass flutes in the first decade of the 19th century
and to Savary's bassoons a few years later, were soon applied to French
clarinets. English makers persevered some while longer with brass.[6]
Two forms are in common use, the flat spring and the needle-spring.
The flat spring is often tapered to work upon a small metal stud

screwed into the joint or, if untapered, in a narrow slot cut in the wood, which may with advantage have an inset of steel.[7] The flat spring works at its best when it is carried some way beyond the axis of the key. It is attached to the key with one or two screws. The needle-spring, an invention of Auguste Buffet, and applied to the flute about 1837, has long been used for clarinets.[8] It is made of fine steel wire tempered to a blue colour. Theobald Boehm recommended fine English sewing-needles suitably tempered for this purpose. Needle-springs are ideal in action, since their strength may be regulated at will with a twist of the pliers. Their only disadvantage is their tendency, already noted, to loosen pillars to which they are attached. This can and should be obviated by anchoring the pillar or providing a separate holder for the spring, another detail for the careful maker. They are of course liable to rust and sudden breakage unless smeared with oil from time to time.

NOTES

[1] *A Treatise . . . on the Flute*, London, 1890, 1928, p. 192.

[2] Louis-Auguste Buffet (d. 1885), also known as Buffet *jeune*, was one of the outstanding Paris makers. His business, established *c.* 1831, had no connection with that of Buffet-Crampon.

[3] Often incorrectly transcribed as *Pakfong*, a common name for the metal.

[4] At least one maker provides a set-screw to keep the point-screw steady and up to its work. Steel bushes are sometimes fitted to the end of the rods.

[5] Recently a compound kid-surfaced pad has been developed which meets the problem well. Some plastic materials have been tried out, mainly in America, and seem to be very efficient. Repair men, however, report that they seem to attract dust and get very dirty. Is this perhaps due to their high electrical insulating properties and the consequent retention of static charges?

[6] Some German makers show a predilection for German silver springs to this day. German silver and brass have only one advantage over steel – they cannot rust. Nevertheless, under the influence of free fatty acids in certain grades of linseed oil, they do tend to produce greenish copper salts. Linseed is still the traditional oil for steeping clarinet joints during manufacture, but it should be absolutely avoided for subsequent oiling of the instrument when in use. In the writer's view [P.B.] only best almond oil should be used in the bore, and that sparingly. In his earlier clarinets Heckel used German silver screws.

[7] Some of the smallest springs in Brod's oboes were fitted at the tip with small wheels. This refinement has not been observed on any clarinet.

[8] The needle-spring was introduced to England by Cornelius Ward in 1842.

CHAPTER 4

Practical acoustics. Tone; compass; registers
The tonal spectrum of the registers
Characteristics of the clarinet. Vibrato

IN THE PRECEDING CHAPTERS some of the material and constructional
features of the clarinet have been considered; the present chapter will
deal with the acoustical system and *practical* working of the instrument.

The flute, acoustically a simple instrument, has been most capably
and fully described by R. S. Rockstro and Professor D. C. Miller, both
flautists, the former a professional musician, the latter an accomplished
amateur and, in addition, a brilliant acoustician. The clarinet has been
less fortunate. Until recently it seldom achieved more than a passing
reference in textbooks, but in the last fifteen or twenty years a crop of
articles in acoustical and scientific journals has indicated an awakening
of interest in the acoustical problem it presents. (These sentences were
written in 1954. Since then the behaviour of flute, clarinet, and oboe
have been investigated in much detail and the effects of their characteristic, and sometimes variable, structures have been expressed in
mathematical formulae.) Some of the more important contributions are
noticed in the bibliography. The notes which follow are written from a
practical point of view. Theory is not infrequently at loggerheads with
practice, and theoreticians are only too often in disagreement among
themselves.

The clarinet, in common with other woodwind instruments, presents
a typical example of a coupled system. The sound-generator is of course
the reed attached to the mouthpiece, while the resonator is the air-
column enclosed within the tube. As Richardson points out, it may well
be considered a tripartite system,[1] if the oral cavity of the player is taken
into account. This human element has so far received scant attention,
certainly not the attention it would seem to merit. Oral cavities must
obviously vary in size; lips, too, in width, strength, elasticity, and thickness; both may contribute powerfully to variety of tone and timbre.
The sound of the reed dissociated from the body of the instrument is,
to say the least, strident and unmusical. Allied to the air-column, the

reed communicates its vibration to it and, provided all joints are properly airtight – an important proviso – harshness will give place to mellowness, noise to music. As every player knows, the partnership of reed and
air-column is at times uneasy. A stiff reed is only too ready to assert its
natural frequency, and in any case will make the player's task painful
and laborious.

The principles upon which the clarinet works are those common to
other woodwind instruments – the shortening-hole system,[2] and harmonics. The air-column is progressively shortened as tone-holes are
opened by the raising of key or finger and, when the limit of the fundamental scale is reached, harmonics are brought into play and the fingering is repeated. It is in its operative harmonics that the clarinet differs
radically from other woodwind instruments. Whether the reed actually
closes the orifice in the mouthpiece or not is a matter of dispute among
acousticians, the balance of opinion being against total occlusion. It is
in any case an academic question. What is indisputable is that the
aperture is virtually closed, and that a node is formed at the top of the
tube. The bore being in part cylindrical, the clarinet behaves as a
stopped cylindrical pipe. The operative harmonics are therefore the odd,
not the even, series; the instrument overblows not in octaves but in
twelfths, and requires only half the length of tube demanded by other
instruments to sound a given note. Two examples. Middle or two-foot
c', the bottom note of the flute, is produced by the clarinet with little
more than 12 inches of tube, and a contrabass clarinet requires less than
9 feet for its lowest note, D in the 16-foot octave.

If the clarinet has the advantage of other woodwind instruments in
range and compactness, it is at a disadvantage in ease of fingering. The
fact that it overblows in twelfths makes for considerable complexity of
fingering and mechanism. Plainly two extensions to the fundamental
scale *f* to *g'* are necessary, one at the top, another at the bottom of the
instrument, the former to carry the scale on from *g'*, the last note of the
fundamental scale, to *b' flat*, the latter to supply the missing *b' natural*.
And further, both extensions are necessarily in continual use, being,
so to speak, in the very centre of the instrument's effective compass. In
flute, oboe, and bassoon there is of course but one extension, and that
at the bottom of the fundamental scale. To gain facility of fingering for
the player has been the aim of the inventors and makers for more than
a century. No instrument has been made with greater variety of mechanism, and it would be idle to pretend the problem is even now completely
solved. To take but one point, far too much work still devolves upon the
left hand. There is further a subtle danger bound up with difficulty of

technique. Unless the student is carefully watched he may set himself
to win the mastery over technical and mechanical difficulties at the
expense of tone. And to acquire a beautiful tone is surely as difficult as
to master technique; it is certainly more important. The clarinet is
essentially a melodic, a singing instrument. Much of its technique is
akin to singing. No one in his senses would attempt a career as a singer
unless he had considerable natural endowment or would continue with
it unless his voice was pleasing to the public. Why should clarinettists
be less sensible in imagining that facility of technique will cover up a
poor or disagreeable tone.

To define a good tone is far from easy. To begin with, many of the
adjectives commonly applied to tone have no precise meaning or,
worse, mean different things to different people. Again, ears differ in
sensitivity; some may be better tuned to higher harmonics, others to
lower; there is no reason to suppose that we all hear alike, and none
whatever for supposing that we shall all admire precisely the same
qualities of tone. But some qualities must surely win general approval.
Rockstro has some illuminating remarks upon the subject in his treatise
on the flute, and much of what he says is applicable to the clarinet.
Some of the constituents he selects are power, volume, brilliancy,
sweetness, and clearness. The first two might in the case of the clarinet
be coupled together as sonority as opposed to thinness or poverty of
sound. The French might call such a tone *bien nourri*; fullness without
harshness. Brilliancy would have as its antithesis dullness, and sweetness stridency. Clearness to the writer means purity not only of sound,
but of intonation: being right in the middle of the note, not just border-
ing on the fringe. Above all, the tone must be alive. Every effort must
be made to breathe life and movement into it, to vary it by every means,
by every trick of articulation, to avoid stagnation and monotony at all
costs. The clarinet is the most expressive instrument in the orchestra;
let full use be made of its capabilities.

This brief digression on the general subject of tone may fitly lead to a
short examination of its harmonic texture. It has long been accepted that
different qualities of tone or of timbre may be explained by the particular series of overtones present in any note, and particularly by their
intensities. The timbre of a clarinet is easily distinguished from that of
an oboe or a flute because, generally speaking, the partials which pre-
dominate in its tone are different from those found in the oboe, and far
more numerous than those of the flute. Recently considerable research
has been devoted to clarinet tone in the U.S.A. and more than one
important paper has figured in the *Journal of the Acoustical Society of*

America. Nor has interest been wanting in Britain; several recent analyses are now available to the student. The pioneer in this research was indeed an Englishman, D. J. Blaikley, an acoustician, associated with the firm of Boosey for more than sixty years as technical adviser. He began his experimenting in the 1870s and summarised the fruits of his research in a paper read to the Musical Association in 1878–79 upon 'The Tone of Wind Instruments'. By means of carefully adjusted Helmholtz resonators inserted in the ears he detected the existence of the even series of partials in the clarinet, and published a short table of his findings. His analysis was essentially qualitative since he did not, in fact he could not with the instruments at his disposal, go far in estimating the intensity of these partials. But he did show conclusively that they were present, and that they played a by no means negligible part in forming the tone of the instrument. Here the matter rested for a generation until the great acoustician Professor D. C. Miller resumed research into the tone of wind instruments with his newly-invented *Phonodeik*.[3] Miller made many photographs of clarinet tone and subjected them to meticulous and painstaking analysis.

The results amply bore out the accuracy of Blaikley's pioneer work. Miller demonstrated that 'clarinet tone may contain 20 or more partials, of which 12 are of importance, with the 7th, 8th, 9th and 10th predominating; the 7th partial contains 8 per cent of the total loudness, while the 8th, 9th and 10th contain 18, 15 and 18 per cent respectively'.[4] This was the first attempt at *quantitative* analysis of musical tone. Miller's investigations are generally regarded as classic and have not been entirely superseded by modern and possibly more sensitive electrical techniques. A typical example of the latter, which eliminates much of the laborious analysis required by the *Phonodeik*, is the *search-tone* method, simply described by Dr Hague in a paper read before the Royal Musical Association in April 1947.[5]

To particularise further is beyond the scope of this work. Useful material for study will be found in the bibliography appended to Dr Hague's paper. As has been said, several analyses both qualitative and quantitative are available, and no more than a rough synthesis of them has been attempted in the following section. While it is disconcerting to find little agreement among them in detail, it is at least encouraging to find that investigators are at one in emphasising the following points: (1) that the tonal spectrum differs from register to register and from note to note within the same register; (2) that the spectrum grows progressively more complex as the clarinet is lowered in pitch; the B flat for example is richer in harmonics than the C, and the A than the

—5 • •

B flat, while the basset-horn and bass are considerably richer than both the preceding; (3) that the richness of texture is attenuated as the intensity of sound declines from a double *forte* to a *pianissimo*. In other words tone-quality is largely conditioned by wind pressure; (4) that the tone-holes have a filtering action.

Before turning to an examination of the individual *registers* we may consider the *compass*. This embraces three octaves and a sixth, from *e* to *c''''*. It has been and frequently is extended. The B flat clarinet is not seldom taken down to *e flat*, and some modern tutors extend the compass up by a tone or a minor third.

The *primary* object of the downward extension is to enable parts for the A to be played on the B flat clarinet, to free the player from the necessity of maintaining two instruments. There are obvious advantages in this. Every orchestral player is only too familiar with the annoyance of changing from a warm to a cold and flat instrument. Only too often little time is allowed by the composer for the change and mouthpiece and socket are apt to jam at critical moments. A mouthpiece, too, will often shed its reed and ligature when it is hurriedly grasped in a moment of agitation. A further advantage is that the player is freed from the considerable trouble of tuning two instruments to a nicety and finding a mouthpiece and reed which are suitable to both. To offset these gains there is the additional weight which the extension entails and a certain loss of balance. Some players, too, detect a loss of brilliancy occasioned by the extension of the tube. The *secondary* object of taking the compass down a semitone is to obtain a purer middle *b' flat* by using for it the twelfth of *e flat*, the bottom note. The note, however, thus obtained is of rather different quality from those adjacent to it and is not to be recommended. The practice of using *only* one instrument is less common

Fig. 11   The Registers

today than it was some forty or fifty years ago – with orchestral musicians, that is. Some conductors are faddy and like their clarinettists to play on instruments of the same tonality; and modern orchestral parts are not always encouraging to transposition. A well-known French player, however, has disclosed (H. Sarlit, *Woodwind Magazine*, January 1952) that he habitually plays on one clarinet only. He has chosen not the B flat but the A, extended by a semitone, for the purpose, because he finds the tone of it warmer and richer in harmonics. He finds, too, that reeds are more easily adaptable to the A than to the other. (See also note 1, p. 164.)

The compass of the basset-horn is always lowered to written *c*, and that of the bass usually to *e flat* and even occasionally to *c*. The contra-bass shares both these extensions. This extensive compass is divided into *registers*, sometimes three, sometimes four, according to the fancy of the writer. The fourfold division seems the more convenient (see diagram). The registers are *chalumeau, throat* or *intermediate, clarinet*, and *extreme* or *acute*. In the *chalumeau* the predominant partials are 1, 3, 5, and 7. The lower evens (the *octave* and *super octave*) do not count at all. On the other hand, the 8th (the *twenty-second*), 9th (the *twenty-third*), and 10th (the *twenty-fourth*), are all strong. Partials above a frequency of 2,000 c.p.s. are ineffective. This for the B flat clarinet. In the case of the A, the lower evens are more telling. There results from this texture a hollow reediness which has been turned to excellent account by the composer. It can be greatly varied at the discretion of the player. It may be harsh and threatening – the Freischütz tone – or merely ominous and foreboding. It may even be smooth and warm.

The *throat register* from *g'* to *b' flat* is a favourite subject for abuse in textbooks of instrumentation, not that composers have much heeded the warnings of theoreticians, since many orchestral solos are centred round these notes. It is an extension upwards of the fundamental scale, the three semitones *g' sharp, a,* and *b' flat*, being governed by closed keys and manipulated by the left hand. It is the dreaded 'break', the first technical obstacle to be overcome by the student. Here the sounding length of air-column is very short and the tone in consequence meagre and poor in harmonic content. No notes, however, are more sensitive to clever manipulation by lips and fingers. As every clarinettist knows, the orchestral second clarinettist in particular, whose part lies often in these regions, the tone may be much ameliorated and steadied by placing the fingers on tone-holes 2 and 3. And this short neutral register serves a most useful purpose in linking the dark-toned powerful *chalumeau* to the brilliant middle register – the *clarinet*.

This is in some ways the most satisfactory register. It is limpid, clear, and crystalline, entirely lacking in bite or roughness; it may be brilliant or placid according to the requirements of the music; and it possesses, or should possess when required, a ringing quality. Here the operative harmonic is the *third*; the fundamental scale is repeated a twelfth higher from *b′ natural* to *c‴* or *c‴ sharp*, and with the same fingering. Since it is all but impossible to overblow the clarinet by lip pressure alone, aid is provided by the speaker-key. This covers a small vent-hole, too small to act as an effective note-hole, some 6 inches down from the mouthpiece. When opened this 'encourages' an antinode and divides the air-column into the necessary segments. This vent-hole must remain open for all notes above *a′*. In this register the fundamental is far stronger than in the *chalumeau*; so too the lower even terms, all but missing in the lowest register. Thus hollowness is replaced by clarity and a bell-like quality of tone, while brilliance is added by the 11th and 12th harmonics which are particularly strong in this section of the compass.

The natural scale of the clarinet has by some been considered to end with *c‴ sharp*. For the first fifty or sixty years of its history the clarinet was seldom taken above *c‴ natural*, but with the developing skill of the player the scale was extended upwards. A high *g‴* occurs in the clarinet concerto of Mozart (1791); it had in fact occurred some fifty years earlier in the concertos of J. M. Molter. By the turn of the century this limit had been exceeded, and in the first decades of the 19th century high Cs are found. Lefèvre's tutor of 1802 gives a fingering for this note and it occurs a few years later in the concertos of Spohr. Such heights held no terrors for virtuosi of the class of H. J. Bärmann and J. S. Hermstedt. But a writer in the A.M.Z. of March 1808 deplores the extension of compass beyond *g‴* which was good enough for Mozart. Most players and listeners will agree with him. Had extreme notes been reserved for virtuosi alone they might have been tolerated. But now they are expected of the orchestral musician too. These sorely tried players are expected to play with perfect tone, impeccable intonation, and evenness from top to bottom of the compass. High Cs are found in Wagner's *Das Rheingold*, *Die Walküre*, in Strauss's *Guntram* where there are three bars of it, and in Busoni, Elgar, Delius, Moeran, and Britten. Some modern tutors give fingerings for *d″″* and *d″″ sharp*, and some players can ascend as far as *e″″* beyond. One can only hope the modern composer will not get to hear of such *tours de force*. For it is idle to pretend that the clarinet is at best above *g‴*. The sounding length of the air-column is far too short and the bore of the instrument too large to assist the harmonic. The spectrum of the *extreme* register from *c‴* sharp to *c″″* is meagre and jejune, entirely lacking the rich texture of the *chalumeau* and *clarinet*. Fundamental and octave are very prominent, but there is little else to give it warmth, interest, and colouring. The operative harmonics, as analysed from accepted fingerings, are the 5th (the *tierce* or *seventeenth*), the 7th (the *flat twenty-first*), and, for the last semitone or two, the 9th (the *twenty-third*). See Fig. 12. Execution is

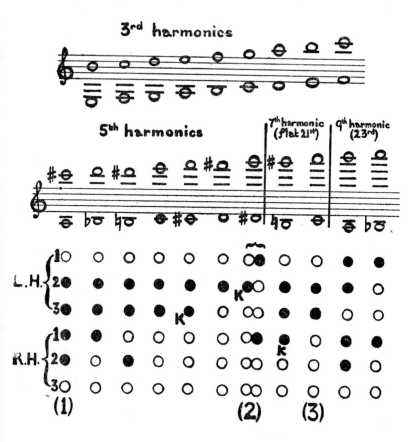

Fig. 12   Harmonics

Note a. 'K' indicates an open key
b. The fingerings are for the Boehm Clarinet
   1. The usual fingering
   2. There are 10 or more fingerings for this note which may well lie within a formant's area of resonance
   3. This note is really a *flat b''' flat*

particularly difficult. Some modern tutors give us as many as forty fingerings for this last octave; g''' alone has ten or twelve. The player selects those best suited to his instrument, to its bore, its mouthpiece, to the strength of reed he employs, to his embouchure, and looks to purity of tone and intonation and security rather than to ease of manipulation. But even with the best of players the tone of this register above d''' or e''' will lack warmth and sweetness. This is not to say it will be necessarily harsh, piercing, or uncontrolled. It seems to lack power and interest, especially in the notes above g'''. And there is often an uneasy feeling of brittleness and insecurity.

In these cursory notes upon tonal structure attention has been drawn to the presence of even partials, especially in the *clarinet* and *extreme* registers. How, it may be asked, do these even terms find their way into a closed cylindrical pipe which, according to the textbook, should show in its composition only the odd numbers of the harmonic series, and which is operated by the latter alone? One explanation may well be that the clarinet is only theoretically a cylindrical pipe. In practice the bore is far from a true cylinder; more than a third of it is definitely conical, the bell, the lower joint, the mouthpiece in particular. Another theory is that the even harmonics are due to wavelets or to beat-waves. Some of the main harmonics, not being completely in tune or phase, quarrel with one another and thereby give rise to subsidiary oscillations in the air-column.

Before leaving this section some account must be taken of the *formant* in which many modern authorities find a powerful determinant of timbre and tone-colour. They would agree that the predominance and intensity of certain partials go far to define the character of tone; they would not agree that these are the sole determinants. An important place must in their opinion be assigned to the formant. Briefly defined, the formant is an area of resonance which powerfully reinforces all partials falling within its limits, whatever the fundamental may be. The theory is fairly generally accepted in the case of the oboe and bassoon. The former would appear to have formant regions in the neighbourhood of 1,700 and 2,000 c.p.s., the bassoon around 500 c.p.s. In the case of the clarinet the theory has found less general acceptance; or rather, while many authorities would accept the general theory they would not agree in fixing the precise position of the formant. No doubt the lack of any close agreement in quantitative analysis, to which allusion has already been made, is responsible for this hesitation. Formant frequencies around g''', b''' *flat*, and c'''' have been suggested, and there we must leave it. The formant theory is attractive. It is, to quote

Richardson,[6] 'an absolute pitch theory of timbre, as opposed to the older relative pitch theory'. And further, by analysing formants we could determine what range of formant is required to produce a good-toned instrument. This last is a very practical point, and would justify to the player a mass of theory which might otherwise seem to him irrelevant and merely academic.

To deal very shortly with some of the *characteristics* of the clarinet. The most obvious and remarkable is its control of dynamics. This is phenomenal, far greater than that possessed by any other orchestral instrument. It is this quality which gives the clarinet its unequalled expressiveness. It is unnecessary to quote examples; they abound in every score and solo work. And not less striking is the rapidity with which the transition from *forte* to *piano*, from prominence to nothing-ness, can be accomplished. It is all but instantaneous. And no instru-ment can speak more clearly in a whisper. One example may suffice, the unforgettable, if hackneyed, passage in the first movement of Tschaikowsky's *Pathetic Symphony* where the fourfold *pianissimo* of the A clarinet is carried down an octave lower in a whisper by the bass clarinet which in this passage often replaces the bassoon to great advantage. This control and expressiveness is no less marked in the lower-pitched members, the basset-horn, bass, and contrabass. It is perhaps even more striking. Agility is another characteristic. No wind instrument thinks less of leaps of two octaves or more. This device, initiated by the composers of the Mannheim School, was developed by Mozart, and to the maximum effect. Two well-known leaps of two octaves and a fifth occur in the slow movements of the Concerto and the Quintet, both striking and most happily timed. And then there is the second concerto of Weber where the solo instrument enters on high *f'''*, drops three octaves to *f* in the *chalumeau*, begins the next bar a semitone lower with *e*, and rises on the second beat to *c'''* above the stave. This was, of course, virtuoso music of the period, written for Stadler and the elder Bärmann.

Fluency and powers of *staccato* may be taken for granted; they are only equalled by the flute. And fluency is ever increasing with the enormous strides made in technique within the last half-century. There may be danger here both for player and composer, as has been already suggested. More than 150 years ago Spohr complained that his friend Hermstedt's great and ever-increasing volubility was not always accom-panied by an increase in his musical taste. The greatest assets of the clarinet are beauty of tone and power of expression. Should they not remain the greatest and most desirable? But even beauty of tone may prove monotonous and cloying without warmth and constant variation of intensity. Especially is this true of wind instruments. Every device of phrasing and articulation[7] – and the clarinet has many – every variation of tone-colour must be brought into play to combat monotony, to impart interest, warmth, and vivacity to interpretation. And here we may ask whether the use of *vibrato* is desirable or even legitimate to achieve these ends. This is plainly a controversial question. By *vibrato* is meant, of course, studied regular oscillation of tone produced by the diaphragm, the throat muscles, or the lips, not the momentary quiver or flickering of tone caused by the player's passing and natural reaction to the emotional content of the music. It has been for some centuries an essential part of the technique of the string-player – string-tone would be dead without it – and no innovation even in wind music. It has long been known to the flautist; Nicholson and other early 19th-century flaut-ists were much given to 'vibration', though recently it has fallen somewhat into desuetude. It is a striking feature of certain schools of oboe-playing; organs have for many centuries possessed not only the tremulant, but *Unda Maris* and *Voix Célestes* stops in which two ranks of pipes are slightly mistuned to give a shimmering effect. Nor is it entirely un-known to the clarinet. Glinka, for instance, instructs the clarinettist to use it in two of the movements of his *Trio pathétique* of 1827. But only of very recent years has the use of *vibrato* in clarinet-playing been revived, if indeed it ever existed to any extent. It is quite unknown east of the Rhine, where a perfectly straight even tone has ever been and is still insisted upon. It had a passing vogue in France, but to the best of the writer's knowledge is now less used than it was; it is in fact only in England and particularly in America that the employment of it has become quite recently a burning question. It is, of course, firstly and lastly, a matter of taste in both player and listener. If *vibrato* is used at all, it is hardly necessary to say that it must be used sparingly and with great discretion. Excessive, even regular, use of it cannot but offend in calling to mind the worst excesses of jazz technique and of the theatre organ. Other obvious dangers are damage to purity of tone and particularly to accuracy of intonation and to the musical line in classical music. Further, it may be suggested that any oscillation of tone is far more marked in wind than in stringed instruments, since the pulsations are necessarily wider, slower, and more obtrusive. It may be suggested, too, that *vibrato* is more suited to wind instruments of tenuous or stringy tone, the flute or oboe, than to the clarinet with its complex and highly charged harmonic texture. Only in certain registers of the basset-horn and the bass clarinet is any approximation to string-tone discernible.

But it is plainly first and last a question of taste. *Vibrato* should be ideally a matter of intuition, of natural sensitivity and response, not of simulated or forced emotion; it must never degenerate into a mannerism. A shimmering or wavering of the *voix célestes* variety is quite a different matter. This may well add an ethereal quality to the tone. It may be observed not infrequently in military music when many clarinets are playing together in unison. It is all but an impossibility to tune all the instruments exactly to each other, and so there results from this slight mistuning an undulation of tone which is by no means unpleasing in the open air. It is not to be encouraged, however, in the concert hall and some conductors insist upon their clarinettists using not only carefully matched instruments by the same maker, but identical fingerings as well.

NOTES

[1] E. G. Richardson, *Acoustics of Orchestral Instruments*, London, 1929, p. 54.

[2] A. Carse, *Musical Wind Instruments*, London, 1939, p. 22.

[3] Described and illustrated in his *The Science of Musical Sounds*, New York, 1922, pp. 78 *et seq.*

[4] ibid. p. 201.

[5] P.R.M.A., LXIII, 1946–47, pp. 67 *et seq.*

[6] op. cit., p. 50.

[7] Here C. Forsyth, *Orchestration*, 2nd edn. London, 1935, may be consulted with advantage.

CHAPTER 5

The bore; tone-holes; influence of materials on tone
Problems of pitch and intonation

THE SUMMARY review of the constituents of tone which occupied the last chapter may lead in the present to an examination of the resonator and some problems of pitch and intonation. And first the *bore*. This is the heart of the instrument, the part to which the maker should and usually does give the best of his skill. In textbooks it is described as cylindrical, a rough generalisation and far from the truth. It is seldom cylindrical for more than two-thirds of its length and more often than not for considerably less. To take a B flat instrument of modern manufacture as an example.[1] It is 67 cm. in length from the tip of the mouthpiece to the bottom of the bell. The mouthpiece itself is conical, wider, that is, at the base than at the top; this is succeeded by a reversed cone which extends from the barrel to the speaker-hole, then a cylindrical portion, succeeded in turn by a longer and more pronounced cone ending in a widely flared bell. Here are the measurements:

> Total length – 67 cm.
> Length of conical mouthpiece – 7 cm.
> Length of barrel and reversed cone in upper joint – 8·5 cm.
> Length of conical portion of lower joint and bell – 15 cm.

The non-cylindrical portions, it will be seen, add up to 30·5 cm., the cylindrical to 36·5, little more than one-half of the whole. Some makers omit the reversed cone which follows the mouthpiece, others extend, others shorten, the cone at the bottom. Fifteen centimetres may however be taken as an average length.[2] The internal diameter is of the very greatest importance. The early clarinets had a bore of 13 mm., rather less than more, and sometimes narrowed at the lower end.[3] By the 19th century the diameter had been increased by a millimetre, and by the middle of the century to 14·75 or 14·85 mm., which may be taken as an average of modern bores. Eugène Albert, the famous Brussels maker, favoured a still greater diameter, 15 mm. or more. One or two modern

makers have followed his example, but most of them are faithful to
14·85.[4] Two points must be borne in mind. Bores are measured in thou-
sandths of an inch, in fractions of a millimetre, and every bore is a
compromise. An organ-builder, planning a stop to give the compass of
the clarinet, would alter his scale (i.e. the ratio of bore to pipe-length)
at frequent intervals. A commonly adopted scale (bore) is $1\frac{1}{8}$ inches at
middle (2 feet) c; 1 inch at (1 foot) c''; $\frac{7}{8}$ inch at (6 inches) c'''. In common practice the bore is changed with every seventh and twelfth pipe;
some six or seven variations of bore, it will be noticed, within the
compass of the orchestral instrument. The clarinet-maker plainly cannot
do this. Guided by experience, by rule of thumb if you like, he selects
a bore which will give the player maximum intensity and evenness
throughout the entire compass. As with all compromises the results are
not entirely happy. It may be said that in general the bore is too small
for maximum power and vigour in some parts of the *chalumeau*, and far
too large for most of the *extreme* notes. It is well suited to the *clarinet*
register. The bore is always circular or, rather, is contained within a
circular tube, for ease of manufacture. Given the same capacity it
might just as well be oval or even square. A square body-tube would in
some cases be better adapted to take the mechanism, particularly when
the keywork is complicated, as in the Schaffner clarinet. Here the inventor relies on long thin tracker rods of steel, five on each side of his
square-bodied instrument, to close the 20 tone-holes, which are located
in line along the top. Such intricate, closely-fitting mechanism could
not be adapted with any success to a round body-tube. Another cogent
reason for the exact precision of the bore is that the length of the instrument is determined by its diameter. It has been observed that, with any
given length of tube, and a given mouthpiece, the narrower the bore the
lower in pitch the resulting note and, further, the richer in harmonics.
The converse is also true: the wider the bore the sharper the pitch and
the poorer in texture. A B flat clarinet, 67 cm. in length, with a bore of
13 mm., would be well below normal pitch and it would overblow with
great facility to the top of the compass. With the hole dimensions now
customary, wide bores tend to sharpen harmonics and to make others
refractory, notably the fifth. The present bore is, as has been said, a
compromise, and is designed to do the best possible for the player in all
registers.

It is a point of honour with the best makers to finish the bore with the
greatest care, leaving it not only exactly dimensioned but with a mirror-
like polish. Experience shows that this careful finish does add greatly
to the flexibility of tone and ease of production. And it is to the player's

profit to maintain this careful finish. Any deterioration or swelling inwards of the bore owing to excess of moisture may have devastating effects on intonation, so carefully are its proportions calculated.

When the finishing reamer has completed the cylindrical portion the cones are put in. The bore at the top may be enlarged by two or three reamers to the extent of a millimetre, while the joint is running in the lathe. The cone at the end of the bottom joint is more pronounced, increasing in 8 cm. of length from 14·85 mm. to 22 mm., while the flare of the bell increases from 22 to 60 mm. in 7 cm. of length. The cone may be gradually and smoothly developed or made in a series of overlapping cones according to the practice of the maker. Generally speaking a conical enlargement at the top of a tube has a flattening effect, placed at the bottom it sharpens the general pitch, but perhaps more importantly the upper one widens the twelfth, while the lower closes it up. The bottom cone, too, may be, and generally is, made in the lathe, but a conscientious maker may add final touches with a hand-reamer when the instrument is finished. This conical enlargement is not nearly so pronounced in early clarinets. In the earliest there is no flaring at all and furthermore no bell. With the development of the modern bell at the turn of the 18th century there is at first a very short enlargement, but this did not attain its present proportions till midway through the 19th century.

The bore of the B flat and A clarinets is in common practice the same. With the C it already begins to decrease, and in the high A flat, only 36·5 mm. in length, it is seldom more than 9 mm. in diameter. Conversely, as the clarinet is lengthened so the diameter of the bore is increased. But the increase is much less than might be expected. Thus a modern basset-horn, 42 inches in length, has a bore of only 16 mm., and a bass clarinet, at least double the length of the soprano B flat, is provided with a bore only some 9 mm. wider.

To pass to a consideration of the tube. The resonant body in all wind instruments is *imprimis* the air-column. The chief function of the tube is to define this column within exact geometrical limits by means of a bore of accurate dimensions. Secondary functions are to provide toneholes, by means of which the column may be shortened or lengthened, and to carry the mechanism by which this process of shortening and lengthening may be achieved. Some considerations affecting the material of which the tube is formed have already been discussed. There remains the vexed question of the influence of the material of the tube on the air-column and ultimately upon the tone. On no other question is there such diversity of opinion among acousticians, or such divergence between theoretician and player. Opinions of 18th- and early 19th-century writers[5] are distinctly in favour of the material exercising no small influence on the tone, but the great mid-Victorian authorities, Mahillon and Blaikley, were vigorous opponents of the theory. Since both were practical musical instrument-makers of repute their opinions are entitled to respect. Of recent years, however, a considerable body of opinion has declared in favour of the material exercising subtle influences upon the tone. The player has never had any doubt of it. It is only necessary to study any 18th- or 19th-century woodwind tutor to find the author, frequently an eminent player, expressing his preferences in the matter of various materials. And if the question is no longer discussed in modern tutors it is presumably because the clarinettist is satisfied with the tone he gets from African blackwood, the most widely used material, or is indifferent to further experiments.[6]

Two quite distinct problems are involved – the effect of the material on pitch and intensity of sound, the *quantitative* effect, and the effect of the tube on timbre or tone-colour, the *qualitative*. The alternate and continuous condensation and rarefaction of the air-column within the tube set up a certain measure of vibration in the surrounding walls, and these may obviously be encouraged or restrained by the material of the body. Every player is aware of this; of the difference between a body-tube which is alive, and one that is completely dead and devoid of any vibration. Plainly a thick-walled tube of dense hardwood will not lend itself to easy vibration and will give a dull flat tone devoid of brilliancy. On the other hand, a thin-walled tube will vibrate too readily. In both cases much of the energy of the player will be wasted; in the first, in trying to extract tone from a heavy inert piece of wood or metal, in the second, in striving to gain intensity and carrying power from a tube which is too weak to produce it. The best results will be obtained from an instrument in which the thickness of the walls is proportioned to the density of the material. Wood varies considerably from billet to billet but the standard gauges of the maker are seldom modified to suit individual cases. This is one of the chief disadvantages of mass production. Many instruments would benefit by thinning and not a few with additional weight. In general, tubes of the softer woods should be rather thicker than those made from the harder and denser varieties. At present thicknesses vary from maker to maker, from rather over 5 mm. to 7 mm. Recent experiments have shown that at least one part of the instrument will take with advantage a greater weight of wood than it usually receives. This is the bell. It has been demonstrated that a bell of substantial, but carefully adjusted, thickness will give better nourished bottom notes than one of more meagre proportions. Here too the form of the cone is more important than is usually supposed.[7] In this connexion a note kindly supplied by a Dutch correspondent, M. Will Jansen, is of particular interest. In speaking of the Dutch mid-19th-century instrument-maker Geisler of Amsterdam, he says: 'The bell-joints of his clarinets were very particular. Many clarinets that had not volume enough and were of moderate timbre were at once enormously improved by fitting a bell-joint of Geisler to them.'

Much of the foregoing will be well known, at any rate, to the player. The *qualitative* effect of material presents a more elusive problem. We have seen that quality of tone or timbre is determined by the presence and intensity of certain partials, whether low or high, within a note, aided to some extent by a formant. Is it not possible that the varying molecular structures of various woods have subtle influences which favour certain partials at the expense of others? It has long been the experience of organ-builders that certain tone-qualities can only be obtained from certain metals or certain alloys. Thus, to emphasise lower partials lead alloys or pipe-metal are necessary; to gain brilliance from higher partials zinc is employed. Pure tin again gives an entirely characteristic tone.[8] Where mixed ranks of wood and metal pipes are employed it requires all the skill of the voicer to conceal the junction of the two materials. Wood is not metal, it is true, but to endow various woods with varying degrees of resonance and of structure is not perhaps too fanciful. Experience, however, is a surer guide than theory. It has long been known that of all woods boxwood, unsuitable though it be for other reasons, gives the sweetest, most expressive, tone, and cocus and African blackwood the fullest and most brilliant.

To sum up, the formula for a good-toned instrument is, in the writer's opinion, that the material of which it is made should be homogeneous. If the body cannot be made in one piece, the joints should be cut from the same log; failing that, they should be carefully matched. It is also desirable that the wood should be split and not sawn, and that the thickness of the walls should be most carefully proportioned to the density of the material.

The tone-holes of the earliest clarinets numbered ten – seven in front, and one behind for the left thumb and two, closed by keys, just below the mouthpiece. By the first decades of the last century the number had risen to twenty, and by the mid-century to twenty-four. Here it has remained constant, though some complex systems of fingering have added four or five more. It might be supposed that the holes would be of equal size and placed at equal distances along the tube. Nothing is further from the truth; their placing and sizing are both empirical, the result of the maker's and player's long experience. It would seem that in theory a tone-hole should be of the same diameter as the bore so that the air-column may be cut off exactly and completely at any given point; in practice it is very considerably smaller, small enough to be covered easily with the finger-tip. Further, these compromise-sized holes form a graduated series, since it has been found empirically that this makes for good intonation in the twelfths. Large holes of flute-size would necessitate the fitting of finger-plates, which have never been popular with clarinettists. The holes are circular from tradition and for ease of manufacture and stopping. On one clarinet, however, the Schaffner, they are of quite divergent shape and size. Here the holes are narrow oblongs which increase in area with mathematical gradation from the mouthpiece to the bell end. Twenty finger-plates are required to cover them. The padded plates would absorb much of the tone were the holes of normal size.

The distance between the holes for successive semitones is fairly uniform on the upper joint; on the lower, the distances gradually increase, so too the size of the holes, till the bell is reached with the largest aperture of all. If the holes near the mouthpiece are too large, the tone will be coarse and uneven; if too small, the tone will be muffled and veiled for lack of venting. The larger holes on the lower joint cannot be taken beyond a certain diameter in the interest of brilliance without serious risk of wildness of tone. The experienced maker seeks uniformity and evenness of scale above all else, and is not prepared to sacrifice it to brilliance. Briefly, the smaller hole keeps the harmonics in, the larger lets them out. This crude, unscientific statement is amply borne out by the example of the bassoon. Here attempts to enlarge the oblique holes in the wing-joint have always resulted in denaturing the tone, in robbing it of all interest.[9] The phenomenon has not, so far as the writer is aware, been explained by acousticians. But, if a small or medium hole gives better tonal results than a large one, it must be adequately vented.[10] The tone must at all costs be clear, crisp, and unmuffled. By adequate venting we mean that the air must have unimpeded egress, not only from the speaking hole, but from as many holes beneath it as possible. If only one hole is available for the escape of the air, the tone will be not only veiled but flattened in pitch. Two open holes beneath are generally sufficient, and two or three small holes are of better effect than one of larger diameter. Further, it is found in practice that, if for constructional reasons it is necessary to misplace a hole, it is better to locate a smaller hole higher up the tube than a larger one lower down.

Not unconnected with the foregoing is the question 'does a wind instrument improve with age?' Certainly a fair or good one will improve, but no amount of use will make a good out of a bad instrument. However well matched or chosen, however well seasoned the joints, regular use will season and temper the wood still further by alternating heat and cold. Further, the enclosed column of air exercises a subtle, but certain, effect upon the molecular structure of the body, causing the tone to become more and more flexible and smoothing away any asperities which may have been present in the new instrument. Intonation is quite a different matter. In a well-cared-for instrument this should remain constant, or even improve, as the structure of the wood adapts itself to the methods and fingerings of the player. But should the bore swell inwards at the top – a not uncommon occurrence – should tone-holes be lessened in diameter by accumulation of dust, so intonation will suffer and the tone become dull and flat. Sharpening is far less common. This can only be caused by an enlargement of the bore through careless cleaning with mop or pull-through or by the hollowing or wearing of the wood round the tone-holes through constant pressure of the fingers.

Tone-holes are very seldom of uniform diameter from the surface of the body to their junction with the bore. The holes of 18th-century clarinets, deceptively small to the eye, will be found to be two or three times larger at the bottom than at the top. This is a very ancient practice in wind-instrument manufacture. It was found no doubt that, while a small hole was easier to cover, a conical hole gave better tone and more of it. Further, when playing strongly, undercutting makes for easy blowing and for increased flexibility. The tone seems more directly under control. It is, too, a valuable means of sharpening a note without enlarging the hole at the surface. The practice is still commonly employed in making high-grade instruments. It is very necessary in an instrument with the thick walls of the clarinet. The modern method of removing the wood is to insert a fraise pivoted on a rod up the bore. This is rotated from outside by the shank of a vertical drill. Thus the hole may be enlarged to any extent, as the fraise is drawn while rotating towards the surface. In boring the tone- and pillar-holes the modern maker makes use of a 'setting-out machine'. This is a combination of a drilling and milling machine. In essentials it consists of a table which can be traversed longitudinally beneath a vertical drill. The joint is mounted on the table, so that the cutter may be brought to bear at any point. There is no lateral motion, but the joint may be rotated, an elaborate dividing head giving any desired degree of angularity. It is a perfect instrument for mass production. The results are accurate and uniform, and satisfactory too, if the keenness and profile of the cutter are carefully maintained. The older makers employed a simpler device. This was a perforated tube or sleeve of brass, familiarly known as the *chemise*, which was slipped over the prepared joint. The holes in the tube gave the exact position of every hole to be drilled.

Inseparably linked with the dimensions of the bore and the tone-holes are the problems of pitch and intonation. Pitch presents few problems to the maker, but many to the player. Briefly, a clarinet is built and tuned by the manufacturer to one pitch, and to one pitch only. At the time of writing the standard international pitch, fixed in 1939, is $a' = 440$ cycles per second, at 68°F.[11] Within living memory there have been at least two other pitches in Britain, viz. *Old Philharmonic* or High Pitch and the pre-1939 *New Philharmonic* of Flat Pitch with a' fixed at 452 and 439 c.p.s. respectively. In France and Germany, before the international agreement, *Diapason Normal* with a frequency of 435 c.p.s. was nominally in force with a tendency to rise to 436 or 437 cycles. For orchestral pitch always rises; it never sinks, and this is where the problem for the player comes in. Say the strings, ever in search of brilliancy, rise higher and higher to 443 or 444, as is often the case, what is the clarinettist with his instrument tuned to 440 to do? If he replaces his standard barrel with a shorter he will merely sharpen the throat notes and the top joint of his instrument. Lipping or tightening the embouchure will effect some slight sharpening of the lower notes, but he cannot maintain the strain for long, and in any case his tone will suffer. Conversely, should the temperature of the hall fall below the temperature at which his instrument is tuned he will never be able to get up to pitch at all. Quite shortly, the pitch of the clarinet is immutable. The player cannot, like the flautist or oboist, vary his pitch appreciably, without devastating effects upon intonation and embouchure. One vibration, or possibly two, up or down is all that can be contrived with safety. A clarinet tuned to *Diapason Normal* cannot possibly play at 439 or 440, nor can an instrument tuned to 440 be forced up to 444 or 445. A considerable shortening of the tube with drastic reboring and re-location of the tone-holes would be necessary to bridge even this small lacuna in pitch. What, then, is the remedy? Surely to impress two things upon conductors. Firstly, that the clarinet must take over the hereditary office of the oboe in tuning the orchestra in virtue of its immutability and, secondly, that the pitch once given should be maintained at a perfectly uniform level. But unfortunately conductors look for brilliancy in their orchestras, and are not inclined to sympathise too readily with the troubles of clarinettists.

—6 * *

If a fine tone is the first requisite of a good player, correctness of intonation is a good second. Most in fact would reverse the order. To provide the player with a correctly tuned instrument is the primary duty of a conscientious maker. And it is no easy task to elicit 45 well-tuned notes of even quality and intensity from a tube little more than two feet in length. It is only fair to the maker to state the magnitude of his task and to give him all due praise when he achieves success. Stated quite briefly, the basic problem is to tune the twelfths to the fundamental; the *clarinet* register is the chief source of trouble. It is not difficult to build a clarinet with a good *chalumeau* and *throat* registers from written *e* to *b′ flat*; nor is it difficult again with all the wealth of fingering at his disposal for the experienced player with a good embouchure to ascend from *c‴ sharp* to *g‴* or beyond with satisfactory intonation. It is far more difficult to achieve satisfactory results in the *clarinet* register, tonally the best part of the instrument, and the region in which the player is expected to excel. At least one writer, a clarinettist of the highest repute, states definitely in his tutor that, if the *chalumeau* register is correctly tuned, the twelfths must be flat. He counsels the player to make his choice of a sharp *chalumeau* and well-tuned twelfths, or of flat twelfths and an accurate *chalumeau*.[12] At least one clarinet has been devised in which the depression of the speaker-key opens a series of small vents alongside the finger-holes to sharpen the harmonics.[13] These are desperate courses and a careful maker will go far to smooth out the discrepancies of pitch. The basic cause of the trouble is the speaker. The air-column cannot be divided into the segments necessary to give the twelfths without a speaker, and strictly every separate note requires a different position of the speaker for perfect results. This is of course impossible without mechanism too complex to be practical. So one speaker in one fixed position has to do the duty of several. This is bad enough, but the problem is aggravated by the necessity of using the speaker as a note-hole for middle *b′ flat* as well. For this purpose the hole, to give an adequate note, must be of a certain diameter, and this diameter does not happen to be the ideal for overblowing. It is in fact far too large. And so the maker is as usual forced to compromise in making the speaker-hole of a size to serve its dual purpose as adequately as possible. It is in effecting a satisfactory compromise that his skill and experience will be shown. But with all his skill some discrepancy in certain twelfths will be discernible; and a tendency to flatness will be aggravated at the bottom of the instrument by inadequate venting. Generally speaking the least satisfactory notes in this register are *d″* and *e″*. The next open hole to the hole speaking *d″* is some two and a half inches distant, and it is only by a clever manipulation of the bottom cone or very judicious undercutting of the tone-holes that the maker makes these notes sound other than veiled and muffled. To overcome these deficiencies in intonation, to which he is often more sensitive than the hearer, the player has various means at his disposal. He can tighten his embouchure for some of the lower notes; for some of the higher notes he can open lower keys to give some additional ventage to the hole speaking. On the upper joint, too, he has some variety of fingering to help him. In any case a badly veiled or defective note will only be really noticeable in a solo passage in slow time. The real bug-bear is the middle *b flat*, particularly prominent, for instance, as a sustained note in the slow movement of Beethoven's Septet. Here he can use the side *b flat* trill-key or, in many clarinets, he can extract strength from weakness by dropping the second and third fingers of the left hand upon their appropriate holes, though not with equal success on all makes of instrument. The maker has done his best to help him here. Many mechanical devices have been patented to improve this note. In most of them a separate note-hole of suitable size is provided which is opened when the speaker-key is depressed in conjunction with the a' key. Thus the usual fingering is preserved. The mechanical problem would seem a simple one, but demands quite elaborate mechanism if its action is to be instantaneous and reliable. So far no mechanism has been found to satisfy these conditions, especially that of unfailing reliability; and the innate conservatism of the player, always opposed to the smallest innovation, gives little encouragement to the maker. It is, however, a prime desideratum. For, if the speaker-hole could be relieved of its dual purpose, it could be moved higher up the instrument to a position better suited to the production of the twelfths. It could, too, be reduced in size, also to its advantage. (See also p. 118, note 12.)

The method of tuning varies from maker to maker. Many clarinets will not be tuned at all. These *instruments de pacotille* are exact copies of a standard model and, if the model is a good one and if the materials agree in density and texture with the prototype, the results may be satisfactory or fairly satisfactory. The conscientious manufacturer, however, will test and, if necessary, tune each instrument individually by tuning forks, harmonium, or stroboscope. The method matters little, whether by thirds, fifths, octaves, or twelfths, provided the tuner has an accurate ear and infinite patience.[14]

The general methods of tuning are well known. A note is raised in pitch by underboring or enlarging the tone-hole with a reamer; in other words by shortening the air-column or, alternatively, by enlarging adjacent holes below it. To flatten a note the hole must be diminished in size, a less satisfactory process, involving the use of shellac or the insertion of a bush in bad cases. It is seldom possible, however, to improve one note without impairing the quality of others, since tone-holes often serve for two or three notes or more. To take two examples. The first finger-hole on the upper joint serves amongst other purposes as the tone-hole for *f'*, for its twelfth *c'''*, for *f'''* *sharp* in a widely used fingering, and also, a most important purpose, as a vent-hole to aid in the production of many of the extreme notes by means of the 5th harmonic. The utmost caution must be used in enlarging this hole to raise a possibly flat *f'* or *c'''*, or more harm than good may be effected. In any case, there are other ways of sharpening these notes. Again, the sixth finger-hole from the top serves as the tone-hole for *a* in the *chalumeau* and for *e* in the *clarinet* register. The latter is apt only too often to be weak and veiled, and, since it is a vital and prominent note in many solos – its importance, for instance, as the sustained opening note in the obbligato to Schubert's *Der Hirt auf dem Felsen* will leap to mind – it is tempting to enlarge or to undercut the tone-hole. The results will be not seldom disastrous to intonation. The *chalumeau a* will be found impossibly sharp, so too *b* and its twelfth, *f''* *sharp* in the *clarinet* register, as well as *c'''* *sharp*, the fifth harmonic of the funda-mental. One weak note will be replaced by three or four of impossible sharpness. The reamer must then be used with the greatest discretion and sure experience. The maker will often prefer to gain his effects by adjusting the top and bottom cones, or by manipulation of the mouth-piece. Undercutting or fraising of the tone-holes has its peculiar dangers. This method of shortening the air-column may well impair the uni-formity and exact dimensions of the bore. Wisely used, the flaring of the tone-holes makes for increased dynamic flexibility; used to excess, it may damage quite seriously the crispness and definition of the note. Where the excavations are considerable and adjacent the tone may become fuzzy and indeterminate. As a rule the holes of the upper joint are less undercut than those of the lower.

Considerable adjustments may be made by varying the mouthpiece. This too calls for expert guidance or great experience, since it is a generally received principle that the bore of the mouthpiece must be identical with that of the body of the instrument. (But see p. 61, note 3.) The bore of the modern mouthpiece is usually conical. This was not always the case. Some of the earliest clarinets were fitted with cylin-drically-bored mouthpieces, and this form of bore was long popular in England, Belgium, and Germany. And to some extent it still is. Speaking quite generally, when coupled to a large bore of 15 mm. or thereabouts, the cylindrical mouthpiece will give excellent twelfths, but it is less kind to the higher harmonics which are apt to be rather sharp and piercing. To replace a conical mouthpiece with a cylindrical without upsetting general intonation, it is usually necessary to shorten the barrel by the width of a ring. Every player will have his own formulae to deal with this difficult problem of intonation. In the writer's experience a mouthpiece with a bore slightly smaller than that of the instrument will tend to sharpen flat notes at the bottom of the instrument, while a bore only a hair's breadth bigger will have the opposite effect. But embouchures, lays, and strength of reeds, vary so much from player to player that it is hazardous to lay down any definite rules. Nevertheless, it is the duty of the conscientious player to have some understanding of these matters, at least as far as they affect himself. Recently the present writer [P.B.] was told by a music-teacher, in a responsible position, that she used a No. 3 mouthpiece by a very well-known firm with their No. 3 reed, without having any idea what sort of lay was implied, or whether the reeds mentioned were 'hard', 'medium', or 'soft' in the rather loose terminology of commerce.

Not the least important of the maker's duties is to attend to the careful regulation of his product. It is often neglected, and this neglect is frequently responsible for dull tone or imperfect notes. By regulation is here meant the careful adjustment of the rise and fall of keys and the fitting of suitable pads. Pads are a necessary evil, and the ideal pad has yet to be designed. It is surprising how much tone a bulging pad, poised too near the tone-hole, can absorb. For this reason covered-hole clarinets have never been popular with professional players. Pads should be as flat and thin as is consistent with the proper occlusion of the hole.

NOTES

[1] It now seems a pity that F.G.R. did not name the clarinet from which he took these measurements. In recent years the internal dimensions adopted by different makers vary so markedly that it is hardly possible to cite an average example. Further, the coning-out of the top joint is omitted by many makers except as a device to adjust parts of the scale (i.e. Selmer, Leblanc, and Boosey and Hawkes instruments produced during the last two or three years). On the other hand, the coning of the lower may extend the length of the whole joint, or it may not continue beyond the *f sharp/c sharp* hole.

[2] But a selection of well-made clarinets of 1969 showed a bottom cone length of 18·5–21 cm. As in many other matters, stability has not yet

come to the clarinet, and no doubt future makers will continue to make adjustments – unless all should agree to adopt a standard formula which nowadays *could* be derived from recent mathematical analyses and the application of the computer!

[3] This contraction was arrived at empirically, and had the effect of widening the twelfths in instruments with relatively small holes.

[4] Again the most recent tendency is to increase the cylindrical part of the bore to 15·05–15·25. As is mentioned in various places in this book, German makers favour a slightly smaller average bore than the French or British, and at present this stands at 14·8–15·0 mm. (Hammerschmidt, Püchner, Uebel). *Per contra*, a brand new Buffet-Crampon measured in 1969 had a bore cylinder of 14·6 mm. and a throat-cone and barrel of 14·8 maximum.

[5] Rockstro, op. cit., Section 242.

[6] The now accepted difference in 'feel' between instruments of different materials is explained by the modern theory of boundary-layer effects between air-columns and their containing walls. As a result of his own experiments, A. H. Benade states that in the laboratory a 2 per cent difference in these effects is detectable between a tube of wood and one of gold, but that the player is immensely more sensitive than the present exploratory techniques. As a player himself, he judges that a mere ½ per cent difference is sensed.

[7] In this again the practice of different makers varies considerably. The inner profile of the bell may be a simple cone, a series of cones, or a smooth curve. This must be considered in relation to the tube profile as a whole, and there are many ways of obtaining similar results in respect of tone colour and internal tuning.

[8] The work of C. P. Boner on organ-pipes tends to cast some doubt on this point; nevertheless the opinion is widely held among organ-builders and pipe men.

[9] Alterations to the traditional dimensions of the wing-holes on the bassoon have changed the 'cut-off' frequency and thus affected the harmonic content of the complex tones.

[10] This is indeed true. In modern theory it is not possible to think of holes singly; one must think of a *set* of holes in their mutual relationship.

[11] In the U.S.A. the standard is established at 72 °F.

[12] This appears almost a counsel of despair which many players and teachers would nowadays challenge. There is more than one factor involved. A general flatness of twelfths can be blamed on the existence of the taper which leads to the bell, but it is quite possible to construct an overall well-tuned clarinet which appears to have wide twelfths at either end of the scale. This is due to the influence of the speaker-hole, which tends to widen the interval when its situation is, so to speak, 'off the node'. The extent to which this occurs has been determined from actual examples and can be expressed mathematically, and some improvement can be secured by adjustment of the relative diameter and depth of the speaker-tube. As a rule, if an instrument be adjusted to give good played twelfths the tone will suffer somewhat, so once again we are faced with

a compromise, though not that suggested by the eminent player mentioned in the text above. There are more ways of killing a cat – etc.

[13] The Charles E. Potter clarinet, British patent 264, 180.

[14] Detailed instructions for tuning 13-key clarinets are given by Iwan Müller in his *Méthode* and by the Belgian maker Tuerlinckx, in his papers edited by R. van Aerde in his *Les Tuerlinckx, luthiers à Malines*, 1914.

CHAPTER 6

Cane; reeds; mouthpiece

LITTLE IS KNOWN of the reed in the 18th century or of the provenance of the cane from which it was manufactured. Of its size we can form a fair opinion from the examination of old mouthpieces. The mouthpiece of the early C clarinet by Klenig, illustrated in Fig. 2, takes a reed 15 mm. in width. It need hardly be said that this size of reed is excessive for a bore of 12 to 13 mm. and was soon drastically reduced. A 4-key English clarinet by an unknown maker, which may be dated *c.* 1765, shows a substantial reduction in width to approximately 12 mm. Even this width may be considered generous when the size of the bore seldom exceeded 13 mm. As the bore was increased in the early 19th century, so the reed was enlarged until in mid-century both were more or less standardised, the bore at 14·85 mm., the reed at 13 mm. These measurements are for the B flat and A clarinets. As the clarinet is raised in pitch and shortened in length, so the reed is narrowed. Conversely, as the clarinet is lengthened, so the reed is enlarged. Thus the high A flat requires a reed only 10 mm. in width, while the bass cannot manage with less than 18 mm. Some standardisation of size was obviously a necessity as soon as the mass production of reeds by machinery was introduced. No doubt mechanical methods were introduced about the middle of the 19th century, since already in 1869 Oscar Comettant in *La Musique et les instruments de musique* alludes to 'nouveaux procédés mécaniques' employed by Kroll of Paris. Massabo (*c.* 1867?) on the other hand still employed the more laborious methods of hand manufacture. In the 18th century, if many players preferred to make their own, commercial reeds nevertheless were obtainable. *Circa* 1750 John Johnson of London was advertising his reeds for bassoons and hautboys, and some thirty years later Longman & Broderip had added reeds for 'clarinets, vaux humanes and bagpipes' to the above. Churchwardens' accounts, too, show constant purchases of reeds for church bands at prices of three-pence and fourpence apiece for the clarinet and of one shilling for the bassoon. Today the vast majority of clarinettists rely on the commercial machine-made product and on their acquired skill or on the knowledge kindly imparted by others to make good its defects. Here and there will be found the player who prefers to fashion his own or will send his mouthpiece to the small maker to have reeds made to his own lay and his own design. This, so the writer is informed, is still a not uncommon practice in Germany, where, too, reed-making is looked upon as part of the clarinettist's curriculum. But whatever the process of manufacture may be, the material is the same – *Arundo donax*.

This cane grows in all parts of the world, in the tropics and in more temperate climes, choosing by preference alluvial soil, marshes, or the banks of rivers. It grows better than anywhere else on the shores of the Mediterranean, and best of all round Fréjus in the province of Var. The siliceous, micaceous soil of the alluvial plains, dry on the surface but with water only some two or three feet below, produces a robuster, more virile, and resilient cane for reed-making than richer soils elsewhere. There may be some rare elements contained in the soil – some growers are confident that there are – the climate, constant sunshine tempered by the dry and intensely cold *mistral*, may be peculiarly suitable, or the growers may have secrets in seasoning their cane unpossessed by others. It is the case of the grape-vine over again where the soil of France produces a better grape for wine-making than the more generous soils of other countries. Around Fréjus the growing of *roseaux* is a long-established industry, not, perhaps, the main industry which is fruit- and vine-growing. The cane grows freely everywhere, along the banks of streams and rivers, and in hedgerows to provide shade and shelter for gardens and orchards. It is cultivated for reed-making as a rule in unenclosed plantations, traversed with alleys to provide free circulation for the air. The cultivations are weeded regularly and furnished with irrigation trenches. The canes reach their maximum thickness after a year's growth and their full height, 15 to 20 feet, after another year or so. In January or February they are harvested. There follows a period of seasoning. The canes are gathered into bundles a foot or so in thickness and stacked out of doors to dry. The bundles may be propped against trees or buildings or built into a wigwam; they may be stored in a roofed but wall-less shed. During their second summer of seasoning the bundles are undone and the canes are sorted out. Only those of the best quality are selected for reed-making; inferior growths are set aside for fishing-rods, walking-sticks, or assigned to baser industrial purposes. Cogolin, some miles to the south-east of Fréjus, produces cane of the most suitable thickness for clarinet reeds. The growths selected for musical purposes are next cut into four-foot lengths and laid on trestles for a week or so to ripen in the sun. Thus the green cane acquires the rich golden or sometimes mottled hue which shows that it is ready for

reed-making. Two years at least should elapse between the harvesting
and the making of the finished reed. These processes of growing, cutting,
and seasoning are curiously akin to those practised by the Greeks close
upon 2,500 years ago. No one could be more exacting in the choice of
cane for his double reed than the Greek *auletes*. The cane was obtained
from the shores of Lake Copais in Boeotia or from the banks of a lake
in Phrygia. It was cut down after two years of growth in September or,
at a later period, in the summer solstice, and allowed to season for at
least three years. Only then was it judged suitable for making up. A
further period of seasoning was usual for the finished reed. The secret
of good cane lies of course in the seasoning, in the slow natural ripening.
This cannot be hurried or abbreviated, nor can it be replaced by artificial
drying without disastrous results to the user.

At no time has the cane situation been worse than at the present.
Great damage was done to the plantations during the Second World
War, while the demands are enormous and ever increasing. And other
industries are competing for the cane. So to meet current needs much
partially seasoned cane has been released. It may comfort the harassed
clarinettist to know that cane has long been deteriorating; the decline
has not been sudden. As early as 1802 Xavier Lefèvre, quoted by J.-F.
Malot in his *L'Art de bien faire une anche de clarinette*, 1820, complained
of unseasoned green cane, and in 1869 Comettant in the work already
quoted says: 'les anches de hautbois, de clarinettes et de bassons sont,
à l'époque actuelle, inférieures à ce qu'elles furent autrefois, bien qu'elles
soient mieux faites'. Many other similar statements could be cited. In
passing it may be noted that Malot ranked Italian cane above the
French.

How is the situation to be improved? Two obvious courses suggest
themselves. To grow better cane elsewhere, or to find a substitute for
the natural product. The late war gave a fillip to both these remedies.
Some success was gained in finding or providing new sources. More
perseverance might have freed the musician from a tiresome monopoly;
but with the termination of the conflict the clarinettist, as might have
been expected, returned automatically to his old sources of supply.
Surely suitable sites for cane cultivation are to be found? The product
of them could hardly be worse than the cane at present available.[1]

The synthetic reed has long taxed the brain of the inventor. Experiments, too, have been made with other materials. Tradition reports the
early use of ivory, of bone, of whalebone, of lance and other woods, and
later of ebonite. The writer has been unable to check the evidence for
these assertions which find their way into print from time to time. They

are not inherently improbable, reflecting as they do the unceasing and pathetic efforts of the player to free himself for ever from the problems and unreasoning behaviour of cane. The recent development of plastics has produced the plastic and semi-plastic reed, the reed of plexiglass and perspex. Recently, too, a return has been made to metal, to silver in particular, with some success. A very obvious disadvantage of all these non-vegetable products is that they are uncommonly unkind to the lips, and have an uncomfortable feel about them.[2] They lack responsiveness, too, and the player is inclined to suspect them, not without reason, of a harsh, metallic tone. No, the fact must be faced; there is no substitute for cane. No other substance has the necessary resilience and responsiveness or gives vibrations so happily adapted to those of the wooden tube. Various small improvements may be noticed in passing. Some players have found the width of the modern reed too great, and have reduced it to the advantage of tone and ease of blowing by a millimetre or so. A big reed does not necessarily mean a bigger tone; it may mean a tone of less brilliance and clarity. The basset-horn is an instance in point where a soprano reed often gives better tonal results than the tenor reed which is more usually employed. Commercial reeds have been marketed with kinks cut out of the sides, with holes cut through the heart or centre, with ribbed or fluted bodies, the object in each case being to promote vibration and resilience. Whether successful or not such efforts are to be encouraged. They show that some makers at least realise that the reed is capable of improvement. Moisture is, of course, the enemy of the reed; hence many attempts at waterproofing and a host of *anches imperméables*. None of the attempts would appear to be entirely happy. The oil with which the cane is impregnated or the varnish with which it is covered deprives it of some of its resonance and vibrancy. Players differ in their treatment of reeds after playing. Some will flatten them under pressure on glass, others again will leave them on the mouthpiece. Chacun à son goût.

The choice of reeds, of their cut and strength, will depend on the player's choice of mouthpiece, or rather on the type of 'lay' or facing he adopts. This will again depend on his shape and strength of lip, on his embouchure, on his methods of blowing, on his mental approach. Such questions are beyond the scope of this work. Quite briefly it may be said that there are three standard types of lay: long, medium, and short. The oblong opening into the tone-chamber or bore is usually about 32 mm. in length. The long lay will begin some 22–24 mm. from the tip of the mouthpiece, the short lay not more than 8 or 10 mm. from the same point. The medium lies approximately halfway between. In any case

the lay begins as an almost imperceptible deviation from the plane surface and only assumes a bolder curve as it nears the tip. Every measurement is of the greatest importance to tone and ease of blowing, even to
intonation, and is gauged in fractions of a millimetre. The long lay is all
but unknown outside Germany; it requires special hand-made reeds
which are in general rather narrower, longer in the blade, and heavier
in build than those of commerce. Most players will be best suited by a
medium or short lay. The depth of the chink between the reed and the
mouthpiece is a matter entirely of individual choice, once the initial
steps have been passed and the embouchure is formed. The object of
the curved lay is to enable the player, by altering his lip pressure, to vary
the length of reed which is free to vibrate, making the natural frequency
of the reed more nearly equal to the wave frequency of each note. The
lips, unconsciously it may be, perform the function of the tuning-wire
in the reed pipe of the organ, where the vibrating length of the brass
tongue is shortened or lengthened by sliding the wire in or out, and the
reed is thereby tuned to resonance with its pipe. The free end of the
reed never completely closes the orifice; if it did, the stability of the
sound-wave in the tube would be seriously impaired.

The materials of the mouthpiece have already been discussed. Where
measurements of extreme fineness and accuracy are involved, the importance of a durable and immutable material need hardly be stressed. It
may, however, be repeated that the tone-chamber and bore are primarily
the concern of the maker and form an integral part of the acoustical
design of the instrument. The player may be as fussy as he pleases in the
matter of the lay or the material of his mouthpiece provided that he
leaves the interior alone. Allusion has already been made to the standardisation of mouthpieces by the various makers. Few clarinets, sad to
relate, are now tuned with the mouthpiece which will accompany them.
Such is the maker's confidence in his tools and gauges. There is no need
to distrust the accuracy of these appliances, or the care of the maker,
but the fact remains that standardised mouthpieces *do* differ, that out
of a batch of a dozen one or two will be quite obviously better than the
others.[3] With a material so variable as wood differences in quality are
understandable; in the case of ebonite they are inexplicable. Nevertheless they do exist. The experience of cor anglais and bassoon players is
precisely similar. Out of a batch of 20 crooks one, maybe two, will be
found to be superlative, the majority will be fair, and one or two
definitely unsatisfactory. Yet all have been made from the same metal,
very possibly from the same sheet, and formed upon the same mandrel.

NOTES

[1] It is reported that attempts to grow suitable *Arundo donax* in Cornwall have met with some success, though not on a scale which could compete commercially with a long-established foreign industry, and one, moreover, in which capital outlay has to wait a long time for returns. About 1945 a small quantity of the reed was discovered growing wild in Bermuda, and samples showed it to be of fine musical quality. Nothing, however, seems to have been heard of any commercial exploitation of this fortuitous growth.

[2] Recently this objection seems to have been largely overcome.

[3] In spite of what one might suppose to be the obvious advantages of using a mouthpiece matched to the instrument during construction, it is common knowledge that some players do change mouthpieces round and get satisfactory results from very unlikely partnerships.

CHAPTER 7

History to 1800

THE SINGLE beating reed in alliance with a cylindrical tube of cane is of very ancient origin. Such instruments were in use in Egypt at least as early as the beginning of the third millennium; Egypt may in fact be the country of their origin. In its most primitive form a flexible tongue is cut in a piece of rush or cane and thinned down either at its free end or at its point of attachment to facilitate its vibration. The knob of the natural cane is left at the end. Such rude instruments in which the sounding reed is formed in the substance of the tube are known as *idioglot*. A later development is to form the sound-generator from a short separate piece of cane and to insert it into a longer body. The pipes were usually double to reinforce the sound or, in some cases, to produce a strong beat-tone when the pipes were purposely mistuned. Modern representatives, hardly changed at all in the course of centuries and still commonly found in the Near East, are the *arghul* and the *zummarah*. In the former the two pipes are of unequal length, in the latter they are even. A much more elaborate form is represented by the Sardinian (Cunzertu de) *launeddas*, a triple pipe with rectangular tone-holes and members of unequal length. A still later development was the provision of a capsule of horn, of wood, or of a gourd to enclose the reed. At first this was possibly designed as a protector for the delicate reed, later it was taken into use as a wind reservoir for the player, enabling him to sustain and steady his tone. The Basque *alboquea* and the Slav *brelka* are of this type. All the foregoing, it may be noted, were sounded with a single beating reed. With the Welsh *hornpipe* or *pibgorn* we are brought a stage nearer to the modern clarinet. This folk-instrument, which survived well into the 18th century in North Wales and in Anglesey, is provided with a bell of cow-horn at the lower end, cut up in front and finished with a *serrated* edge; and further, cane being all but unprocurable in Britain, the body was made of bone or elder-wood and provided with seven finger-holes. One of these for the thumb is on the underside. The reed of *arghul* type, inserted at the top of the resonator, is enclosed within a piece of horn which is smoothed for the lips. The *pibgorn* was plainly an advance on some of the preceding in having a detachable resonator pierced with seven holes, including a *thumb-hole*, and a definite bell. Three specimens are known to survive. Of these one has twin pipes, and is fitted with a wooden mouthpiece bearing the date 1701; the others have single tubes and horn wind-chambers. Here are the measurements of the specimen presented to the Society of Antiquaries by the Hon. Daines Barrington, and described and pictured in *Archaeologia:*[1] *resonator* with six equally spaced finger-holes – $6\frac{1}{2}$ inches; *horn bell* – $7\frac{3}{10}$ inches; *horn reservoir* – $4\frac{1}{2}$ inches; length of *beating reed* – 1 inch; diameter of *bell* – 2 inches; *bore* of tube – 6/7 mm. The tube of elder is slightly curved and irregularly bored, but the small holes are drilled with great precision. The little instrument gives a scale of f' major. The instrument must have enjoyed some popularity in the Middle Ages, since it figures in a painted glass window in the Beauchamp Chapel, St Mary's, Warwick, *c.* 1440,[2] and a year or two later in the inventory of one Symon Beryngton, a scholar of Oxford.

A very similar pipe is found in Scotland, where it was known as the *stock-and-horn*.[3] This, too, had a resonator of wood or bone, pierced with eight finger-holes and a horn bell, but the air-reservoir was formed not of horn, but of wood. Of two surviving specimens one, preserved in the Museum of Scottish Antiquities, Edinburgh, has a double bore formed in a single stock of ebony. The length of the stock is 9 inches, and the diameter of the bore is $5\frac{1}{2}$ mm. That such instruments are not autochthonous was pointed out by the late Henry Balfour, Curator of the Pitt Rivers Museum, Oxford, in his 'The Old British Pibgorn or Hornpipe and its Affinities' (*Journal of the Anthropological Institute*, vol. xx, 1890), who drew attention to the existence of very similar instruments in both the Near and Far East. In the islands of the Greek Archipelago, for instance, the *serrated* horn bell is commonly found, but here the resonating tubes are usually double. The resemblance between this Greek type and the double-tubed Welsh *pibgorn* is very remarkable. In the Far East the *pungi* of the Indian snake-charmer is typical of many similar instruments. In this the horn wind-chamber is replaced by a globular gourd or calabash into which two, occasionally three, cane pipes are fixed. The chanter may have seven or eight finger-holes. The *pungi* approximates to a bagpipe, the *pibgorn* more nearly to a clarinet. There is a tradition, too, of the existence in China in the dim ages of a double clarinet. This is stated to have resembled the *pibgorn* in having a bell and wind-chamber of horn.[4] It is generally assumed, quite reasonably, that the Welsh *pibgorn* and the Lowland *stock-and-horn* belong to a large family of primitive reed-pipes which, originating in the East, were introduced into the British Isles by the Celtic immigrations. It is significant that the type long survived in the Celtic fastnesses of Wales and Scotland.

There is every evidence that throughout the Middle Ages and beyond them well into the 17th century the single reed was confined to the music-making of peasants. There is no evidence whatever that it was ever adopted for more serious purposes. There were, of course, cylindrically-bored instruments in plenty, but these were invariably sounded with a double reed. Such were the *sordoni* and *doppioni* with their low humming tone and the soft-voiced *cromornes* which were particularly popular in England and made in as many as six different sizes. Why the single reed was so little favoured it is difficult to say. Little of course can be done with it without mechanism; it cannot be overblown without a speaker and keys are needed to bridge the lacunae in its scale. But 16th- and 17th-century musicians were not particularly concerned with the extent of an instrument's compass at a time when the economics of the concert room had not begun to operate; players with instruments of many sizes were always available.

The exclusion of single-reed instruments from all but bucolic music-making has been stressed, because the statement is frequently made that such instruments were available in Western Europe in the 17th century in various pitches and were commonly called *chalumeaux*. There is a further suggestion that the name *chalumeaux* is reserved to single-reed instruments, *schalmeyen* to double. No concrete evidence has been found for either suggestion. *Chalumeau*, derived from the Latin *calamus* or *calamellus*, is merely the French form of *shawm* or *schalmey* and a generic name for any *small* reed-blown pipe. No single-reed instrument is described in the *Syntagma musicum* of Praetorius (1619) and none in Mersenne's *Harmonie universelle* (1636–37), the latter a veritable encyclopaedia of organological knowledge. It is quite unthinkable that an instrument of such a distinctive type would have escaped the notice of these acute observers. To Mersenne and later to B. Borjon in his *Traité de la Musette* (1672) *chalumeau* was the chanter of a bagpipe, fitted with a double reed.

We now approach the turn of the century, the early 1700s, a crucial time in the history of the clarinet. At least as early as 1706 Estienne Roger, the Amsterdam publisher, in a catalogue of his music appended to Félibien's *Recueil historique* was advertising 'Fanfares et autres airs de chalumeau à 2 dessus' by J. P. Dreux and, further, *chalumeaux* for sale at 3 florins apiece. And two years earlier, in 1704, parts for the *chalumeau* begin to appear in numerous scores. Here are some of them: M. A. Ziani, *Caio Pompilio* (1704); A. M. Bononcini, *Conquista delle Spagne*;

and A. Ariosti, *Marte placato*, both of 1707. The series is continued by Keiser, Bonno, Hasse, Telemann, Handel, Fux, Zelenka, Dittersdorf, Molter, Graupner, and Harrer down to Gluck in the Paris and Vienna editions of *Orfeo* and *Alceste* of 1764 and 1769. There are many others. The instrument would seem to have found its way to Hamburg at an early date. Graupner, no doubt, made its acquaintance here during the years from 1709 he spent as harpsichordist to Keiser at the opera, and Telemann, who settled in Hamburg in 1721, would naturally avail himself of all local resources. The parts are usually of short duration and often comprised within a ninth or a tenth. They seldom descend below middle c; they are in fact more or less confined to the treble stave and seldom occur more than once or twice in a work. For what instrument were these parts intended? Surely not for a double-reed instrument when oboes were available at this pitch. The inference in inescapable that a single-reed instrument was intended and that *chalumeau* had acquired within a decade or so a new and additional meaning. This is confirmed by the illustration of a *chalumeau* in Diderot and d'Alembert's *Encyclopédie* of 1767 which shows a two-piece instrument, consisting of a cylindrical body without a bell, pierced with eight finger-holes, and a detachable mouthpiece fitted with a single reed. Further confirmation is found in the fact that Gluck's *chalumeaux* were replaced by clarinets in later editions. And then in 1716 or just before Roger was advertising 'Airs à deux clarinettes ou deux chalumeaux'. The two instruments may just as well be equivalents as alternatives. In passing it may be mentioned that this is the first occurrence of the word *clarinette* which has been noticed. In 1730 the two instruments are again associated in J. G. Doppelmayr's *Historische Nachricht von den Nürnbergischen Mathematicis und Künstlern*, when, in speaking of the flute-maker, J. C. Denner, he says:

> 'At the beginning of the present century [Zu Anfang des lauffenden Seculi] he invented a new sort of pipe, the so-called *Clarinette*, to the great satisfaction of music-lovers . . . and finally produced *chalumeaux* in an improved form.'

The date is significant; it coincides with the first appearance of *chalumeaux* parts and with Roger's first advertisement. It may be noted that many historians – F. J. Lipowsky in his *Übersicht der deutschen Geschichte*, 1794, may not be the earliest – put the date of Denner's invention back to 1690. There may be good authority for this or it may rest upon tradition which is not always to be disregarded. 'Denner's

—7 * *

invention' – what exactly did he do? It would appear from a literal reading of Doppelmayr's statement that he did two quite different things – that he invented a new instrument and improved another whose existence was already known. The modern interpretation is rather different. It is that the writer was guilty of an ambiguity or at best of a hendiadys; that what he really intended to imply was that Denner invented the *clarinet* by improving the *chalumeau*, i.e. by giving it a separate mouthpiece, by adding keys to it, by developing the bell, and by making available for the first time the third and fifth harmonics; in other words that he added the *clarinet* to the already existing *chalumeau* register. It is of course not impossible that Denner was himself the inventor of the keyless *chalumeau* in or about 1690 and had time to add to its resources before his death in 1707.

There would seem no reasonable doubt that for the first two or three decades of the century the clarinet was in Germany, and in Austria even later, known as the *chalumeau*. The word *Clarinette* seems to occur for the first time in German in the passage of Doppelmayr already quoted. Possibly this use of the word *chalumeau* was deliberate, an act of kindness on the composer's part, to distinguish the new instrument quite clearly and unequivocally from the *clarino*, a very necessary distinction. J. G. Walther in his *Musicalisches Lexicon* of 1732 makes it quite clear that we have to deal with no more than a matter of nomenclature when he defines *chalumeau* (1) as a *Schäfer-Pfeiffe*, a shepherd's pipe; (2) as the chanter of a bagpipe; (3) as a small wind instrument with seven holes; (4) as a small wind instrument, made of boxwood, with seven holes on the top, two brass keys, and one hole beneath. The last is quite clearly Denner's clarinet and the penultimate quite possibly Roger's 3-florin *chalumeau*. It is not impossible that the simple keyless instrument depicted by Diderot and d'Alembert had a short-lived existence parallel with Denner's elaboration of it. Some of the simpler orchestral parts, contained within a ninth, may have been played upon it; but no specimen of it is known to survive in any public collection,[5] a fact which does not argue a vigorous or prolonged existence. There are on the other hand (or were before the late war) at least twenty 2-key clarinets extant, five or possibly six by Denner or his sons.

It may be asked why the clarinet was used so sporadically in the first half of the 18th century, and why parts of such restricted compass were assigned to it. The answer to the first question may very well be found in the imperfections of the new instrument, some of which will be examined later in this chapter, to the second in the probability that the occasional *chalumeau* parts were entrusted to oboists or flautists, who, seeing no latent possibilities in the new instrument, did not bother themselves to acquire a new technique.

We may now turn from uncertainty and speculation to the inventor, Johann Christoph Denner, whose claims have never been disputed. He was born at Leipzig in 1655, the son of Heinrich Denner, a horn-turner, who specialised in making bird and animal calls. While still a child he migrated with his family to Nuremberg, where he learned not only his father's craft, but music as well, and applied his specialised knowledge to improving woodwind instruments, especially in intonation. He excelled especially in the manufacture of *flûtes-à-bec* or recorders which soon gained for him celebrity outside his own country. The flautist A. B. Fürstenau relates that his sons travelled with his instruments to the farthest corners of Europe. Missionaries, it was said, took them even to China. At least fifty instruments made by Denner and his sons survive. They include flutes, both fipple and transverse, oboes, bassoons, a rackett, and five or six 2-key clarinets. He died in 1707, and the business was continued by his sons, one of whom, Jacob, 'stadt musicus und flötenmacher', died in 1735. From the foregoing it will be seen that Denner was just the sort of maker, with his keen instinct for the improvement of wind instruments, to have created the clarinet; Doppelmayr's statement has in fact never been questioned. The instruments made by the family are branded with two stamps: I. C. DENNER and I. DENNER, the latter with a fir-tree. It is usual to ascribe instruments branded with the former stamp to Johann Christoph, the father; but the presence of this stamp on an oboe (Berlin 1071) which must be later than 1707, the year of the elder Denner's death, has thrown doubts on the correctness of such attributions. C. Sachs in his *Beschreibender Katalog* (Nachträge, col. 2) suggests (a) that J. Denner was the father and J. C. Denner one of the sons, (b) that both were sons. It seems equally possible that J.C. was the father, and that one of the sons inherited his stamp. The practice is not unknown.[6]

To turn to an examination of J. C. Denner's Clarinet, No. 20 in the Baierisches Nationalmuseum, Munich, of which Brussels 911 is a facsimile. In externals it resembles a treble fipple-flute or recorder, of which Denner was, as we have seen, a noted maker. It is approximately the same length, 50 cm., giving *f*, an octave lower than the recorder, as its bottom note. It is in three pieces, a mouthpiece and a slender barrel in one, an undivided body-joint with six equally spaced holes in front and one behind, and a foot-joint with two small holes pierced side by side. The device of boring twin holes was adapted from the oboe and recorder. With all holes covered, the bottom note, *f*, would be sounded;

with one of the twin holes uncovered by a roll of the little finger, *f sharp* would result. The foot-joint, being movable, could be accommodated to suit either a right- or left-handed player. Above the first hole a raised ring is left in the turning; in it are mounted two keys, covering two small holes bored *diametrically* opposite to each other. The bore is approximately 13 mm. There is no widening or flaring at the lower end; there is on the contrary more than a slight contraction.[7] Four almost identical specimens, two by Klenig, two by Liebav, are preserved in the Musikhistoriska Museum, Stockholm (Nos. 141, 142, 139, 143). Nothing is known of these makers. The mouthpieces of all these instruments are abnormally large and are obviously intended for a 15 mm. reed. The facing is long and wide with little curve, while the opening into the shallow tone-chamber is narrowed at the lower end; the bore is *cylindrical*. It is necessary to take the mouthpiece well into the mouth to sound the instrument with ease. The reed was placed against the upper lip, a practice surviving from the old idioglot instruments. The keys, opened singly, give *a'*, opened together, *b' natural*; *b' flat* was presumably produced by slackening the embouchure and stopping the tone-holes of the upper joint. Either key may be used as a speaker to produce the twelfths. Two other specimens of this early type with *diametrically* opposed keys may be noted, both in the Berlin collection. They are No. 2870 by J. W. Oberlender and 223 marked I. Denner.

The next stage in development to be noted is the moving of the thumb-key nearer to the mouthpiece and a great reduction in size of the hole it covered. This had two important results: *b' flat* was produced with both keys open, while greater security and purity were imparted to the harmonics. Other improvements were the substitution of a flared bell of larger dimensions for the recorder foot-joint and a slight reduction in the size of the mouthpiece and reed. These improvements are often attributed to Jacob Denner. The attribution is apparently based on Brussels 912, which is stamped I. DENNER, and shows these modifications (see Plate I*e*). There is no other evidence. Nor is the date known. That it was before 1721 may be inferred from F. Bonanni's *Gabinetot armonico*, published in 1722, but licensed for printing in 1721. The pertinent passage reads:

'An instrument similar to the oboe is the *clarone*. It is two and a half palms long and terminates in a bell like the trumpet three inches in width. It is pierced with seven holes in front and one behind. There are in addition two other holes opposite to each other, but *not diametrically*, which are closed and opened by two springs pressed by the finger.'

He adds that the tone of the instrument was deeper than that of the oboe, and that no writer mentions the name of the inventor. Doppelmayr, of course, had yet to write. Two interesting points arise from this: the early arrival of the clarinet in Italy and the obscurity which already, only some twenty years after its invention, veiled its origin.

The primitive 2-key clarinets described above were made in several tonalities. And here a word of caution. The pitch or key of a modern clarinet may be assessed by the simple process of measurement in cases where it is impossible to sound it. In the case of old clarinets measurements of length are most misleading, since bores vary wildly in diameter. A clarinet measuring some 50 cm. in length with a bore of 12 mm. might be assumed to be pitched in C; with a bore enlarged to 14 mm. the pitch might well be raised to D. Allowance, too, must be made for some warping of the bore after at least two centuries of disuse. Examination of some twenty specimens shows that the favourite pitches were D and C, with B flat rather a bad third. At least two are in higher pitches, Munich 19 (Brussels 906) in high A, and Brussels 916 in high G. The former is anonymous, the latter by I. B. Willems. No 2-key clarinet has been found pitched in A, the pitch of the modern orchestral instrument.

The tone of these early clarinets is far from satisfactory. Disparaging remarks occur as early as 1713, when J. Mattheson in his *Neu-eröffnete Orchester* speaks of 'chalumeaux with their howling symphony', and Walther's statement that 'the clarinet sounded from afar like a trumpet' points to some stridency of tone in the higher register. The ill-proportioned reed and mouthpiece, and the narrow bore, rob the *chalumeau* of vigour and clarity. The tone in this register is less harsh than feeble and buzzing. An ivory 2-key instrument in D by Scherer preserved in the Donaldson Collection, R.C.M., is an exception. Here a bore, measuring 14 mm. and enlarged at the bottom, gives a far more open and robust tone. The twelfths are better in quality and better in intonation. The overall measurement is 53 cm. The compass given in J. T. Eisel's *Musicus Autodidaktos* of 1738, and repeated in Majer's *Neu-eröffneter Musik-Saal* of 1741, is from f to c'''. Higher notes would have been possible – Eisel in fact hints at the feats of *Virtuosen* in playing higher – but would not have been easy without a drastic reformation of the mouthpiece. There were of course no tone-holes for the semitones. These were obtained by cross-fingering, the normal practice on all woodwind instruments of this date.[8] To take the fundamental register of an early C clarinet. Bottom *f* with all fingers on and *g* with little finger removed would be satisfactory, *a* less so owing to bad venting; *f sharp*, *a flat/g sharp* would be non-existent, unless the maker had provided twin holes for these notes; *b flat*, obtained by 'forking', i.e. with R.1 and 3, would be very muffled and sharp, since it was in reality an insufficiently flattened *b natural*; *b natural* fingered with R.1 alone, and unaided at this period with a vent-key, would be too flat, or too sharp when fingered as *c' flat* with R.2,3; *c* would be good; *c' sharp*, fingered as *d' flat* with L.1,2 and R.1,2 would be wretched; *d'* and *e'* good, but *e' flat* forked with L.1 and 3 would be sharp and feeble; *f' sharp* fingered with L. thumb would be good if somewhat flat, but flattened to *f' natural* by the imposition of L.2 less satisfactory. Open *g'* with all fingers off would be a pure note, but, raised to *g' sharp* by opening the speaker, would be too sharp. As has been said, the twelfths would be better, more resonant, and more clearly defined. In fact, on some modern instruments forked *c'''* is a standard fingering and forked *g'' sharp* (L.1 and 2 + R.1 and 2) a most useful auxiliary.

An obvious fault of all 2-key clarinets was the lack of a hole to give a proper *b' natural*. This was soon provided by lengthening the bell and piercing a hole just above it. The new hole was controlled by an open key; the long shank to close it was carried at the rear of the instrument in some early specimens and manipulated by the thumb. Thus the instrument could still be played with left or right hand on the bottom joint. But as soon as the key was moved to its present position on the left side of the joint, the position of the hands was fixed once and for all. A further advantage of the new key was to extend the compass down a semitone to *e*. No precise date can be assigned to this innovation which is often ascribed to one of Denner's sons. The suggestion is probably based on Brussels 913, which, although stamped 'LINDNER', has been attributed, possibly through misreading of the stamp, to Denner. This clarinet, which from its appearance cannot be much later than 1730 and may be earlier, is pitched in A. It is the first clarinet in this pitch which has come to the writer's notice. Two-key instruments were evidently produced well after the mid-century. This is the only instrument illustrated in Diderot and d'Alembert's *Encyclopédie* of 1767. Other makers of 2- and 3-key clarinets, in addition to those already mentioned, were J. W. Oberlender, G. A. Rottenburgh of Brussels, T. Boekhout, Walch of Berchtesgaden, I. S. W[alch], G. N. Kelmer, C. Kraus, J. W. Kenigsperger, and T. W. Joseph of Triftern. There were no English makers. No clarinet by T. Stanesby, father or son, the English Denners, has yet come to light.

The joints of the earliest clarinets were seldom provided with tips. A moulding of some thickness is sometimes left at the top of the R.H. joint to reinforce the socket. The tip of ivory or, in cheaper instruments, of bone, was of fairly late introduction. The bell, too, was often unmounted. The division of the body into three pieces became common practice as soon as clarinets in several tonalities were required, to permit the interpolation of the *pièces de rechange* of varying dimensions. The middle joint was as a rule unprovided with a thumb-rest, an uncomfortable omission; it was possibly less necessary when the instrument was played reed upwards and held perforce in a higher position than now obtains. The details of the keywork and of its mounting have already been treated in a previous chapter. Generally speaking, the clarinet was not as yet a popular instrument with wealthy dilettanti. Hence it was made plainly and soberly on workaday lines. One or two essential keys were still missing, the closed keys in particular for *g sharp* and *f sharp* on the lower joint. The *g sharp*, which for the future will be known as the *a flat/e flat* key to distinguish it clearly from *g' sharp*, an octave above, appears to have been the first addition. No doubt it made its appearance early in the third quarter of the century, since this and the *f sharp* key are both found on a 5-key clarinet by T. Collier of London, dated 1770, and now in the Keighley Museum. The credit for adding these keys is frequently given to Barthold Fritz, an organ-builder of Brunswick. The statement is found in Lefèvre's tutor of 1802 and has been repeated in countless dictionaries ever since. It may be traditional; it may be untrustworthy, but on more than one occasion attention has been drawn to the inventiveness of organ-builders.

Before passing on to the musical history of the clarinet it may be of interest to discuss some details of construction. The material was almost invariably wood, although at least two ivory clarinets by Scherer are known, and generally boxwood, in its natural state or stained to a dark brown with acid. Occasionally the wood was burned to imitate tortoise-shell;[9] less often some of the harder fruit-woods, plum or pear, were employed. The use of ebony or cocus was very uncommon for body-joints, but mouthpieces were sometimes made of these materials. The three joints of Denner's clarinets were generally by the third decade of the century increased to five or six, namely:

(1) The *Mouthpiece*. This had now been considerably reduced in width. It was now generally tapered, and after the mid-century was fitted with a reed rather narrower and shorter than that now in use.

(2)   The *Barrel* or *Socket*. This was now piriform. Hence the German
      Birne. English makers were still inclined to make it in one piece
      with the mouthpiece.

(3)   *Upper* or *Left-hand Joint*. This carried the four finger-holes for
      L.H. and the *a'* and speaker-keys mounted in rings left in the
      turning or in knobs.

(4)   *Right-hand Joint* carrying three finger-holes for R.H.

(5)   *Lower Joint*, carrying the *g* hole for R. little finger and the three
      keys. These were mounted in a swelling in the wood, which
      enabled the finger-hole to be bored obliquely to secure some
      approximation to correct intonation and at the same time to
      bring it within reach of the finger. Clarinets so made were
      known in Flemish as *Klarinet met eksteroog* (i.e. oeil de perdrix).[10]

(6)   The *Bell*. This was sometimes made in one piece with the
      preceding.

It may be assumed, then, that the 5-key clarinet was known in 1770.
That it must have enjoyed considerable popularity is indicated by the
large numbers still surviving. A sixth key, for middle *c sharp*, was
added not much later to X. Lefèvre's clarinet by Baumann, the Paris
maker. An approximate date of 1790 is assigned to this addition. This
was possibly not the first 6-key clarinet, if we may credit the statement
in the *Supplément* (1776) to Diderot and d'Alembert's *Encyclopédie*
that a player with a 6-key instrument had just passed through Berlin.
The new key was of vital importance; without it no true *c' sharp* was
possible unless twin holes were provided. It is surprising therefore that
for many years English makers replaced it with the *a'/b'* trill-key as the
sixth key. The statement is often made that it was for the 5-key clarinet
that Mozart composed his major works. This is quite probable; at the
same time it is not impossible than Anton Stadler, who played them,
had a more elaborate instrument. For it is well known that he had an
extension to written *c* fitted to his B flat clarinet and possibly to his A
as well, an extension of which Mozart made full use in *Così fan tutte*
and *La Clemenza di Tito*. The extension is described in Gerber's
Lexikon, 1814, I., 248, quoting the *Modenjournal*.

We may now review briefly the musical history of the clarinet in the
18th century. With all its glaring imperfections Denner's 'invention'
could not be expected to gain an enthusiastic welcome from musicians.
Nor did it. It was vastly inferior to the contemporary oboe and flute in
tone, intonation, and agility, and there is no reason to suppose that
musicians of the period were particularly interested in new voices or

orchestral tone-colour. The occurrence of *chalumeau* parts was, as we have seen, sporadic rather than constant. Outside Germany the new instrument was more often known as *clarinet* than *chalumeau*, and there is reason to think that its use was not uncommon in the Netherlands. In the early 1720s J. A. J. Faber, organist and choirmaster of Antwerp Cathedral, included a part for a C clarinet in his often quoted Mass 'Maria Assumpta'. The work is now lost, but F. A. Gevaert reproduced 21 bars from the 'Qui tollis' in his *Nouveau traité d'instrumentation* of 1885. There is no reason to doubt the authenticity of this Mass since the information was communicated to Gevaert by the Chevalier L.-P.-M. de Burbure, a noted and learned musicologist. The solo contralto is accompanied by two flutes, clarinet, and cembalo or organ. A most unexpected feature is arpeggios for the clarinet in the *chalumeau* register, descending to *f*, at that time the lowest note.

As we have seen from the description of it in Bonanni, the clarinet was known in Italy under the name of *clarone* at least as early as 1721. So it is not perhaps surprising to find it used by Vivaldi in three recently discovered concertos.[11] Two (F. xii. 1 and 2) are in C major; the third 'Per la Solennità di S. Lorenzo' (F. xii. 14) is in D major. In the first and second 2 clarinets are associated with 2 oboes, strings, and cembalo; in the third 2 flutes and a bassoon are added. The range of the clarinet is from *g* in the *chalumeau* to *c* above the treble stave. The writing is mainly diatonic in *clarino* style, and abounds in short semiquaver scale passages, rapid triplets, and easy trills. The missing *b'* natural and doubtful accidentals, the two *e flats* and *f sharps* in the treble stave excepted, are carefully avoided. In the *Largo* of the second work oboes and clarinets play together without the strings. The composer had evidently made a careful study of the 2-key clarinet. No precise date can be assigned to these interesting works. Vivaldi, it may be noted, died in 1741.

To return to Germany. There is evidence that about this time, the later 1730s, the name *Clarinette* was coming into commoner use. On 13 October 1739, for instance, an advertisement in a Frankfurt paper announced the presence in the city of 'Zwey gute Clarinettisten' who were ready to display their talents.[12] And clarinets began to figure in inventories. In the detailed list of instruments in the possession of the Court of Sayn-Wittgenstein at Berleburg, dated 1741, 'Zwey Paar Clarinetten' are included; and again in the *Inventar des Stiftes Krems-münster*, a year or two earlier, '2 buchsbaumerne Klarinetten' appear.[13] And then there are the manuscripts of two little-known Concertos by J. M. Molter, preserved in the Landesbibliothek at Karlsruhe. Both are for 'Clarinetto concertato' in D with accompaniment for strings and harpsichord. 1740 has been plausibly suggested as a date for these interesting compositions. The solo part lies almost entirely in the *clarinet* and *acute* registers, ascending not infrequently to *g'''*. The lowest note employed is *c'*, and that but seldom. The writing is in *clarino* style, and mainly diatonic; naturally, since the clarinet could do little else at this period, and the *acute* register was far more easy to force into tune than the *chalumeau* and lower middle register. It is perfectly playable clarinet music, unexpectedly brilliant for the time, in which accidentals impossible on a 2-key instrument are carefully avoided.[14]

Of only one early clarinettist do we know the name. This is 'Mr Charles' who was active in London and the provinces in the 1740s and 1750s. He is a shadowy figure, described variously as 'the Hungarian', 'the famous French-Horn', or the 'Music Master from London'. In March 1742, he came to Dublin, and on 12 May, in addition to horn duets with his 'Second', played a Concerto on the clarinet and 'a select piece on the Shalamo', accompanied by 'the best Hands in the city'. A note to the announcement in the *Dublin Mercury* of 24 April 1742 adds that the 'clarinet, the hautbois de Amour and Shalamo were never heard in this kingdom before'. He gave a very similar programme at Salisbury in the following year, where his wife joined him and his 'Second' in a French horn trio, and he appeared in a concert at Edinburgh in 1755. He composed music for the horn and harpsichord but so far as is known, none for the clarinet. Handel, it will be remembered, was in Dublin in the spring of 1742. Did Handel hear him here, or had he heard him previously in London? There appears little doubt that he knew the clarinet and composed for it. The question has recently been ably handled by R. B. Chatwin in his article 'Handel and the Clarinet', contributed to the *Galpin Society Journal*, March 1950. Here it can be only summarised. In the undated Granville MS of *Tamerlano* (1724) the original two cornetti which accompany the singer in the pensive 'Par che mi nasca' are replaced by Clar. 1° and 2°. The plaintive character of the song rules *clarini* out of court; it is just the sort of music which calls for woodwind tone. Again in *Riccardo primo* (1727) *Chaloumeaux* are introduced to accompany 'Quell' innocente afflitto'. The parts extend from *d'* to *c'''*. It would seem, as Mr Chatwin suggests, as if Handel were trying out the instrument, then known to him under its old German name. If doubts remain about Handel's knowledge of the instrument, his autograph *Ouverture* in D for clarinet 1 and 2 and corno di caccia should dispel them. A tentative date of 1740 was assigned by Dr A. H. Mann to this work, which was originally thought to have been scored for strings as well.[15] It is now looked upon as complete in itself, a trio in fact for clarinets and horn. Is it too fanciful to suggest that it may have been written for Mr Charles, his 'Second', and his wife? To avoid the non-existent *c″ sharp* the clarinet parts were no doubt played on the D clarinet, a not uncommon pitch for the early clarinet, as we have seen.

To turn to France. In Paris the *Mercure* of February 1728 informs us of the performance of a 'Concerto de Chalumeau avec accompagnemens de la Simphonie'. The solo instrument is described somewhat equivocally as 'cet instrument qui est fort en usage en Allemagne imite le hautbois et la flûte a bec'. In tone or in appearance? In France the clarinet was constantly considered a relation of the oboe, and as late as 1780 Laborde described it as an 'instrument du genre des Hautbois'. And there the matter rests for twenty years until in 1749 the archives of the Opéra reveal the use of clarinets in Rameau's *Zoroastre*.[16] They figured again in 1751 in *Acante et Céphise* by the same composer. The scoring is unexpectedly original and shows Rameau as a pioneer in orchestration. There are in particular some arresting dialogues between clarinets and horns, which must have come as a revelation in skilful use of tone-colour to contemporary audiences. Two of the earliest clarinettists to be heard in Paris were Gaspard Procksch and Flieger. We know nothing of their origin or when they came to France. It has been suggested that they were brought to Paris by Johann Stamitz when he assumed charge of the tax-farmer La Pouplinière's private orchestra for a year in 1754, but it is known from the researches of L. de la Laurencie that they were engaged for *Acante et Céphise* in 1753. It is quite possible that they were the clarinettists in *Zoroastre* four years before, since Rameau had charge of La Pouplinière's orchestra from 1731 to 1752–53. They may, too, have been fellow countrymen of Stamitz and have come to Paris at his suggestion. Procksch was a composer as well and, in addition to symphonies, wrote *Recueils d'airs pour deux cors ou deux clarinettes*, dated by Cucuel 'vers 1776'. Other works by him are advertised in Breitkopf's catalogue of 1777, viz. *Sei Terzetti per Clarinetto, Violino è Violoncello*, op. IV.; *Sei Sonate a Clarinetto è accompagnemente di Violoncello*, op. V., all Paris publications. Procksch is described as 'Primo Clarinetto della Musica di S.A.S. il Principe di Conti'. *Six Quatuors concertante à une Clarinette, Violon, Alto & Violoncelle* attributed to Gaspard in the same catalogue were no doubt also works of Procksch. In the same list appear four quartets for the same instruments by C. Stamitz and six by Kichler. When the tax-farmer's orchestra was dispersed in 1762, Procksch and Flieger passed into the service of the Prince de Conti. Procksch was still alive in 1785 and Flieger visited London in 1791. Notices in the *Mercure* keep us informed of the progress of the clarinet in Paris. In March 1755 a symphony by J. Stamitz with horns and clarinets was included in a programme at the *Concert Spirituel*. In April 1757 several symphonies with clarinets were given; one, the *Nova Tempesta*, was by Filippo Ruggi, another, given in November 1761, was by Schencker. The clarinet found a place, too, in religious music. On Sundays and festivals La Pouplinière's band played for an hour in the forenoon and provided the music for the Mass which followed; on every day of Holy Week the clarinets were heard alone. By 1760 the clarinet may be assumed to have been well established in Paris. It was first heard at Lyons in July 1763. According to Gossec the Seven Years War brought many clarinettists to France and especially to Paris. In 1762, as Cucuel observes, the clarinet received a form of official sanction; the Gardes Suisses were allowed to form a band of four bassoons, four horns, four oboes, and four clarinets; in 1767 or thereabouts clarinets and horns were at last admitted to the *Chapelle du Roi*. No one did more to propagate the use of the new instrument than Gossec. He had been director of La Pouplinière's band from 1752 till its dispersion, one year excepted, and passed with many of its members into the service of the Prince de Conti. He began to write parts for it in his symphonies from 1760–61 on. In his *Messe des morts* of 1760 clarinets are joined by horns and trombones; the 'Tuba mirum', in particular, includes three trombones, four clarinets, four trumpets, four horns, and eight bassoons, the first complete use, as Cucuel observes, of wood and brass. In January 1764 was published by Le Menu of Paris the first theoretical study of the instrument, Valentin Roeser's *Essai d'instruction à l'usage de ceux qui composent pour la clarinette et le cor avec des remarques sur l'harmonie à deux clarinettes, deux cors et deux bassons*. Only one copy is known to exist, that in the Bibliothèque Royale of Brussels. Roeser was described as 'musicien de M. le prince de Monaco', and elsewhere as 'Maître de clarinet'.

A more important work was published a few years later, in 1772 according to Fétis: L.-J. Francoeur's *Diapason général . . . des instruments à vent*, subsequently revised (and published) by A.-E. Choron in 1813. Francoeur, quoted by Laborde in 1780, gives the compass of the clarinet as ranging from *e* to *a'''*, dividing it into three registers, *chalumeau, clarinette ou clairon, sons aigus*. The tonalities then commonly in use were A, B flat, B natural, C and D, F, and E natural. There was also 'la grande clarinette' in low G.

Of the instruments used by these early French clarinettists we know nothing. The 2-key clarinet with a developed bell is alone illustrated in the *Lutherie* section of Diderot and d'Alembert's *Encyclopédie* published in the mid-1760s. The principal Paris woodwind-makers in the third quarter of the 18th century were Lecler, Charles Bizey, Paul Villars, and Thomas Lot. No clarinet by any of these is known in any collection. The first mention, indeed, of a clarinet by a Paris maker is the *basse-tube* of Gilles Lot, an early bass clarinet, and this is known only from an advertisement and description in the *Avant-Coureur* of 11 May 1772. In the *Almanach Dauphin* of 1777 Lot was mentioned as 'renommé pour les clarinettes'. The making of woodwind instruments did not emerge as a great national industry of France until the 19th century was well advanced.

In London in 1751 and again in 1752 'clarinette' concertos were included in concerts at the New Theatre in the Haymarket. The performer's name is not given. A year or two later Carl Barbandt, a southern German from Munich, a well-known harpsichordist, organist, and oboist, was advertising concerts with clarinets, horns, and kettle-drums. It is sometimes assumed that he was a clarinettist as well, as many oboists were. It is not improbable. The combination of horns and clarinets, already exploited by Rameau, was particularly popular, especially in the pleasure gardens of Marylebone and Ranelagh. The names of the players at Marylebone were Frickler, Henniz, Seipts, and A. Rathgen. The last-named wrote for his instrument as well. *Seven Sonatas in five parts for two Clarinets, two Horns and a Bassoon* were published in London and advertised by Breitkopf in 1777. In 1763 clarinets were introduced into the festival orchestra at Gloucester and were heard at York in 1770. The principal performer was Carl Weichsel, originally an oboist. His wife, a pupil of J. C. Bach, was a well-known singer at Vauxhall. Their daughter was the celebrated Mrs Billington, most famous of English sopranos. It has been suggested that Bach may have written his clarinet music for his friend's benefit, and that much of Mrs Billington's excellence may be attributed to the accompaniment of her father's clarinet. In passing it may be noted that not a few of Bach's clarinet parts are written in the tenor clef.

The combination of horns and clarinets was used by Arne in his *Thomas and Sally*, produced at Covent Garden in November 1760. C clarinets appear again in *Artaxerxes* (1762), replacing flutes and oboes in occasional numbers and being chosen to provide the accompaniment to Miss Brent, and later to the famous male soprano Tenducci in 'Water parted from the Sea'. D and B flat clarinets were used in the same year by J. C. Bach in his *Orione*. By this time clarinets may be taken to have been well established in London and available when required; in fact by 1770 English makers were turning to their manufacture. It has been suggested that it was in London in 1764 that Mozart first heard his favourite wind instrument. Certainly K. 18, his transcription of Abel's symphony, contains clarinet parts.

It is not improbable that many of the early players were, if not Germans, of German extraction, converted oboists or double-handed players. Two British players may now engage our attention, John and William Mahon. Possibly of Irish extraction, both were born at Oxford, John in 1746, William about 1750, and were members of a famous musical family.[17] Both were well-known clarinettists, concerto-players, and orchestral musicians. William died in 1816, at Salisbury, John in 1834, in Dublin. Both were violinists as well, as was Richard Mühlfeld more than a century later. John wrote several concertos in the last quarter of the century and the first important English tutor for his instrument in 1803. A 'Mr Mahon' took part in every Three Choirs Festival from 1773 to 1811, and from 1778 to 1823 in the Birmingham Festival and other provincial gatherings. Since he did not play after the 1815 season, it was probably William who was chosen with Oliver and Kramer as clarinettist to the Philharmonic Society, founded in 1813. The following is extracted from his obituary in the *Gentleman's Magazine* of June 1816:

> 'his celebrity in the musical profession had long rendered him one of its greatest ornaments. He was leader of the concerts in Salisbury upwards of 30 years, and his eminent talents were duly appreciated at the Opera House, where he had been many years engaged, and was esteemed the first performer on the clarionet in England. His scientific knowledge, and fine execution on the violin and other instruments, were also of the first description.'

The clarinet figured in a concerto in the Oxford Music Room as early as 1772, and in a symphony by Gossec played there in 1774. Cambridge was rather later; it is not till 1789 that we hear of the activities of a local clarinettist, Peter Hellendael junior. By 1790 probably many provincial towns could produce a local player to support the imported London musician. A London directory of 1794 supplies some statistics of the numbers of wind-players at that date. Clarinets number 26, bassoons 49, flutes 20, oboes 36, serpents 5, and horns 36. The number of clarinet-, bassoon-, and horn-players is surprising. It may well have been increased by military players in London. The clarinet was introduced into the military band in 1763 or soon after, the well-tried combination of two clarinets and two horns being added to a like number of oboes and bassoons. The military musician played no small part in popularising the clarinet, and many an early player attained fame after graduation from the ranks. John Mahon was for some time a bandmaster both in Oxford and in London.

To return to Germany and to Mannheim in particular. It was here that the possibilities of the clarinet as an expressive instrument were first realised. By the 1750s the Elector's orchestra, under Johann Stamitz, had acquired an immense reputation for sensitivity and refinement. The Mannheimers did not, it is true, invent the *crescendo* and *diminuendo*, for which they were famed, but they carried gradation of tone and expression to a degree undreamed of before. The clarinet was obviously the wind instrument of all others for such purposes. Its control of dynamics was a conspicuous virtue among its many and obvious imperfections, and it was included in the symphonies of C. Stamitz, the younger, Cannabich, Holzbauer, Beck, Toeschi, and others. Where clarinets were not available the parts would be played by oboes, flutes, or violins. But by 1775 clarinets would have been available, as we have seen, in many centres, in Paris, in London, in Oxford, in Lyons, in Milan, in Munich, but not apparently in Vienna,[18] in Dresden, Berlin, or Leipzig; unless of course they were kept well in the background and considered unworthy of particular mention. Several of the cities where clarinets made a belated appearance had included *chalumeaux* in their orchestras; Hamburg for instance had them in 1738 in a curiously assorted band. It is possible that many local musicians considered the clarinet not worth persevering with and were blind to its latent possibilities.

Did Johann Stamitz compose for the clarinet? Mr Peter Gradenwitz, his biographer, thinks he did and attributes to him a manuscript 'Concerto a 7 stromenti, Clarinetto Principale Toni B . . . del Sigr. Stamitz', which is preserved in the Central Archiv, Regensburg. The attribution is made on grounds of style and subject. If Mr Gradenwitz is correct, the work must have been written before 1757, the year of Johann's death. The work is unexpectedly agreeable in performance, the lyrical *Adagio* and gay *Presto* in particular. In little more than twenty years the clarinet had developed from a shrill voice, capable only of the brilliant *clarino* parts of Molter, into the expressive instrument dear to the Mannheimers and later to Mozart. The first clarinet-players at Mannheim were Michael Quallenberg, a Bohemian trained in Vienna, and Johannes Hampel, both installed between 1758 and 1759. A few

years later they were joined by Jacob Tausch. It was no doubt Quallenberg and Tausch senior and junior who so impressed Mozart when he
heard the clarinets in the orchestra for the first time. Or had he heard
them in London as a child? The important name is Tausch. Of Tausch
the elder we know little. He is best known as the father of Franz (1762–
1817), a great virtuoso and an infant prodigy, who played before the
Elector at the age of eight. After a long period of service at Mannheim,
and after several concert tours, he settled as a Court Musician at Berlin
in 1789. It is known from the elder Rellstab that the Berliners had not
taken kindly to the clarinet which Joseph Beer had introduced to them,
until Tausch arrived to reveal to them its full powers of expression and
beauty of tone. Gerber, who heard him in 1793, was enthusiastic in his
praise. 'What versatility in gradation of tone. At one moment the low
whisper of leaves borne along by the soft breath of the zephyr; at
another his instrument soared above all the others in a torrent of
brilliant arpeggios.'

Franz Tausch was not the first well-known virtuoso. This was
Joseph Beer (1744–1811), also a Bohemian, sometimes known as Baer,[19]
who spent much of his prime in Paris where he was clarinettist to the
Duke of Orleans and made many successful concert tours. He played
his first concerto in Paris in 1771. He had a lucrative sojourn in England
in 1772 and was again in London in 1774. For him Carl Stamitz wrote
the majority of his dozen concertos between 1770 and 1784, of which
Sieber published six. In addition he wrote not a few concertos himself.
His particular importance lies in his propagation of the clarinet as a
brilliant solo instrument in the furthest parts of Europe and in his
formation of a typically French school of playing. Among his pupils
were Michel Yost (1754–86), the master of X. Lefèvre and a prolific
composer of concertos and chamber music for his instrument, Rathé,
and Solers. He made the clarinet the popular instrument in France
which it has always remained. There is every evidence that the style of
Beer was vastly different from that of Tausch. The latter put beauty,
expression, and gradation of tone first; Beer, we may infer, placed them
a good second to brilliance and volubility. The latter were long the
characteristics of the French school until Frédéric Berr effected a
reformation some fifty years later. In the early 1780s Beer left Paris and,
passing through Belgium, heard for the first time, so Fétis relates, a
German clarinettist named Schwartz.[20] Struck by the superiority of his
tone over his own, especially by its soft expressive quality, he applied
himself to reform his style and possibly his embouchure. After some
months of study he was able to add the German tone to his considerable

technique and brilliance. Wherein lay the difference of tone? Had Tausch and other German players already adopted the practice of playing with the reed downwards? We do not know. In 1818, it may be noted, a writer in the A.M.Z. counselled all clarinettists to play with the reed downwards. 'By so doing,' he says, 'they may lose some of the high notes, but will gain the whole instrument.' From this it may be inferred that some at least of the German players had already adopted the modern embouchure. The best qualities of both schools were united in H. J. Bärmann, the elder, a virtuoso who will be considered later.

Franz Tausch was not without importance as a composer. The concertos of C. Stamitz were sound musicianly works of the Mannheim school, not less important as music than as pioneer works in this field. Beer and Michel wrote, as might be expected, mainly to display their execution. Tausch in his compositions combined the better qualities of both Stamitz and Beer – virtuoso music, but not without considerable musical merit, though a critic in the A.M.Z. took him severely to task for writing octave passages in the *acute* register. Tausch wrote two concertos, an *Andante* and *Polonaise* for solo clarinet, and a *concertante* for two clarinets.

It is noticeable that all the concertos by Stamitz, Beer, Tausch, and Eichner were, with one or two exceptions where the C clarinet is indicated, written for the B flat instrument. This seems to have been selected quite early as the virtuoso's instrument, at once brilliant and mellow in tone. The A clarinet appears not to have been used as a solo instrument until Mozart revealed its quality in the Stadler Quintet of 1789, and later in the Concerto, K. 622, of 1791. This, the best-loved concerto in the repertoire, needs no description, but calls maybe for a few comments. Sketched originally for a basset-horn in G, K. 584b, it is not by any means the first clarinet concerto, as we have seen; it is, however, an easy first in musical quality, and has survived for that reason, while its many predecessors, once more popular, have been forgotten. It is often said that Mozart was the first to use the *chalumeau* register. This is not quite true. It is used in Faber's Mass, in the Vivaldi concertos, and to some considerable extent by Carl Stamitz. The latter also employed leaps from register to register, an innovation often ascribed to Mozart. But Mozart was wise in curbing the upward extension of the compass. He never wrote about g'''. Would that later composers had shown equal prudence. His concerto does not seem to have enjoyed any immediate popularity and little, if any, outside Vienna. No contemporary of Stadler appears to have played it; Beer preferred Mozart's *Variations on the March of the Samnites* 'of which he alone

—8 * *

possessed the manuscript'. This was presumably an arrangement of his variations on a theme from *Les Mariages Samnites* of Grétry, K. 352. Bärmann and Hermstedt, of a later generation, showed more liking for Weber and Spohr. It was not played in London till 1838, and was only rescued from comparative neglect in recent years. Mozart's clarinet works were composed primarily for Anton Stadler (1753–1812), the first Viennese clarinettist of note, a bosom friend of the composer from 1781 to 1791, and a fellow Mason. Stadler's outstanding qualities were those of Tausch, to whom he was considered but little inferior – charm and vocal quality of tone and refinement of style. Stadler stood in the same relationship to Mozart as Beer to Stamitz and later, the elder Bärmann to Weber and Hermstedt to Spohr. J. F. Schink in his *Litterarische Fragmente* of 1785 speaks of him as a 'braver Virtuoso' and has enthusiastic praise for the soft vocal qualities of his tone which no one with a heart could withstand. He praises especially his performance in the Serenade in B flat for thirteen wind instruments, K. 361. In his description, it may be noted, the basset-horns appear as 'Basset-Corni', while the double bassoon part was taken by a string bass. Stadler seems to have had a peculiar affection for the *chalumeau* register. This is indicated by his extension of the compass downwards and by the prominent use of these notes in works written for him by Mozart. He is sometimes described as an instrument-maker. There is no evidence for this.[21] Anton's younger brother, Johann (? 1756–1804), was also a clarinettist and basset-hornist of quality, though he never attained to the fame of his brother as a soloist. Anton played second to him in the Imperial Court Orchestra, which both joined in 1787.

To revert to Paris. Here the *Almanach Dauphin* of 1785 lists thirteen clarinettists, of whom six played the flute or oboe as well. The best known are Ernest (1ᵉ clarinette au Concert Spirituel), Gaspard Procksch, Klin, Michel Yost, Rathé, and, of course, Jean-Xavier Lefèvre. Stamitz is described as 'compositeur pour clarinette'. To these might be added A. Vanderhagen and M. F. Blasius, the former a Belgian of German parentage, the latter an Alsatian. Both wrote much music as well as serious tutors for their instrument, the former's *Méthode nouvelle et raisonnée* appearing in 1785, the latter's *Méthode* and *Nouvelle Méthode* respectively some ten or fifteen years later. Undoubtedly the greatest player was Lefèvre (1763–1829), a pupil of Michel Yost and an improver of his instrument. He was professor at the Paris Conservatoire from 1795 till 1825, composed much music for his instrument, including six concertos, and in 1802 wrote an extended tutor. This was long a standard work and was translated into several languages. Lefèvre was faithful throughout most of his brilliant career to the simple 6-key clarinet, refusing to adopt the many improvements which were made during the first quarter of the succeeding century. It was only in 1824 that he acquired a 13-key instrument. His tone was voluminous in the traditional French style, having none of the German mellowness, which according to Fétis he despised. He considered that the piercing of holes for more than six keys was injurious to the nature of the instrument.

In London no players appeared to rival John and William Mahon as concerto and orchestral players, itinerant foreign virtuosi excepted. In addition to Beer, Lefèvre paid at least one visit in 1790, and Flieger a year later. In 1789 David and Springer, two well-known virtuosi, had performed on the basset-horn, apparently the first appearance of this instrument in London. That interest in the clarinet was increasing is shown by the appearance of at least three anonymous tutors during the last twenty years of the century; not very serious or informative works, it is true, but indicative of current taste. Fingerings for the 5-key clarinet are followed by a collection of popular tunes and preceded by an engraving of a fashionably dressed dilettante performing in his garden. From about 1780 the clarinet began to figure in church bands. Church-wardens' accounts of this period show frequent purchases of clarinets at prices averaging just over 30 shillings apiece. Many of these 5-key instruments are still preserved. The English makers of this period are T. Collier, G. Miller, and T. Cahusac, all of London. Among the French makers were Prudent, Porthaux, Baumann, and Amlingue of Paris and, rather later, Cuvillier of St Omer, while Tuerlinckx of Malines and Raingo of Mons were the most distinguished Belgians. Of German makers the best known were the Grensers and Grundmann of Dresden, Gehring of Adorf, and Riedel. It is curious to note that, although clarinets were of late introduction to Dresden orchestras, A. Grenser was making them as early as 1777. They were none of them makers on a large scale, Tuerlinckx and Amlingue excepted, who supplied many instruments to the continental armies in the last fifteen or twenty years of the century.

Before passing on to the 19th century we may sum up very briefly. The clarinet still mainly made of boxwood had attained the dignity of at least six keys, but 5-key instruments were the more common. Intonation was still poor in the *chalumeau*, but passable in the *clarinet* and *acute* registers. The tone was what the player made it: soft, sweet, and agreeable or voluminous, brilliant, and penetrating. The former was the ideal of the German, the latter of the French, school. By 1800 few orchestras of any pretension would have been without it, and symphonists could write for it without hesitation. In military bands it had long won its tussle with the oboe. In chamber music its place had been assured by Mozart. As a solo instrument it had already had by 1800 a fairly long career. The unembellished *clarino* parts of Vivaldi and Molter, and, no doubt, of 'Mr Charles', had been greatly enriched and developed by the Mannheimers. In 1791 Mozart had written his imperishable concerto.

NOTES

[1] Vol. III, 1775. The three specimens are described and illustrated by Dr I. C. Peate in 'Welsh Musical Instruments', *Man*, February 1947.

[2] W. Bentley, 'Notes on the Musical Instruments figured in the windows of the Beauchamp Chapel, St Mary's, Warwick', *Birmingham Archeol. Soc.* Trans. LIII, 1928.

[3] Not to be confused with *stockhorn*, a forester's horn; see also L. G. Langwill, 'The Stock-and-horn', *Soc. of Antiquaries of Scotland*, Vol. LXXXXIV, Session 1949–50.

[4] C. Sachs, *The History of Musical Instruments*, New York, 1940, p. 212.

[5] Or possibly one, a small idioglot instrument of cane, covered with red leather, formerly No. 916 in the Snoeck Collection and described and pictured in R.M.E. catalogue, No. 221. This has six holes in front and one behind and is some 8½ inches (21 cm.) in length. The upper end is closed by the natural joint of the cane. It is very similar to the *chalumeau* described in Reynvaan's *Muzijkaal Konst-Woordenboek* of 1795, but this instrument is rather longer and has one key above the first finger-hole. In both the reed is on the upper side.

[6] At the time of this edition 68 instruments by the Denners are on record. See Philip T. Young, 'Woodwind Instruments by the Denners of Nürnberg' in *G.S.J.*, Vol. XX, March 1967. No fresh light is shed on the mystery of the Denner sons, but some interesting comparisons are made between the types of instrument which bear the two recognised versions of the Denner mark.

[7] This is particularly noticeable in the Klenig instruments, where the bore beginning at 13 mm. is narrowed down to 11·5 mm. before its junction with the foot-joint. Klenig's barrels are pear-shaped, while Liebav's, like Denner's, are slender and undeveloped (see Plate I).

[8] In cross-fingering the tone-hole immediately below that speaking is the note stopped with the finger. It is essentially a process of flattening.

[9] The 6-key clarinets by G. Miller of London depicted in Zoffany's painting (1781) of the Sharpe family are so treated. Wooden recorders were often covered with tortoise-shell. See also p. 13.

[10] V.-C. Mahillon, *Catalogue du Musée instrumental du conservatoire*, Brussels, Vol. III, 1909, p. 347.

[11] Ed. A. Ephrikian.

[12] C. Israel, *Frankfurter Concert-Chronik von 1713–80*, 1876.

[13] C. Mennicke, *Hasse und die Brüder Graun als Symphoniker*, 1906, where these instruments are erroneously stated to be in the Oberöster-reichisches Landesmuseum, Linz.

[14] This reference to the Molter *concerti* in the first edition of this book has stimulated much interest both in England and abroad. Today four *Concerti* for Clarinet in D by Molter are known and have been published by Breitkopf and Härtel. Recordings of all by distinguished British and continental clarinettists are listed by some of the specialist recording companies. Dating from about 1765, two *Concerti* for B flat clarinet by Franz Xaver Pokorny are also published under the same imprint.

[15] *Catalogue of the Music in the Fitzwilliam Museum*, Cambridge, 1893.

[16] G. Cucuel, *Études sur un orchestre au XVIIIe siècle*, Paris, 1913, p. 17, footnote.

[17] At least four sisters and a niece were soprano singers of the first rank.

[18] Vienna had long known the *chalumeau*, possibly Denner's 2-key invention.

[19] Baehr, an Austrian clarinettist, much praised by Chladni, has not been identified.

[20] According to Fétis, Schwartz was 'maître de musique du régiment de Kaunitz'.

[21] Oskar Kroll in his *Die Klarinette*, Kassel, 1965; English translation Hilda Morris, edited Anthony Baines, London, 1968, p. 19, says, 'The Vienna clarinettist Anton Stadler sought to increase the compass of the lower register. In co-operation with the maker T. Lotz he lengthened the clarinet . . . etc.' and again '. . . he performed a concerto on this so-called "bass clarinet".' The *Journal des Luxus und der Moden*, 1801, p. 543, reported, 'Herr Stadler . . . played a clarinet with modifications of his own invention.' At the time of writing (1970) there is a great revival of interest in this extended clarinet among the younger generation of players who, following the lead of Jiri Kratochvil in his extensive Mozart researches, have adopted the distinctive term 'basset-clarinet'.

CHAPTER 8

History from 1800

DURING THE FIRST sixty years of the 18th century the clarinet had had
a severe struggle to survive at all. As an orchestral instrument it had not
been welcomed with any particular enthusiasm. Wandering virtuoso
clarinettists had failed to impress more than a few composers with the
potentialities of their primitive instrument, and it was the Mannheim
School which had assured the new invention a place in the orchestra.
And then had arisen a new school of virtuosi to grapple with the
numerous concertos and chamber works written to display their talents;
or rather two schools, a German and a French. Towards the close of the
century the battle had been won; the clarinet had arrived and was on
the threshold of a brilliant career as a solo instrument. It was indeed the
demands of virtuosi which led to the great improvements in mechanism
with which this chapter will deal. Surveyed in the briefest and most
summary fashion the years from 1800 to 1970 may be divided into
periods as follows:

(1) 1800 to 1840, a period of soloists and concerto players, and from
1810 onwards of mechanical development.

(2) 1840 to 1860, continued mechanical improvement. Solo works
for wind instruments make rarer appearances in concert pro-
grammes.

(3) 1860 to 1900, solo works almost disappear: on the other hand
clarinet sonatas and chamber works become more frequent in
performance.

(4) 1900 to 1925, great advances in technique due to the increasing
demands of composers.

(5) 1925 to date. This period is marked by the re-emergence of the
wind soloist, a revival due in large measure to radio and sound
recordings.

As has been said, this division into periods is rough and ready and the
limiting dates are arbitrary.

By 1800 the clarinet had achieved six keys, though the large number
of surviving instruments suggests that many players were content with

five, the more popular model. More elaborate instruments were no doubt available. Simiot of Lyons claimed to have made a 12-key clarinet as early as 1803, and thirteen keys were fitted to a bass clarinet made by Desfontenelles of Lisieux in 1807. This interesting instrument is described in a later chapter. The great Heinrich Bärmann was playing on a 10-key instrument by Griessling and Schlott of Berlin, in 1810, at the height of his career. Reading downwards from the mouthpiece the indispensable six keys would be: the *speaker*, *a'* key, *c' sharp* key; and on the lower joint the open key for *e*, the *f sharp*, and *a flat/g sharp* keys.

Fig. 13   The 6 keys of the 18th-century clarinet
numbered in order of addition

Additional keys to assist purity of tone and intonation would be: on the *upper* joint, a *g' sharp* key for L. first finger, an *f'* key, the latter placed crosswise just under the first finger-hole or against the right side of the joint, and a cross- or side-key for *e' flat*. Without a key this note hardly existed. On the *lower* joint a cross-key for *b flat* might be added and a side- or cross-key to vent the flat and impure *b natural* obtained with R. first finger. The long trill-key on the upper joint, essential for the trill *a'–b'* for R. first finger, was more commonly found on English than on continental clarinets. The player would no doubt make his choice from the six additional keys offered to him. A late 9-key specimen by Stengel of Baireuth, *c.* 1825, in the writer's possession has, in addition to the six indispensables, keys for *g' sharp*, *e' flat*, and *b flat*. It is, of course, of boxwood and fitted with a short R.H. joint to allow the insertion of a longer piece to change the tonality from B flat to A. It has, too, an ivory thumb-rest. This adjunct seems to have come into use rather late in the instrument's history, probably about the turn of the century. In German boxwood clarinets it is often an integral part of the R.H. joint, carved from a ring of wood left from the turning. In modern instruments, it may be noted, the thumb-rest is of metal. In the best practice it is not let into the joint, but screwed to the surface so that it may be moved up or down to suit the player's hand.[1] An 11-key instrument, formerly owned by the famous Finnish virtuoso B. Crusell

(1775–1838) and made by Grenser of Dresden, has all the keys we have mentioned, less that for *b natural* on the lower joint. This note could be produced by stopping the fifth and sixth holes, as a flattened *c′*, or by forcing up with the lips the flat note obtained from the closing of the first four holes. The latter is of course the normal fingering on the older models of today. The *forked f′* obtained by stopping the second finger-hole L.H. (in reality a flattened *f′ sharp*) is still a widely used fingering on German clarinets. As has been said in the previous chapter, forked fingerings are invariably better in the *clarinet* register than in the fundamental. For instance, *c‴*, the twelfth of forked *f′*, is perhaps the best note on the old clarinet, pure and capable of infinite gradation. *Forked f″*, too, on the lower joint often speaks more freely than the note obtained by the cross-key; on the other hand its fundamental is weak and sharp. One key remained to be added, an open key to close the *g/d″* hole controlled by the R. little finger. This hole, it will be remembered, was bored obliquely through a swelling in the wood to reach the bore at happy. The oblique hole was much too small and, placed an inch or more too high, afforded very inadequate venting to the notes immediately above; it compared very badly in fact with the semitone just above it, the hole for which was far too large and placed too low. An open-standing key, with its shank sunk and pivoted in the wood or carried

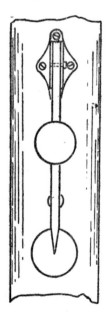

Fig. 14   *Left:* Müller's open *f* key mounted in a saddle.
Right: A saddle mounting

in a saddle, allowed the traditional swelling to be dispensed with for ever and the tone-hole to be enlarged and located in its correct position.

Fig. 15   The 7 keys added 1800–10

The credit for all these improvements, for the addition of the seven additional keys, was claimed by Iwan Müller. The claim has never been disputed. The improvements of Simiot and Desfontenelles were probably not widely known, since both were provincial makers. Müller, who was an itinerant virtuoso of Russian extraction – he was born at Reval in 1786 and was described as a *Russische Kaiserliche Kammermusiker* in the A.M.Z. – had initiated his improvements at least as early as 1808. In October of that year he was using a 16-key basset-horn by Grenser of Dresden, and in the following year the A.M.Z's Vienna correspondent informed its readers that these improvements could be applied to the clarinet, enabling it to play with certainty and accuracy in all keys and registers. Merklein, a Viennese maker, had carried out his ideas. According to Kees, *Darstellung des Fabriks-und-Gewertwessens*, 1803, II, pp. 166 *et seq.*, Merklein himself devised a new type of clarinet under the title of 'Orphinette'. The provision of leather under the keys to minimise the rattling is also mentioned. Gyrowetz singled out for special praise the ability of the new clarinet to play in all keys with ease and security without change of joints. The inventor had already begun to claim that his model was *omnitonique* and that only one instrument, the B flat, was necessary for the orchestral musician. The claim has been repeated many times since then. In 1811 or 1812 Müller had migrated to Paris and had had another instrument made by Gentellet. He had, moreover, secured a wealthy patron in a banker. But Gentellet's order-book was not to be filled for some time, since an official commission of musicians and players, appointed in 1812, reported unfavourably on the new invention. The loss of the distinctive tone-colour of clarinets in various tonalities was deplored, so *pièces de rechange* continued in use for several years to come. No doubt it was the innate conservatism of Lefèvre and Duvernoy, who sat as professional advisers with Méhul, Cherubini, Gossec, Sarrette, and Catel, that swayed the balance. The verdict may be quoted in part.

'Nos clarinettes par leurs différentes proportions produisent différents caractères de sons; ainsi la clarinette en *ut* a le son brillant et vif; la clarinette en *sib* est propre au genre pathétique et majestueux, la clarinette en *la* est propre au genre pastoral. Il est incontestable que la nouvelle clarinette de M. Müller, si elle était exclusivement adoptée, priverait les compositeurs de la ressource que leur donne l'emploi de ces caractères très-distincts.'

The priority of Müller's invention is an academic question. What is undisputed is that he had made an honest and practical attempt to improve intonation by re-location of the tone-holes. He was a pioneer in stressing the principle that holes must be placed in their correct position at all costs and that keys must be made to cover them. Theobald Boehm carried these principles further some twenty years later. It was one thing to allot a key and hole to each semitone, but quite another to arrange an easy passage from key to key, especially in the case of those appropriated to the two little fingers. This has been the main concern of makers ever since. To take but two examples, the passage from *b'* to *c'' sharp* and from *c''* to *e'' flat* in the *clarinet* register. In the first, the little fingers of both hands are engaged and, while the right hand remains static, the L. little finger must move instantaneously down or sideways to the second long key beside it; in the second, the R. little finger must move instantaneously from the head of the *c''* key to that of the *e'' flat* just above, *not* an easy movement, if an intermediate note is to be avoided. Müller made the operation somewhat easier by soldering a branch, to be manipulated by the R. thumb, to the shank of the long *e* key to the left of the joint. This made possible the trill from *e* to *f sharp*, and gave some facility in rapid passages between the two. Another branch for the R. thumb provided an additional lever for the *e'' flat* key. So the passage from *f* to *g sharp* or *c''* to *e'' flat* was somewhat facilitated. Neither of these innovations was popular, and clarinets so equipped are seldom found. Rollers fitted to two adjacent keys are a neater expedient. These are stated to have been the invention of César Janssen, a clarinettist of the Paris Opéra, and were applied to the bassoon and flute as well. They may be made of ebonite, ivory, or metal and are still in occasional use. They may, however, be an obstruction to execution, unless they are carefully made and fitted.

The adoption of Müller's invention was only checked for a time by the adverse verdict of the Commission. Before 1820 it had been taken

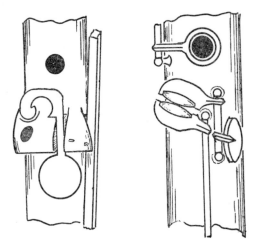

Fig. 16   *Left:* The misplaced *a flat/e″ flat* key of early clarinets. *Right:* Modern rearrangement of *f* and *a flat* keys

into use by J.-B. Gambaro and Frédéric Berr in Paris and was attaining popularity in Germany. Bischoff of Darmstadt was a notable maker, so too Wünnenberg of Cologne, Geisler of Amsterdam, and Schott of Mainz who advertised clarinets of the 'nouvelle invention' with silver keys at 75 florins in boxwood, and at 85 in ebony. But no maker made it to greater perfection than Simiot of Lyons. This city was for many years a rival of Paris in neatness of workmanship. In addition to Simiot we may mention his pupil, Piatet, and Tabard, Benoit, Brelet, and Muller, who all found markets in Switzerland and Italy. The writer is fortunate in possessing one of Simiot's 19-key clarinets, a beautiful piece of workmanship, and possibly an exhibition model (see Plate 4*c*). It is made of ebonised light wood and is riveted against cracking. The mounts and the keys, which are mounted between pillars on foot-plates sunk in the wood, are of pure silver. In addition to Müller's thirteen keys, it possesses on the *lower* joint an additional lever for *a flat/e flat* between the two long keys for L. little finger and a second key for *b natural*; on the *upper*, the open *g* hole is moved round towards the top of the joint and controlled by a thumb-plate. There are in addition three supplementary trill-keys. The speaker is of an improved form. The orifice, pierced on the top, is controlled, by means of a ring contrived in a groove in the wood, by a lever at the back. This neat and precise action was copied by S. Koch of Vienna, and is found in the boxwood instrument made many years later by Vinatieri of Turin for Ferdinando

Busoni (Berlin, 1442).[2] Müller's levers for R. thumb were replaced by two ingenious hinges. An extra joint in A was provided, a late example of a *corps de rechange*, and to extend the lower joint a rack and pinion were fitted. Another elaborate model is illustrated in J. Fahrbach's *Neueste Wiener Klarinetten-Schule, c.* 1840. This has at least three keys to be added to Müller's thirteen. It has an *f' sharp* key on the upper joint mounted on the left side, a short side- *e' flat* key in addition to the cross-key, a key of great utility, and a long *a flat* for the L. little finger as found in Simiot's design. A lug is soldered to the *c' sharp* key on the upper joint so that it may be fingered with R. 1, an improvement preserved in modern German clarinets, while another short touchpiece is fitted to the long *e* key, enabling the same finger not only to close the fourth finger-hole, but to depress the key as well. Thus the difficult trill *e/f sharp* could be safely performed. English makers made a rather different 13-key clarinet. T. Key, R. Bilton, and other London makers for long rejected Müller's *f* key, retaining the swelling and the misplaced oblique hole for R. little finger. Their additional key was a cross *b natural* placed just below the fourth hole. T. L. Willman added a lever for R. thumb to the long *e* key, thus permitting easy transition from *e* to *f sharp*. But Müller's innovations were put completely in the shade by a little-known clarinet patented by William Gutteridge of Cork in 1824. The specification (No. 4890) reveals an instrument which far surpasses Müller's in ingenuity and ran it close in time, since it was devised as early as 1813. The designer's military service in the Peninsula delayed the realisation of his ideas till 1824. In its complete form the instrument was equipped with eighteen keys. It went far to tackle two problems which Müller left unsolved – the difficulty of playing across the break and the gliding of the little fingers from key to key in rapid passages. The latter problem was met by a logical, if complicated, rearrangement of the keys of the lower joint, the former by the provision of a closed key for *b' natural* for L. thumb alongside the speaker and the extension of the downward compass by two semitones. These gave *a* and *b' flat* as their twelfths. The same idea occurred to Adolphe Sax some sixteen years later. But the ingenuity of the designer, which called for light, well-contrived mechanism with pillar mountings, outstripped the skill of the maker, Clementi of London, who published a method for the new invention, At this point we may leave the development of the instrument for a time to consider some of its players.

The period 1800 to 1840 was the heyday of the soloist and touring virtuoso. Iwan Müller (1786–1854) was typical of the latter. Apart from a longish stay in Paris, during which he visited London and played in a quartet by the elder Bochsa and in the Beethoven Septet, his restlessness drove him to every capital in Europe. It was only towards the end of his life that he settled down as a court musician at Bückeburg. Judged by contemporary criticisms his playing was impetuous, fiery, and brilliant, but somewhat lacking in delicacy. He was particularly fond of displaying his ability in the *acute* register to the detriment of his tone. Generally speaking his qualities were, as might have been expected, less appreciated in Germany than elsewhere. Müller wrote a quantity of brilliant solo pieces for his instrument. His best remembered work is his *Méthode* published about 1825 in French and in a German translation. It was dedicated to George IV. The statements that he set up as an instrument-maker in Paris, and was a professor at the Conservatoire, have not been substantiated. A player of equal, if not superior, attainments was Johann Simon Hermstedt (1778–1846). Most of his life was spent as conductor of the court orchestra at Sondershausen, where he was fortunate in the encouragement which he received from the Duke, himself a clarinettist (see Plate 3*f*). For him Spohr wrote his four concertos, his *Fantasie sur un thème de Danzi*, and, no doubt, his *Sechs deutsche Lieder* with their telling obbligati, and his chamber works in which the clarinet plays a prominent part. Hermstedt's execution was brilliant in the extreme; he shared with Müller a partiality for the *acute* register and for dramatic gradations of tone and striking *crescendi*. On at least one occasion his rather exaggerated *crescendo* led to an amusing mishap as readers of Spohr's *Autobiography* will remember. Hermstedt is stated to have composed concertos himself and to have written a tutor. He performed upon an elaborated 13-key clarinet, fitted with tuning-slides between the joints and with an ivory barrel. His mouthpiece was of gold and silver.

With the two preceding may be contrasted three players of a different order, all renowned less for fire and brilliance than for the delicacy and beauty of their tone. They are H. J. Bärmann, F. Berr, and T. L. Willman. Heinrich Joseph Bärmann (1784–1847), the greatest of them, inherited the best of both the French and German schools from Beer and Tausch. He excelled in the soft velvety quality of his tone and in the refinement of his nuances. Weber was charmed by his musicianship when he met him at Munich in 1811, and was immediately inspired to compose his *Concertino* and his two great concertos for him. The Quintet, op. 34, and the *Variations on a Theme from Silvana*, op. 33, followed; only the *Grand Duo*, op. 47, was not dedicated to him, but to his rival, Hermstedt. From 1807 he was resident as a court musician at Munich, making constant concert tours all over Europe, often with Weber. Nor were Mendelssohn and Meyerbeer less charmed by his personality and musicianship. It was for him and his son Carl that the former composed his two *Konzertstücke* for clarinet, basset-horn, and pianoforte, op. 113 and 114. In 1819 he came to London to play two of his own works at a Philharmonic Concert. In Paris he was especially popular, even idolised. He composed close on forty works for his instrument. In his tutor his son Carl praised the quality of the tone which he drew from his simple boxwood instrument, contrasting it with that of the better equipped instruments of the 1860s.

Frédéric Berr (1793–1838), born at Mannheim, began his career as a bassoonist, but soon abandoned the bassoon for the clarinet. He held every worthwhile appointment in Paris in succession to J.-B. Gambaro and was professor at the Conservatoire from 1831 to 1838. His influence on French clarinettists was profound, especially in impressing upon them German ideals of tone and refinement. As a first step he insisted on his pupils playing with the reed upon the lower lip. He was an early convert to Müller's improvements and wrote, among much other music, an admirable *Traité complet* which has been many times re-edited.

Thomas Lindsay Willman (?–1840), an English player, was plainly an artist of the highest class. Fétis, who placed Bärmann on a pedestal by himself, put Willman only second to him. The date and place of his birth are unknown. He was possibly the son of John Willman, at one time a bandmaster in Ireland. The son appears to have been a pupil of Christopher Eley, who came to England about 1783 in charge of a band of twelve musicians, recruited in Hanover for the Coldstream Guards. Eley was also master of the East India Company's Volunteer Band, an organisation which trained several fine musicians. Willman, after a sojourn in Ireland, appears to have been associated for some little time with the Coldstreams, a band which turned out many fine clarinettists. Among them were Lazarus, Pollard, Maycock, and Burton, all well known later as orchestral musicians. Willman retired from his military duties in 1825, but before this, in 1817, he had stepped into the places of John and William Mahon. Until his death he remained the idol of the public. He excelled in the beauty of his tone, which was compared to the musical glasses, and in the vocal quality of his playing. He shone especially in obbligati, frequently accompanying Mrs Salmon (a niece of the Mahons), Catalani, Sontag, and Malibran. His association with Mrs Salmon was especially successful. According to the singer Henry Phillips, 'her voice was rich and full like the clarinet, and when Willman accompanied her it was difficult at times to distinguish the voice from the instrument'. It is not perhaps fanciful to suppose that the quality of her voice was influenced by the clarinets of her two uncles, the Mahons. According to Fétis, a very severe critic, no equivocal sound (son douteux) ever came from his clarinet. His execution was probably less assured than Hermstedt's, since, in the words of a critic, the great difficulties of a Spohr concerto, which he played with the Philharmonic in 1838, seemed 'to baffle the skill of the performer'. He played, as already noticed, on a 13-key instrument of English make, for which he wrote an excellent tutor in 1825–26, and favoured the embouchure with the reed against the upper lip. This practice seems to have continued for some years in England, since John Hopkinson in his *New and Complete Preceptor*, published a few years after Willman's death, states: 'Foreigners play with the reed downwards, the contrary is practised in England.'

Other soloists of repute in England during the early years of the 19th century included Edward Hopkins (1778–1859), bandmaster of the Scots Guards and musical director of Vauxhall Gardens. He was long principal at Covent Garden, where he excelled in obbligati; his brother George Hopkins was also a well-known clarinettist; Joseph Williams (1795–1875), a native of Hereford, was a violinist, pianist, and composer, as well as a clarinettist. Coming to London, he was appointed leader of the Queen's private band in 1837 with Eisert as his second and later became a director of the Philharmonic. He was overshadowed in the early years of his career by Willman, in the later by Lazarus. He wrote an excellent tutor in 1855 for Boosey which incorporated many of Klosé's exercises. According to the *Musical World* he had the parts of Mozart's concerto in his possession for twenty years before Willman performed it in 1838. On the continent famous soloists were: J. G. H. Backofen (1768–1839), of Durlach and Darmstadt, who performed on the harp and basset-horn as well, and, in addition to his *Anweisung* (1803 and 1824), wrote three concertos and chamber music; he was stated to have been a maker;[3] A. Beerhalter (1800–52) of Stuttgart, also a noted basset-hornist; J. Bender (1798– ?) and V. Bender (1801–73), brilliant German clarinettists from Bechtheim and notable directors of military bands in Antwerp and Brussels; F. A. Bliesener (1780–1841) of Berlin; P. X. Christiani (1787–1867) of Amsterdam; J. A. Canongia (1784–1842) of Lisbon, a touring virtuoso and prolific composer; B. Crusell (1775–1838) a Finn, of Stockholm, who wrote three concertos and several quartets for clarinet and strings; his clarinet by Grenser is preserved at Stockholm; I.-F. Dacosta (1778–1866) of Paris, a well-known pupil of C. Duvernoy (1766–1845) at the Paris Conservatoire and an early bass clarinettist; W. Farník (1769–1838) of Prague, who, we are told by the A.M.Z., overcame the greatest difficulties with ease and without grimaces; J. Faubel (1801– ?) of Munich, a pupil of Bär-mann; J. Friedlowsky (1777–1859) of Prague and Vienna, credited with a magical tone; J.-B. Gambaro (1785–1828), an Italian, long resident in Paris, composer of two concertos, chamber music, and some excellent studies, was an early devotee of the 13-key clarinet; J. Kleine, of Am-sterdam; J. G. Kotte (1797–1857), Weber's solo clarinet at the Dresden Opera. Caroline Schleicher (1794–185?) was the first recorded woman virtuoso of the clarinet. She was an accomplished musician and made many successful concert tours in Germany, Austria, and Switzerland. She married E. Krähmer, a well-known Viennese oboist, with whom she appeared in double concertos and as a soloist. F. Sebastiani (1803–60) was soloist of the San Carlo and founder of the Neapolitan School. Among the works played by these virtuosi were concertos by Pleyel, Krommer, Cartellieri, Schneider of Berlin, Crusell, Riotte, Winter, Wilms, Stumpf, Friedrich, Müller, Traugott-Eberwein. All have now passed into oblivion after a temporary popularity, together with those of Carl Stamitz and the other Mannheimers. Mozart's great work, strange to relate, seems to have achieved no success during the early part of the 19th century. Willman played it for the first time in London in 1838, when doubts were cast upon its authenticity. It was considered, in the words of a critic, 'a product of the laboratory of André'.

The formative years for the development of clarinet mechanism were the years from 1835 to 1850. From 1825 or thereabouts the skill of the maker had been maturing, less perhaps in Germany than in France and Belgium. In Brussels G. C. Bachmann, professor of the clarinet at the Conservatoire, and Charles Sax *père* had developed a high degree of neatness, and the latter had found in his son Adolphe an apt apprentice. Adolphe was, moreover, a skilled clarinettist, and so it is not surprising to find in his patents of 1840 and 1842 an advanced design. Less bold that Gutteridge, Sax was more practical; in addition he had the ability to carry out his own ideas. He had in view a greater compass and even-ness of tone. By extending the range down to written *d* he completed the scale of E *flat* and hoped to secure a purer *b′ flat* and *a′*. With an addi-tional speaker he provided easier emission and greater security to the *acute* register as far as *c″″* and even to *d* and *e* beyond. By changing the closed *b natural* key for R. 3 into an open key, closed by means of rings for R. 2 and 3, he enabled transitions from *g* to *b* and from *d″* to *f′ sharp* to be played in tune, an impossible feat before. Other improvements were: a covered cup for the open *g'* hole in which Simiot had anticipated him; a gilt metal mouthpiece; a pierced plate for L. 1, to lessen the diameter of the vent-hole and so to facilitate the fifth harmonics; a long tenon between the upper and lower joints, to allow a proper position for the *c' sharp* hole. Some of these improvements survive, among them the ring-keys on the lower joint and the long tenon. The additional speaker and semitone at the bottom are indispensable to the bass clarinet, an instrument which Sax did much to improve. His forged keywork is light and strikingly modern in design, far removed from the crudities of a few years before; it is quite evident that his influence on his immediately successors in Brussels, Albert and Mahillon, was immense. His improved clarinet, with extension, cost 150 francs in 1851, his bass clarinet 200–300 francs.

Sax's patents, however, enjoyed less success than they merited, at any rate in France. In Paris H. Klosé, who had succeeded Berr at the Conservatoire, had been collaborating between 1839 and 1843 with Auguste Buffet to produce a clarinet on Boehm principles. These were first, to place the tone-holes where the laws of acoustics, and not convenience of fingering, demanded they should be; secondly, to contrive suitable mechanism to cover them. It is well to be clear on two points. Firstly, Boehm himself had nothing whatever to do with the new clarinet; he supplied no lay-out of holes or mechanism. Secondly, the inventors called their invention, which was patented in 1844 (brevet 9759), 'clarinette à anneaux mobiles'. The name *clarinette système Boehm* was only applied to it rather later for convenience and brevity. In the notes which follow it will be called the *Boehm clarinet*. The precise parts played by the two inventors are not known. One may suspect that Klosé presented his problems to Buffet *jeune* and that the latter, fresh from his labours on the Boehm flute and oboe, provided a solution. A preliminary model figured in the Paris exhibition of 1839, where Buffet was awarded a medal for a 'clarinette construite d'après la même système mais que M. Boehm n'avait pas cherché jusqu'ici à appliquer à la clarinette'. We have no details of this model; possibly it had the rings on the lower joint which appeared on Sax's clarinet and which are often attributed to Buffet.[4]

The Boehm clarinet will be well known to most readers, and can be accorded no more than a summary description. The standard model has 24 tone-holes, governed by 17 keys and 6 rings. It solved at once one of the problems left over by Müller – the freeing of the little fingers from their task of gliding from key to key. The keys controlling the three lowest tone-holes are duplicated and interlocked, so that the three notes

—9 * *

e/b′, f/c″, f sharp/c″ sharp, can be fingered by *one* finger alone and on *either* side of the instrument as convenience or necessity dictates. Thus economy of fingerwork is achieved; sequences and trills in extreme keys, formerly unplayable, are facilitated; and in theory, if not always in practice, gliding is abolished. Furthermore, the L. little finger is set free on most occasions to finger *middle c sharp*, when this follows on notes formerly employing both little fingers. It was, no doubt, Buffet's inventiveness which devised this simple but ingenious duplication. Above the four duplicate keys for R. little finger are placed the holes for the four semitones *a, b flat, b*, and *c′*, controlled by three fingers. This is made possible by the provision of a padded cup over the *c′* hole, automatically closed by ring-keys placed over the three holes just below it. On the upper joint there is a rearrangement of the tone-holes. The two lowest give, as on the Müller system, *c′ sharp* and *d′*. Owing to the jointing of the instrument the hole for *c′ sharp* is placed too high, unless a long tenon is employed. In this case it can be placed in line with the other holes, in its right position and correctly sized. L. 2 closes two holes by means of a ring soldered to a rod, the hole for *e′ flat* or *d′ sharp* and above it the *e′* hole. The open key above the *e′ flat* hole can be closed by any of the three fingers of the right hand by means of a clutch or *correspondance* between the ring mechanism of the lower and upper joints. This is generally known as the 'long' *e flat* or *b flat*, and is of special service in arpeggios. Above the *e′* hole lies the *f′* hole, smaller than the first finger-hole of the Müller system and of a more suitable size for venting the fifth harmonics. On the Boehm clarinet the thumb-hole speaks not *g′* but *f′ sharp*, L. 1 closing not only the *f′* hole but the small *g′* hole just above by means of a ring-key which controls a padded cup. The latter is also closed automatically by a ring-key surrounding the thumb-hole, an arrangement evidently suggested by Simiot. Above the *g′* hole are the closed keys for *g′ sharp* and *a′*, the former, often provided with an adjusting screw, crossing over the shank of the latter. The speaker retains its traditional position at the rear of the instrument. Four trill-keys are provided at the side of the upper joint, also a closed cross-key to furnish *e′ flat* or *d′ sharp* as on Müller's clarinet. A closed key for *b natural* on the lower, fitted just under the fifth finger-hole, gives an additional fingering for this note. Klosé wrote a tutor for his new model in 1843 which has been many times translated and re-edited.

The use of the Boehm clarinet spread rapidly in France, where its use was imposed in all national conservatoires, far less rapidly elsewhere. It was not unopposed even in France. To meet the challenge of the new invention a few Paris makers brought out improved models of the 13-key clarinet, incorporating keys and rings borrowed from the new instrument. Such was the *clarinette omnitonique* of 1845, a joint product of Buffet-Crampon, a firm shortly to attain considerable fame, and the clarinettist Blancou. This, and a model of F. Lefèvre, introduced in 1853, may have achieved some currency, since both figure, together with the 13-key and the Boehm, in the second edition of Romero's tutor. Lefèvre's model in particular borrowed heavily from the Klosé-Buffet clarinet. Gyssens, a former workman of Buffet *jeune*, had less success with his system which he produced in 1852 and in the end turned to the more profitable business of making collars. No doubt the older generation clung to their simple Müller clarinets, while the younger, finding the task of relearning their fingering less difficult than they had supposed, preferred the full advantages of the new system to the few offered by hybrids. Liverani took the Boehm to Italy without at first meeting with much success. It was not adopted at the Brussels Conservatoire till well on in the 1890s.[5] Gustave Poncelet taught it towards the end of his career, but continued himself to play upon an older system. And so did Henry Lazarus in England, although he recommends the Boehm as more convenient in his *New and Modern Method* of 1881, and possessed a basset-horn with Boehm fingering. The new instrument was advertised in the Rudall, Carte catalogue of 1854 and pictured in Tamplini's *The Bandsman* of 1857. A few were imported for trial in regimental bands, but were presumably found too fragile for military use. No London professional is known to have adopted it,[6] and no London maker turned to its manufacture, though Fieldhouse, cleverer and more enterprising than his fellows, gathered some ideas from its mechanism. It was not in fact until the early 1890s that the use of Klosé's instrument became more than infrequent in England, and it is only within the last sixty years that its use has become common. Spain favoured, as we shall see, at first an instrument of Spanish invention, but has of late years shown a preference for the French clarinet. In Germany, Austria, and other countries under German influence, Müller clarinets have until quite recently been predominant, and some of the improved models of this system will be considered later. Today Boehm players are becoming more numerous east of the Rhine, and some forty years ago there was an established school of them at Leipzig. This is not to say that German makers do not make such clarinets. Some make them very well, notably Schmidt of Mannheim, who has introduced some notable improvements. The Slavs, too, always notable clarinettists, have ever favoured the older types, but recent information suggests that the use of the Boehm is spreading in

Czechoslovakia. The importation of many thousand Boehm clarinets every year from France to the U.S.A. suggests that here, too, the French clarinet predominates. Here and there, however, will be found an artist of outstanding ability who sees no reason to change the system on which he graduated in Germany, Bohemia, or Russia, and near the beginning of the century the influence of such men appears to have been considerable. At that time American firms, as well as French houses with American connections such as Selmer and Buffet, are known to have produced a quantity of the more advanced 'simple system' clarinets for this market.

And here we may fitly compare the two systems, the German and the French. In ease of fingering there is really no comparison; the advantage must rest with the Boehm. The fingers in the first place are far more comfortably placed; the mechanism is quicker and more responsive, in particular the short levers for the little finger L.H., which replace to advantage the long and yielding levers of the Müller; and there are many more duplicate fingerings. There are, for instance, in addition to the duplicated lower notes, three choices for *b natural*, five for *e' flat*, six or seven for its twelfth. There are fewer fork fingerings. But to say the fingering of the Boehm is more logical is to make an exaggerated claim. It is true, perhaps, of the fingering in flat keys; in sharp keys, with the back-fingering for *b*, the claim would be harder to support. In short the Müller calls for nimbleness of finger, the Boehm for nimbleness of wit to select the correct fingering. Nor is the tone more even on the Boehm than on the best Müller clarinets. In fact the latter is better vented at the bottom. In any case the fetish of evenness of tone may be pursued too far. Certain notes are better on one than on the other. To take an example or two. The Müller has an advantage in *b/f" sharp* and in *c'''*. On the Boehm *b flat/f"* is decidedly better, and the emission of the *acute* register is facilitated by the smaller vent. Is there any discernible difference of tone between the two? This is a matter of mild controversy. To nine hearers out of ten there is no apparent difference. The tenth, gifted with a hypersensitive ear, an ear, that is, tuned to discern certain elusive partials, might detect a more open tone in the Boehm, a more veiled tone in the Müller, due to the forked fingerings and the greater number of closed keys. To another the tone of the former might seem less centred, less concentrated, more diffuse than that of the latter. There is certainly less difference between the two than between the French and German bassoons. And the difference in schools and styles must be taken into account. A player will as a rule obtain on any system of clarinet the tone which he admires, which he strives to cultivate, or in which he has been schooled. We may go further; in the writer's experience the tone which a skilled player draws from an antique boxwood instrument is astonishingly like the tone he obtains from his modern clarinet with double or treble the number of keys. Nevertheless, it is now recognised that on average there *is* some difference between the characteristic tones of the Müller and the Boehm types which, by mathematical analysis, can be traced to the configuration of the bore and the disposition and treatment of the holes.

Generally speaking the Boehm player employs a wider mouthpiece and shorter lay than is usual with the Müller, while the long lay of the latter demands a harder, narrower reed. In theory there should be no difference in *intonation*. In practice there is, since some of the duplicate fingerings of the Boehm give varying shades of sharpness or flatness which the experienced player can turn to good account. Excellence of intonation depends primarily on the care expended by the maker. The more elaborate Müller is as a rule built for the orchestral musician or soloist and tuned to a nicety. Mahillon and the Alberts excelled in making and tuning them; so, too, Oskar Oehler of Berlin. On the other hand the Boehm clarinet has suffered from its very popularity. It is not as a rule made by the smaller maker, but by the large mass-producing firms in thousands to a price, a price which seldom permits the luxury of fine tuning. This necessary task is too often handed on to the purchaser.

The Boehm clarinet of 1950 differs hardly at all from that of 1843. The favourite model is still that fitted with 17 keys and 6 rings, known as the 'plain Boehm' or 'Boehm ordinaire'. The touchpieces of the keys are now rather larger, those for the little fingers in particular, and the tone-holes rather smaller. In many early Boehms the holes were unduly large to the detriment of tone and intonation. Some additions have been made from time to time. The more important are: on the lower joint, the *low e flat*, an additional lever for *a flat/e flat*; on the upper the 'articulated' *g″ sharp* key and the 'forked' *b″ flat* device. To consider them singly. The *low e flat* is essential for players who use only one clarinet, the B flat. This practice is now commoner in the theatre than in the symphony orchestra. In theory its twelfth, *b′ flat*, should be a better note than that obtained with the normal fingering; its quality, however, is markedly different. The additional *e″ flat* completes the duplication of the keys for the little fingers, but is of less utility than the *articulated g″ sharp*. The latter presents obvious advantages. It facilitates some passages in sharp keys, and makes possible perfect trills of *b-c′ sharp* and *f″ sharp-g″ sharp*; and it also allows the *c′ sharp/g″ sharp* hole to be located in its correct position and in line with the finger-holes. For this purpose the body is made in one piece or, alternatively, with a long tenon. The key is made in two pieces: a shank, carrying a padded cup and sprung to open, and a touchpiece for L. little finger. The latter is fitted with a stronger spring and, bearing upon the cup, prevents it rising till the little finger exerts its pressure. The shank is attached to the rod which carries the rings for R.H. and moves in concert with them. There are, however, disadvantages. The mechanism, of which there are many forms, is just short of absolute reliability, and one of the best fingerings for *f'''* is removed. Furthermore, the forked *g'' sharp* (L. 1 and 2 + R. 1 and 2), an excellent note on many instruments, removes just as many difficulties as the articulated key. In passing it may be noted that P. Pupeschi, a noted Florentine maker, tackled the problem of the *c'/g'' sharp* key, always an obstacle to fluent technique in keys with more than 2 sharps or flats, in a far more drastic manner. He removed the separate touchpiece altogether. On his improved clarinets, both Boehm and Müller, the key is articulated, but the stronger retaining spring is depressed by pressure upon any of the 3 keys on the left of the lower joint. This allows easy passage from *b'* or *c'' sharp* to *g'' sharp*, without gliding in the case of the old system, without forethought in the case of the Boehm. Carefully made and balanced the mechanism functions perfectly and is of very real assistance to the player. The *forked b'' flat* on the upper joint is probably the most useful addition to the plain Boehm. Another ring is needed for the third hole, raising the number to seven, but the mechanism is simple and satisfactory. It increases the fingerings for *e' flat* to six, those for *b'' flat* to seven. The *low e flat* and additional *a flat/e flat* lever were known, as we have seen, in the 1820s. The *articulated g sharp* and *forked b flat*[7] were fitted to the clarinet in the 1860s.

The clarinet, armed with these additions, is known as the 'full Boehm'. It is less popular now than it was. Symphony players, almost to a man, prefer the plain Boehm, distrusting additions which may let them down, and which add weight to an already heavy instrument. Furthermore, the *low e flat* is considered by many to detract from the brilliancy of the tone. Some additional keys occasionally fitted are a closed key to produce *c' sharp* or *g'' sharp*, fitted below the fourth finger-hole, and trill-keys for *g' sharp* and *a'*. These usually take the form of rod-keys mounted on the right side and worked by R. first finger. An additional trill-key for *g' sharp* is sometimes added to the customary four on the right side of the upper joint.

Before passing on to the variations of the Müller system one drastic reformation of the Boehm may be briefly described. This is the *Romero* clarinet, called after its inventor Antonio Romero y Andía. On his appointment as professor at the Real Conservatorio of Madrid in 1849, Romero introduced the Boehm clarinet, but during the 1850s began to devise a better system to give more facility across the break. He made repeated journeys to Paris, but failed to awaken any interest in Buffet *jeune* and Triébert. Finally Paul Bié consented to realise his invention, and it was with him that Romero took out patents in 1862 and 1867. The perfected model of that year is a miracle of ingenious and compli- cated workmanship. The one-piece body is pierced with 28 holes – with 29 when the *low e flat* is fitted – but has no more touchpieces than the plain Boehm. Romero boldly set out to grapple with the problem of the break by transferring many of the duties of the left hand to the right. The holes for *g′ sharp*, *a′*, and *b′ flat*, re-located in a line above the *g′* hole, were each closed by a key sprung to open. These keys were in turn depressed by levers bearing upon the cups, each actuated by a stronger spring. Pressure was released and the keys were allowed to open by the fingers of the right hand. It is the principle of the *articulated g sharp* which also made its appearance, and possibly its début, on this clarinet. The idea is more attractive in theory than in practice. Pads under constant pressure are apt to cling to their holes and weak springs lose their power when constantly depressed. The lower joint is plain Boehm with a modification in detail which transforms the normally closed *f sharp* into an open key to give aditional venting to *g*.[8] Romero, it may be noted, provided some additional trills, including a useful key for the *b′* to *c″* shake at the top of the instrument. Had the mechanism been entirely reliable the instrument might have enjoyed some popularity. The paucity of extant specimens, however, shows that its appeal was limited. There were some drastic changes of fingering; *b′ flat* for instance, not *g′*, was the open note obtained with all fingers removed. That the mechanism was in constant need of adjustment is shown by the provi- sion of at least 15 adjusting screws. A boxwood specimen in the writer's collection shows signs of considerable use. It has a beautiful tone and in intonation is far superior to the contemporary Boehm clarinets. The price of the instrument was 360 francs in boxwood and 400 in *ébène*, a miracle of cheapness. The idea of manipulating the closed keys at the top of the instrument by the ring-keys on the bottom joint has attracted others in addition to Romero. By a remarkable coincidence Mahillon exhibited a similar, but simpler, model at the Paris Exhibition of 1867, where Romero's invention also figured. Mahillon's design (Brussels 2300) was based on the 13-key clarinet, Romero's on the Boehm. A similar idea is found in G. H. Child's very ingenious and novel system for which a provisional patent was obtained in 1924.[9] Figs. 17 and 18 show the lay-out of the Romero and Child mechanisms.

To return to the Müller. This developed on different lines in Germany, Belgium, and England. In Germany the original model was much

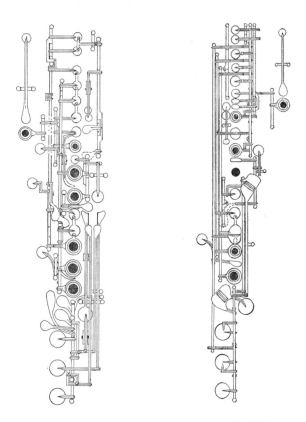

Fig. 17 The Romero key-system (semi-diagrammatic)

Fig. 18 The Child key-system. From the Patent of 1924

improved by Heckel of Biebrich, with whom Müller spent the winter of 1845. At this time rings were added to the lower joint. A much more elaborate model was devised by Carl Bärmann about 1860 in conjunction with Georg Ottensteiner, a Munich maker. This added at least 5 or 6 keys to the original thirteen. Two rings were added to the upper joint, giving an automatic *f' sharp* without the use of the side-key, and duplicate levers for *e' flat* and *f'*. On the lower joint 2 duplicate levers to manipulate *a flat* and *b flat* were fitted on the left side, making 4 touch-pieces for L. little finger. Müller's clumsy, simple-lever *f* key was retained. It was a crude, rather unimaginative model, but notable for two reasons. It produced Bärmann's admirable tutor, written between 1864 and 1873 and fingered expressly for this model, and it was the system adopted by the famous Richard Mühlfeld of Meiningen. It has been replaced in Germany by the *Oehler* clarinet which is the favourite model of most German and Austrian players. This instrument, perfected by the well-known Berlin maker O. Oehler (died 1940), has 21 keys, four more, be it noted, than the Boehm. It is, in effect, an improved Bärmann with lighter mechanism. The L. little finger still has four keys to control. Additions on the lower joint are the 'patent' *c'' sharp* key and the vent-key to improve *forked f''*. On the upper joint a perfect forked *e' flat/ b'' flat* is obtainable; there are four trill-keys for R. 1, one of them for *g' sharp*, and an additional cross-key for *f'*, a traditional German im-provement. A recent model has the *f sharp/g sharp* trill as well. This may be changed at will into the ordinary *g'' sharp* key by turning a lug. In like manner the 'patent' *c sharp* key may be instantaneously disconnected. These facilities call for elaborate mechanism and no less than 15 adjusting screws. The Oehler cannot be called a simple clarinet. It is elaborate in comparison with the Boehm. No attempt is made to lighten the burden of the little fingers and sliding from key to key is not elimin-ated. Simpler models are made with four rings and 16 keys.

In Belgium, Mahillon and E. Albert, established in Brussels in 1838 and 1846, carried on the tradition of fine workmanship inaugurated by Charles Sax *père* and G. C. Bachmann. Both adopted and made to perfection Müller's 13-key model with the usual two rings on the lower joint. The speaker was brought round to the front of the instrument, a loan from Simiot, while a long key for *g' sharp* was fitted independent of the *a'* key and manipulated by L. 2. Many thousands of these finely made and finely tuned clarinets were built. Wuille, a Belgian virtuoso, introduced them to England in the 1850s, where their popularity was immense. The impresario Jullien was the first agent for them in London.

Albert's clarinets, which had a larger bore than Mahillon's, soon received several additions. Of these the 'patent' or *extra c'' sharp* key, which enabled *f sharp* and its twelfth to be made by the L. little finger alone by means of an additional tone-hole, and which gave great facility in sharp keys, was the first. The credit for its introduction, *c.* 1862, was claimed by Mahillon, but it appeared on Albert clarinets too and both Chappell and J. Tyler, a well-known London player, took out patents for very similar designs.[10] This 14-key clarinet was a standard model in British military bands until a very recent date. The addition of a short side-key for *e' flat* and a long trill-key for *a'-b' flat*, both taken from the Boehm, fitted this model for more serious use. It was in fact the clarinet chosen by Henry Lazarus during the last thirty years of his career. The intonation and tone of these instruments were very fine – they have in fact never been surpassed – and were, generally speaking, much superior to those of the contemporary Boehm. Hence the reluctance of Belgian and English players to change their fingering until the increasing demands of composers made it necessary. Another improvement which enjoyed great popularity in Belgium and in England, and some in Italy, was the *Barret* action, adapted from the oboe in the late 1870s. In the case of the clarinet the action is reversed. Two weakly sprung articulated levers for *e' flat* and *f'* on the upper joint are free to rise with the fingers when a side-key, fitted with a powerful spring, is depressed by the R. first finger. This simple and reliable mechanism facilitates many difficult trills and combinations in keys of more than two flats or three sharps, and offers great facilities upon the upper joint. The Barret model, with a lower joint embodying the duplicate *c sharp* and a vent-key for *forked f*,[11] was the model chosen by the brilliant executant George Clinton at the outset of his career. It was made for him by Messrs Boosey of London, who, aided by the great acoustical knowledge of D. J. Blaikley, soon proved formidable rivals to the Brussels makers. The model used by Clinton for some twenty years before his death in 1913 was more elaborate. The upper joint is the same as that of his first model. It is fitted with Barret action, cross-over *g' sharp*, and speaker at the rear, while on the lower joint the unsatisfactory Müller keys for the little fingers are replaced by the rod-key mechanism of the Boehm clarinet. The *forked f* is, however, retained, and on the left side *a flat/ e flat*, not *f*, is duplicated. The *articulated g'' sharp* is fitted, and on the lower joint the 'patent' *c sharp*, so beloved of the older player, remains. This system offers many advantages to the player unwilling to change his fingering and has more facilities than many other systems and is the so-called 'Clinton-Boehm'.

To conclude our brief survey of systems a completely original clarinet may be briefly considered – the *Schaffner*. This was the bold conception of a Florentine surgeon-dentist, H. L. Schaffner, and has been alluded to in a previous chapter. It is made in one piece of ebonite, squared for four-fifths of its length, which terminates at the top in a circular neck and socket to receive the mouthpiece, at the bottom in a tiny bell. The bore is circular, slightly flattened at the top, the upper surface of the body being formed by a long strip of metal. This metal facing is perforated with twenty carefully graduated oblong or rectangular tone-holes. These are at least double the size of the usual round hole, and are closed by bold finger-plates hinged above them. Along the sides run thin steel tracker-rods, five to a side, to close automatically the plates which cannot be directly controlled by the fingers. There is no tuning socket, but two speakers are provided, actuated by a rocking action of the left thumb. The mechanism is a miracle of ingenuity and precision, but the provision of at least 35 minute regulating screws points to the necessity for frequent and skilled adjustment. The specimen roughly described has been kindly put at my disposal by Mr T. K. Dibley. Others are available at Brussels and in the former Heyer collection. Schaffner made oboes and flutes to the same pattern, the latter designed by C. T. Giorgi of Rome. Possibly he designed the others as well.

In the preceding paragraphs a few of the variations of the Müller clarinet have been considered. There are, of course, many more to illustrate the harassed player's struggle to grapple with the difficulties of technique on more equal terms. The modern trend in the face of ever-increasing technical difficulties is towards greater simplicity of mechanism. The 'plain' is generally preferred, as we have seen, to the 'full' Boehm; the Oehler represents the limit of permissible complexity to the old-system player. What of the future? It is difficult to foresee any revolutionary change of design. Among desiderata are a reliable device to give a full *b' flat*, to free the speaker from its double duty, and some securer method than Romero's of relieving the overburdened left hand.[12] Even more desirable is far greater attention to detail on the maker's part to ensure reliability and particularly the noiselessness of the keywork he provides. Many old clarinets with fifty years of use behind them show far less wear than some modern instruments after no more than a year or two. The secret lies in the lightness and hardness of the mechanism; in other words, in handwork and craftsmanship. Is craftsmanship dead? Not dead, perhaps, but certainly moribund. Modern trends and modern economics are all against the small maker with his stock of acquired experience and empirical methods. Handwork and simple tools have been replaced almost entirely by precision machinery and repetition work. The intuition of the old maker, the sixth sense, so necessary to perfect results, now comes a bad second to the blue-print of the modern operative. The results so far are not encouraging. There is little to suggest that the assembly-line can endow the instrument it produces with a soul. The only hope for a rather grim

future would seem to lie in the growth of a body of improvers and
finishers. These men, craftsmen in their own right, would not make an
instrument throughout, but would procure the rough models from the
factory and adapt them for the exacting needs of the soloist and
orchestral musician by judicious refitting, regulation, and tuning.[13]

The musical history of the clarinet during the past century is bound
up with the players. Brief notices of some of the more famous may fitly
conclude this chapter. In England Henry Lazarus (1815–95), after a
short military career, joined Willman in the Philharmonic in 1838 and
subsequently succeeded him in his many appointments. He had been a
pupil of John Blizzard, bandmaster of the Life Guards and later of the
Royal Military Asylum, Chelsea. For fifty years he was the doyen of
English clarinettists, excelling in tone and phrasing. He reached his
prime when clarinet concertos were less in demand and the day of the
sonata had not arrived. It was the heyday of the occasional piece with
piano and of elaborate variations on operatic airs. Many were written
for him and he arranged many himself. His fine phrasing was extolled
by George Bernard Shaw, who began his career as a music critic in the
1880s under the pen-name of 'Corno di Bassetto'. He shone especially
in chamber music. His performance in the Beethoven Septet, the
Mozart Quintet, and the Schubert Octet was long remembered.
Bernard Shaw's opinion of it may perhaps be quoted in part.

'Listening to the Septet it was impossible to avoid indulging in
some stray speculation as to the age of Mr Lazarus. Fifty or sixty
years ago when the great clarinettist was beginning to rank as a
veteran the subject might have been a delicate one. Today it is
difficult to know how to treat him critically; for it would be absurd
to encourage him as if he were a promising young player; and yet
there is no use in declaring that he "played with his usual ability",
because his ability is still, unfortunately for us, as far as ever from
being usual. The usual clarinet player is stolid, mechanical, undistinguished, correct at best, vulgar at worst. A phrase played by
Mr Lazarus always came, even from the unnoticed ranks of the
woodwind at the opera, with a distinction and fine artistic feeling
that aroused a longing for an orchestra of such players. And his
phrases come just that way still. When, in the slow movement of
the Septet, Mr Lazarus would not have it so fast as Madame
Neruda wanted, the question arose whether the difference was one
of taste or of age. But when Madame Neruda led off the final
Presto at full speed without sparing a flash of her Hungarian fire,

Mr Lazarus answered the question by following her spirited challenge without slackening one demisemiquaver.'[14]

He was principal clarinet at the Italian Opera from 1838 to 1883. His first instruments were by Thomas Key, of boxwood with 13 brass keys. In the 1850s he changed to a cocuswood pair by J. Fieldhouse, fitted with a simple and ingenious Boehm mechanism for the little fingers, and in 1865 to a 16-key trio, also of cocus, by E. Albert of Brussels. Plate 3 shows five of his instruments.

A player of similar qualities was Julian Egerton (1848–1945). The son of a clarinettist, he held every worthwhile appointment, succeeding Lazarus as professor at the Royal College of Music. His playing was distinguished by elegance of phrasing, and the beauty of his tone is still a memory. He was for long a member of Queen Victoria's private band. Retiring relatively early, he accepted engagements till the age of ninety-one, and continued to play his beloved instrument until within a week of his death. He played upon a pair of ebonite instruments made by Fieldhouse in 1862, with 13 keys and additional mechanism for *forked f* and *forked b flat*. It is noteworthy that the silver keywork is as tight and sound today as when it left the maker's hands, a tribute to painstaking craftsmanship. These instruments had originally belonged to George Tyler, who died at an early age in 1878. This fine player was a member of the Royal Italian Opera orchestra and of the Philharmonic. The *Musical Directory* spoke of his death 'as an almost irreparable loss'. Two German players, contemporaries of Lazarus and long resident in Britain, may be noticed in passing, Papé and Grosse. Carl Papé (1820–74), considered by Lazarus a very fine player, was principal in the Crystal Palace orchestra for nineteen years. F. W. Grosse (1823–87), a native of Saxony, held a similar position in the Hallé orchestra.

A player of a very different order was George Clinton (1850–1913), the son of a bandmaster and clarinettist, Arthur Clinton, of Newcastle-upon-Tyne. He was long a member of Her Majesty's private band, in which he was enrolled before he was twenty, and principal at the Crystal Palace under A. Manns and in the Royal Philharmonic. He excelled in execution; difficulties did not exist for him, and he played the most exacting flute music with facility. In the 1870s he performed concertos by Weber and Spohr at the Crystal Palace, rescuing these works from temporary oblivion. He was, too, like Lazarus and Egerton, an ardent chamber musician and formed a quintet which gave frequent concerts at the St James's Hall. His instruments have already been noted. Throughout his career he preferred ebonite to wood. As professor at the

Academy, he sedulously taught the old system of fingering, to which he adhered himself. His young brother, James (1852–97), was according to some accounts an even better player, but without his brother's ambition. He was inventive, too, being chiefly remembered for his combination clarinet (in German, *Kombinationsklarinette, Klarinette mit Mutation*).

A definite step in English clarinet-playing is marked by the arrival in London of Manuel Gomez (1859–1930) in the late 1880s. A native of Seville, where he studied under Antonio Palatin, and a *lauréat* of the Paris Conservatoire, Gomez remained in England till his death. From Signor Lago's Opera Company he soon rose to be principal at Covent Garden and in the newly-formed Queen's Hall orchestra under Henry Wood. He later assisted in the founding of the London Symphony Orchestra. His execution was quite exceptional, and the wonder it aroused was increased when it was noticed that he played everything upon one clarinet. This was at first a full Boehm model, with the necessary extension, of normal design. Later he had a special model made by Boosey which had, in addition to the *f sharp/g sharp* shake, an additional trill-key for *g' sharp* on the right hand side. Another modification was that the 'long' *b'' flat* was made with two fingers of the L.H. and one ring-key on the lower joint, thus bringing it into conformity with other fingerings for the same note. The influence of Gomez on the younger school of players was great. It may be said that he introduced the Boehm system to England. And further, he provided a stimulus. In spite of the efforts of Lazarus and Clinton, interest in the clarinet as a solo instrument had been declining. Gomez did much to restore it by inducing musicians to compose for it. Among the works composed for him was Percy Pitt's *Concertino*, op. 22 (1897), which he played with the Lamoureux Orchestra. He may be said to have reintroduced clarinet concertos to the concert hall. Still more was done by Richard Mühlfeld who paid several visits to England in the '90s. Manuel's brother, Francisco (died 1937), was also a fine player. As a bass clarinettist he has never been surpassed. One of Gomez's more enthusiastic followers was Charles Draper (1869–1952)[15] who changed his fingering while still a scholar at the Royal College under Lazarus and Egerton. Draper was an important link between the old and new schools of players. He inherited from Lazarus a fine well-nourished tone and coupled it with a more fluent technique. No one did more for English clarinet-players or more for his instrument. Many works were written for him, notably C. V. Stanford's Concerto, op. 80 (1902), and Sonata (1918). The dedication of the latter he shared with Oscar W. Street, a fine amateur player. The concerto still awaits printing. During his tenure of the professorship, Draper had many distinguished pupils. Among them were the late Frederick Thurston, the well-known soloist and chamber-music player, and Ralph Clarke, both in their turn principals in the B.B.C. Symphony Orchestra, and both professors at the Royal College of Music. None was more brilliant than his nephew, Haydn P. Draper (1889–1934), who had gained virtuosity on his instrument at a pheno-menally early age, holding several appointments before election to a scholarship at the Royal College of Music. The younger Draper com-bined superb technique with highly developed musicianship. Among other appointments he was for long principal in the Queen's Hall Orchestra, and it was for him that Sir Henry Wood wrote the exacting cadenza in his *Fantasia on British Sea Songs*. He was well known to European audiences as the leader of the brilliant team of clarinettists which was the glory of the short-lived B.B.C. Military Band. As pro-fessor at the Royal Academy he formed many excellent pupils; among the more brilliant is Reginald Kell (1906–   ), now resident in the U.S.A. As a chamber musician he was long associated with R. Murchie (flute), L. Goossens (oboe), Aubrey Brain (horn), and F. Wood (bassoon) in the London Wind Quintet. Like his uncle he preferred the plain Boehm clarinet with no additions.

To turn to some continental players of note. Carl Bärmann (1811–85) accompanied his father, Heinrich Joseph, on many of his tours, and finally succeeded him as principal in the court orchestra at Munich. His clarinet and the admirable tutor written for it have already been noticed.

Arnold Joseph Blaes (1814–92), a distinguished Belgian clarinettist, was a pupil of G. C. Bachmann (1804–42) at the Brussels Conservatoire and his successor in the professorship. In early life he made extensive and successful concert tours which he described in his *Souvenirs de ma vie artistique*, visiting England on two occasions and Russia many times. He married Elisa Meerti, a coloratura singer of merit, whom he excelled in accompanying. His playing was more refined and no less fluent than that of some of his contemporaries. The *Musical World* of 1846 was lavish in its tributes of praise. 'M. Blaes is certainly the most expressive performer now living, while his execution is scarcely less facile than that of Cavallini.' Again, 'M. Blaes has no living rival. . . . He is perhaps the first of all virtuosi on the clarinet.' Lazarus, too, paid tribute to his fine musical qualities. He did much to establish the reputation of the Brussels Conservatoire as a fine school of clarinet-playing. He used a pair of clarinets made by his master, one of ebony, one of box, fitted with 14 keys and without rings on the lower joint.

Franz Thaddäus Blatt (1793– ?) was a pupil of Dionys Weber and Wenzel Farník at the newly-founded Prague Conservatoire. He was a virtuoso of the stature of Hermstedt and the elder Bärmann, and was considered by Berlioz the finest player of his day in Germany. Bohemia has ever been a fertile school for clarinettists and, as professor at the National Conservatoire, Blatt took no small part in moulding it. He produced an admirable tutor in 1828, distinguished by the originality of the studies it contains and by its attention to artistic detail. Other distinguished Bohemian clarinettists are: J. Pisařovic, F. Reitmayer, Blatt's successors at the Conservatoire, and J. Sobeck. The latter has written much for his instrument. Blatt played upon a simple 13-key clarinet without additional keys. The date of his death is unknown.

Ernesto Cavallini (1807–74) was a pupil of Benedetto Carulli (1797–1877) who taught the clarinet for fifty-six years at Milan. As H. J. Bärmann was named the Rubini, so Cavallini was known as the Paganini, of the clarinet. His execution was prodigious, so too his volubility and power of lung. And his wizardry was displayed on a simple instrument of yellow boxwood with only six keys. He toured extensively, and was received everywhere with acclamation. Fétis, an exacting critic, praised his tone and intonation, but English critics and Lazarus were less impressed. They had but recently heard Blaes, and Lazarus was perhaps biased by Cavallini's attempts to undercut him in Costa's orchestra at the Royal Italian Opera.[16] Lazarus admitted that his execution was 'unapproachable', but held that he had sacrificed tone to technique. His shortcomings in tone and intonation were very marked in slow movements. Lazarus, it may be noted, attributed the tonal superiority of English players to the solid diet they enjoyed. From 1852 to 1867 he was a star clarinettist in St Petersburg. The last years of his life he spent as professor at the Milan Conservatoire. He wrote a quantity of music of which his *Duetti* and thirty *Capricci* are best remembered. The backwardness of the Milanese school is surprising since the Lyonnese and German makers, notably Stengel of Baireuth, were exporting clarinets with many more than six keys to Italy at this period.

Hyacinthe-Eléonor Klosé (1808–80) came from Corfu and was, as we have seen, in part the inventor of the Boehm clarinet. He succeeded F. Berr at the Paris Conservatoire in 1838, and held the post till 1868. He was in a sense the second founder of the French School, Berr being the first. He was a good musician, writing as a clarinettist for clarinettists. His admirable tutor for his invention has been many times reprinted. He excelled as a teacher and formed many excellent pupils, among them A.-M. Leroy, his successor at the Conservatoire, C. Rose, Grisez, and C.-P. Turban. It is perhaps of interest to note that the composer Augusta Holmès studied not only orchestration with him but also the clarinet, upon which she attained some virtuosity.

Domenico Liverani (1805–74), professor at the Liceo Rossini of Bologna, may be mentioned as the introducer of the Boehm clarinet to Italy. He visited England in 1836.

Aurelio Magnani (1856–1921), professor at the Reale Accademia di S. Cecilia in Rome, was well known as a soloist and teacher. He did much to foster ideals of tone and to raise the Italian school to its present excellence. Among his more distinguished pupils were U. Blonck-Steiner, professor at the Conservatorio of Milan, and C. Luberti, his successor in the professorship in Rome. Magnani was no mean composer, writing, in addition to his excellent *Metodo* for the Boehm instrument and ten *Studi*, three melodious sonatas and other concert pieces.

Richard Mühlfeld (1856–1907) was associated with the Meiningen Hofkapelle, first under Hans von Bülow and later under Fritz Steinbach, throughout his career. Joining it in 1873 as a violinist he became first clarinet in 1876. As a clarinettist he was self-taught, and was perhaps the better for it; for he played less as a clarinettist than as a fine and sensitive musician who, excelling in artistic phrasing and in the finer points of style, had chosen the clarinet as his means of expression. Technically he was no doubt inferior to some of his contemporaries. Opinions of his tone and intonation vary. Some competent critics found him deficient in both; others praised the velvet quality of his lower register. In England he met with special acclamation, but it should be remembered that the pitch at the time of his first visits had not been lowered. To ears attuned to this higher pitch his flat-pitched A clarinet would have sounded as soft and mellow as a basset-horn. No artist has ever had a profounder influence. Not only did he inspire Brahms to write his immortal works for his instrument, but he brought a number of other composers, among them G. Jenner and W. Rabl, under the spell of his art. The clarinet henceforward was looked upon not merely as an indispensable member of the orchestra, but as an instrument capable of the highest range of expression in solo and in chamber music. Further, his influence was salutary in stressing the importance of musicianship and interpretation over brilliance of technique and showy execution.

Henri Paradis (1861–1940) was one of the most famous of Rose's pupils at the Paris Conservatoire, where he was awarded the *premier prix* in 1880. He succeeded his master as soloist at the Opéra and held the position till the age of seventy-three. At the same time he was soloist in the Garde Républicaine and in the Lamoureux Orchestra. He has been described as the best-known French player never to be professor of his instrument at the Conservatoire. Of his many compositions the best known are perhaps the brilliant fantasias on 'Malbrouck' and 'Le Pré aux Clercs'.

Gustave Poncelet (1844–1903) succeeded Blaes as professor at the Brussels Conservatoire in 1872, a position he relinquished to David Hannon in 1901. For the remaining years he was professor of the saxophone. He was an outstanding soloist in the orchestra of La Monnaie. His influence was profound as a teacher and in carrying still further the excellence of the Belgian school founded by Bachmann and Blaes. He formed a notable and brilliant clarinet ensemble in which a contra-basset-horn, made by E. Albert, was included. Among his English pupils was E. Mills, long a well-known clarinettist in the North of England and a most artistic saxophonist.[17] Throughout his career Poncelet adhered to the old system, but taught the Boehm clarinet to his later pupils. These included such well-known artists as Joseph Schreurs, long a distinguished principal in the Thomas Orchestra, Chicago, D. Hannon, A. Bageard, Hublard, and Gustave Langenus. Langenus, after a season or two in London with Sir Henry Wood, migrated to New York where he won an enviable reputation as a player, teacher, and composer for his instrument.

Cyrille Rose (1830–1903) was, like many other French clarinettists, a native of the industrial north. He won his *premier prix* in 1847 and succeeded Leroy as professor at the Conservatoire in 1876. From 1857 to 1891 he was in the orchestra of the Opéra, where he was consulted on many technical points by Gounod, Massenet, and Bruneau. Rose made many contributions to the literature of the clarinet in the shape of studies; he reintroduced Weber to Paris, re-editing the concertos and furnishing them with cadenzas. Less well known are the experiments he made in conjunction with Messrs Buffet concerning the proportions of the bore, the *évasements*, the cones at top and bottom, in particular. Himself a brilliant player and indefatigable worker, he produced a number of fine players, among them P. Mimart, Henri and Alexandre Selmer, R. Verney, H. Lefebvre, E. H. Stiévenard, Paul Jeanjean, and Louis Cahuzac.

Robert Stark (1847–1922), a pupil of the Dresden Konservatorium, was solo clarinet at Wiesbaden before becoming teacher, and later professor, of his instrument at the Royal School of Music at Würzburg. Stark has exercised a considerable influence outside the borders of his own country by his contributions to clarinet music. In addition to three concertos and a quintet for flute, oboe, clarinet, bassoon, and horn, he compiled about 1900 a comprehensive tutor in several parts – *Die hohe Schule des Clarinett-Spiels*. Stark included the basset-horn in his curriculum and did much to revive its use in Germany. He used a clarinet of Bärmann type with some modifications.

Two players of a later generation were Gaston Hamelin and George W. Anderson. Hamelin (d. 1951), who won his *premier prix* under Turban at the Paris Conservatoire, was principal for some years in the Boston Symphony Orchestra and later in the Orchestre National in Paris. He was highly esteemed as a teacher; American players in particular owe much to his tuition both in the U.S.A. and in France. George Anderson (1867–1951), distinguished for many years as an orchestral player and as a successful teacher, preserved his powers up to his death. He was for many years principal in the London Symphony Orchestra and for a time at Covent Garden. He was one of the team of talented clarinettists who raised the B.B.C. Military Band to the heights. One of the later pupils of Lazarus, he adopted the Boehm clarinet early in his career. A feature of his playing was his full, sweet tone and impeccable intonation. As late as May 1941 he was appointed professor at the Royal Academy and held the post until his death.

This cursory sketch of clarinet history over more than two centuries has taken us a long way, from the primitive 2-key boxwood invention of Denner to the modern product of mass production. We have passed on the way many curious and ingenious designs, and cast a backward sentimental glance at the beautifully wrought works of the older maker. We have noticed, too, some of the older virtuosi and giants of the past who travelled so tirelessly the roads of Europe from St Petersburg to Naples to play their now forgotten concertos or pot-pourris to admiring audiences. In this brief epilogue we may do well to consider the present position. At no time in its history has the clarinet been more popular. As we have seen, it enjoyed no small popularity between 1780 and 1840. There were few amateur players, it is true – here the flute reigned supreme – but many competent virtuosi made its beauty of tone widely known. Thereafter followed an eclipse. Piano and violin concertos ousted woodwind instruments entirely from concert platforms, and the orchestral musician, however fine an artist, was little regarded. The arrival of Mühlfeld effected a temporary improvement. The clarinet was again restored to the concert room, but only for a brief space. A period of indifference followed, and it is only within the last thirty-five years or so that the clarinet has really come into its own. This in the writer's opinion is due largely to broadcasting. No instrument lends itself better to recording[18] or is more frequently heard upon the air; there is little doubt that many of its present devotees first heard its voice upon the ether and succumbed to its charm. And musical education has never been more enlightened, more widespread, or more easily obtainable. Instruction is available for all, and only the high price of instruments acts as a deterrent to the would-be musician. Technique, too, has been increasing from year to year. First-year students at musical colleges play with ease passages which Hermstedt and Lazarus would have considered all but impossible of execution. This is not solely due to improved instruments – in too many respects these are worse than they were fifty years ago – but to an innate instinct and capacity for technique which has been maturing through the years. It has been noticed and commented upon by professors of other instruments. It is true to say that there have never been more and finer executants than there are at the present day. And this in every country. It is not proposed to name them. Such a task would be invidious. Every school of playing has its own particular character, its own peculiar excellence. The German differs from the Viennese and both from the French, the French from the English, the English from the American. Each makes its own contribution. Fortunately the wireless and gramophone have made it possible to hear them all; the warmth, vivacity, and perfect chording of the Viennese in Mozart's B flat Serenade; the slickness and perfect ensemble of the Trio d'Anches in modern French music; the classical renderings of the Mozart Quintet by English, French, and American artists, each with its own distinct flavour. These should do much to mould our taste. Another remarkable feature of the present day is the number of women players, both professional and amateur. Two generations ago Lazarus considered it 'unbecoming' in a woman to play the clarinet, although he had two or three women among his pupils. Today he would be astonished at their number. He would find not a few of them in symphony orchestras and at least one a distinguished recitalist.

So far the picture is pleasant, the prospect promising. And the music? There is no lack of it, of chamber music, of occasional pieces, of concertos, commissioned, some of them, by famous players. Much of it is frankly virtuoso music, written for virtuosi and only playable by some of them. There is little, far too little, for the rank and file, for the player whose attainments fall short of this exalted standard. There is little, too, for the clarinettist who is but moderately attracted to modern music, who finds in austerity, ingenuity, and rhythmic subtleties indifferent substitutes for warmth, melody, and feeling. Only too often such a player is necessarily forced back upon his repertoire of older works which, every clarinettist knows, is all too scanty, or upon transciptions. Here it is possible to be too precious and too critical. If 18th century music goes charmingly on the clarinet – and much of it does – what possible objection is there to transcribing it? Tartini, Handel, Cimarosa, and Galuppi, to mention but a few, do not lose their quality when transferred to the clarinet; they are often the gainers by transcription. Here the oboe has shown the way.

NOTES

[1] This is the practice of modern German makers.

[2] A well-known virtuoso clarinettist. His son, F. B. Busoni, it may be noted, was inspired by the playing of the Swiss clarinettist, Edmondo Allegra, to write his *Concertino* (1920) and a cadenza for the Mozart Concerto (1922). A cadenza for an unspecified Weber concerto remains in manuscript.

[3] The writer [F.G.R.] had a neatly made 10-key instrument which bears his name and also a striking resemblance to Bischoff's clarinets.

[4] A ring-key had been fitted by F. Lefèvre to a clarinet in 1826 and was known to F. Berr. C. Welch, *History of the Boehm Flute*, 2nd edn., London, 1892, p. 44.

[5] Gevaert proposed its adoption on his appointment to the Conservatoire in 1871, but was dissuaded, Lavoix tells us, 'sur le conseil des meilleurs clarinettistes'.

[6] James Conroy, a Dublin clarinettist, seems to have been a pioneer in adopting the Boehm. He bought a boxwood pair quite early in the 1860s from Buffet and demonstrated them to Lazarus.

[7] P. Goumas took out a patent for this mechanism in 1865. Goumas, who did much to improve the Boehm clarinet, was one of the partners in the well-known firm of Buffet-Crampon of Paris. In 1885 the business was acquired by P. Evette and E. Schaeffer, but the old name of the firm was and still is retained.

[8] An additional hole for the same purpose is fitted to some modern French clarinets. An open key covers it, which is controlled by the *f* key and closes with it.

[9] In 1959 Rosario Mazzeo of the Boston Symphony introduced a clarinet with a number of important ameliorations. Chief among these is a device whereby a good middle B flat is secured by linking the side trill-key for that note to right-hand rings and little-finger keys of either hand. This arrangement combined with the normal *a* key sounds the new B flat, but with the *a* key closed yields a useful alternative *a*. J. McGillivray in *G.S.J.*, Vol. XVII, 1964, points out that the *b flat* trill-key on the normal Boehm yields a useful *a* if the normal *a* key be kept closed, though few players seem to use this facility much. It is interesting to note that as long ago as 1886 André Thibouville made use of this same trill-key to give a good *b flat* by linking it with the ring for the left thumb and the normal *a* key. The speaker-key thus became completely independent.

¹⁰ The latter in May 1862. British patent No. 1308.

¹¹ The *forked f″* with a vent-key was an early improvement. The tone-hole under R. 2 which speaks the note is placed lower down the body to remove the sharpness of the forked note, and a vent-key which opens as soon as R. 2 is removed assists the purity of the sound.

¹² As long ago as 1894, D. J. Blaikley patented an extremely simple and ingenious mechanism which opened a special hole for the middle B flat with the normal fingering. This was manufactured by Boosey and Co. for a time but does not seem to have found general favour, possibly on account of its employment of opposed springs of different strength – always a feature of some insecurity. Since then a number of makers in Germany and America have brought out such automatic devices on less revolutionary principles than that mentioned in note 9 above, and some of these have found devoted adherents. It would seem then that reliability has been more or less secured.

¹³ This rather grim picture as F.G.R. saw it in 1954 has happily not been entirely realised. Certainly in France and, to some extent, in England, mass production methods now obtain, but both countries *can* still show fine craftsmanship. In the last ten years or so certain German makers have come into considerable esteem and some of their instruments show great individuality. All are small – some very small – firms. No doubt they employ machine tools as facilities, but many of their products show real craftsmanship of a high order.

¹⁴ The *Star*, 23 January 1889.

¹⁵ Died 21 October 1952.

¹⁶ According to Lazarus, Costa refused his offer, remarking that he expected every member of his orchestra to be able to play everything put before him. Possibly Cavallini was an indifferent sight-reader. Certainly Ferdinando Busoni, another itinerant virtuoso, was shaky in rhythm, too, according to his son, Ferruccio.

¹⁷ The saxophone had been introduced to England by the Belgian clarinettist Wuille in the 1850s. It suffered from alternating periods of oblivion and revival.

¹⁸ In the experience of the present writer [P.B.] the clarinet presents rather special problems to the recording engineer. When played 'straight' (i.e. without any *vibrato*) there is no instrument which betrays more quickly any unsteadiness of turntables or tape-feeds.

CHAPTER 9

The clarinet, a transposing instrument
The high-pitched clarinets and clarinette d'amour

THE REMAINDER of this work will deal in rather more detail with the higher- and lower-pitched clarinets. The present chapter is designed to provide some additional notes on the clarinets pitched above the normal orchestral pair, many of which have already been noticed, and on the *clarinette d'amour*; the later chapters will deal with the basset-horn, bass, and contrabass clarinets, with some remarks on their history.

And firstly a question which is often put to the clarinettist may be briefly considered. It is – why is the clarinet built as a transposing instrument; or why is more than one instrument necessary to the orchestral player? Why should he not content himself with one instrument pitched in C like the flautist, the oboist, the bassoonist, and thus save the composer and the score-reader a load of trouble? Previous chapters will have provided at least one answer, it is hoped – the difficulty of fingering. Much of the music with which the 18th-century player had to cope, written though it was in simple keys, would have been quite unplayable had he not had clarinets in many pitches at his disposal – the B flat for flat keys, the A, B natural, and D for the sharp. It is only with the mechanical improvements of the early 1800s that the number of clarinets begins to diminish until the advent of the 13-key clarinet finally reduced it to three or even two. And then the 'full' Boehm made it possible, at least in theory, to play all parts on one. The clarinet was at last *omnitonique*; and not a few players availed themselves of the privilege which was offered to them. Recently, as we have seen, faced with the difficulties of the modern score, the orchestral musician has found the use of one instrument less attractive and has reverted to two (see also p. 164, note 1). Another answer is that the clarinet in C, though not without quality and character, is less pleasing tonally than the two just below it. It was discovered quite early by the Mannheimers that the B flat was the ideal solo instrument, at once mellow, warm, and brilliant. Mozart, and a century later Brahms, revealed the possibilities of the A in concert with strings.

And then there is the question of tone-colour. Once composers had this wealth of clarinets in ranging pitches at their disposal they were loth to let them go. So we are told, and so we may perhaps infer from the report of the Commission appointed to pass judgment on Müller's *clarinette omnitonique*. Or did the conservatism of Lefèvre and Duvernoy put ideas into the heads of the musicians there assembled? The answer may probably be that for more than a century composers chose their clarinet to suit the tonality of their music, thinking less of tone-colour than of the convenience of the player. It is just possible that Brahms and Dvořák had certain effects in view when they wrote for the C clarinet; it is certain that Strauss and Mahler had; but it is fair to suppose that Beethoven and Schubert had more practical reasons for their choice of this instrument.

It will hardly be necessary to say that parts for the sopranino clarinets pitched above C will be written below the key of the piece. Parts for D and E flat clarinets, for example, will be scored a tone and a minor third lower and will remove two sharps and three flats from the signature. Parts for the high A flat, were it used orchestrally, would be written a minor sixth lower. Nor will it be necessary to stress the fact that the sopraninos demand special treatment and technique, special reeds, special embouchure, and great discretion in the performer. The tone of the higher-pitched instruments lacks the body and sweetness of the lower; they are necessarily shriller and more penetrating. But they can be piquant and, with discreetness in blowing, they need not be harsh and unpleasing unless intended to be so.[1] Structurally the smaller clarinets differ but little from the bigger, beyond the fact that the bodies are from the D upwards often made in one piece. In modern practice tone-holes are often smaller, smaller in proportion to the bore that is, than in the larger members of the family, and the mechanism must be fined down to avoid obstructing the fingers. Light forged keys are therefore to be preferred to castings. To turn to details. Octave clarinets in C, a ninth above the normal B flat clarinet, have been made. No existing specimen is known to the writer, but such *ottavini* are mentioned in A. Tosoroni's *Trattato pratico di strumentazione*, of 1851. At least one specimen in high B flat is known. It is by N. M. Raingo, one of a well-known family of makers of Mons, and is preserved in the Brussels Museum (No. 167). It may be dated *c.* 1800, has five keys, and is little more than 13 inches in length. Some clarinets in A natural were advertised by C. S. S. Tuerlinckx of Malines, *c.* 1830. No specimen has come to the writer's notice.

With the A flat clarinet (Ger: *Sextklarinette*; It: *clarinetto sestino*) we are on surer ground. Many specimens of this high-pitched clarinet may be seen, since the instrument is still in use, and still manufactured, at any rate in Italy, Germany, and France. Cav. P. Pupeschi advertises a Barret action model in his 1932 catalogue. It also appears in the catalogues of Rampone of Milan and of Selmer of Paris (1949). The average length of it is 15¼ inches. It is essentially a military instrument, and still figures in continental bands, in Italy and in Spain particularly. A beautifully made specimen in cocus with Boehm fingering by Buffet *jeune*, now in the writer's collection, shows that it was used at an earlier date in France as well. It was long a favourite instrument in Hungarian Zigeuner bands, where it lent itself to considerable virtuosity. The gipsy players preferred few keys and simple models were provided for them by the Hungarian makers. According to Sachs again, it was introduced into the Bavarian army in 1839, and had a fairly long life in the German and Austrian service. Specimens by German makers are quite common. It has never been employed officially in English service bands, and apparently only seldom in America, although Gilmore's band boasted a player in 1878. It has never to the best of the writer's knowledge achieved a place in the orchestra.

Very few instruments would appear to have been made in high G. A 2-key specimen by I. B. Willems of Brussels, dating probably from the first half of the 18th century, is preserved in the Brussels collection.[2] Its length is 17 inches. A few specimens by German makers, by Stengel of Baireuth (Heyer 1464), and a skeleton brass model by Wünnenberg (R.M.E. 243), point to a limited use in Germany. It is, perhaps, worthy of note that Stowasser of Budapest advertised A flat, G, and F clarinets in his 1912 price-list.

With the F clarinet we come to a far more popular instrument. It figures in Valentin Roeser's list of 1764, and appears as late as 1927 in the catalogue of a Paris maker. It had a long career in German military bands and in those of countries under German influence. Adolphe Adam, for instance, noticed German silver clarinets of this pitch in Russian bands in 1840. Beethoven and Mendelssohn included it in their military marches, and the latter in his Overture, op. 24, for military band. It was a popular instrument in England just before and just after 1800, but was superseded a few years later by the lower pitched instrument in E flat, a more useful and practical pitch.

It has made occasional appearances in the orchestra; instances of its use have been noticed in Grétry and Cherubini. It has not been revived by modern composers who prefer the lower-pitched instruments in D and E flat.

A clarinet in E natural is mentioned by V. Roeser, and again by

Laborde in 1780. The latter couples it with the D clarinet as suitable for 'morceaux a grand bruit'.

With the E flat clarinet we come to the most commonly used of all the high-pitched members. It has long been a valuable constituent of, and a not infrequent soloist in, military bands, and has of late years found an increasing use in the orchestra. Parts for it occur in not a few late 18th-century operas of Cherubini, while a prominent part is assigned to it by Berlioz in the *Nuit de Sabbat* of the *Symphonie Fantastique*

More recently the use of it has been revived by Strauss who employs it, amongst other works, in *Salome, Elektra, Die Frau ohne Schatten,* and by Mahler, Stravinsky, Ravel in *Bolero, Daphnis et Chloé,* and *L'Enfant et les sortilèges,* and Elgar in his Second Symphony.

Other examples will be found in A. Schoenberg's *Pelleas und Melisande,* op. 5, and in his Violin Concerto, op. 36, and in A. Casella's *Scarlattiana* of 1926. The use of it by older composers was probably an act of kindness to the player to free him from embarrassing flats; its use by Berlioz and later composers is no doubt prompted by its incisive, mordant tone. Forsyth in his *Orchestration* draws attention to R. Strauss's telling use of this instrument, particularly in *Till Eulenspiegel* and *Ein Heldenleben,* where it is employed to vulgarise, to deride, to sneer. It may be noted that in writing for it three flats are removed from, or three sharps added to, the key-signature.

A far less legitimate use of it is to replace the clarinet in D which is little known and used this side of the Rhine. This is a very old member of the family. Not a few of the oldest clarinets, as we have seen, were made in this useful pitch, not in the interests of tone-colour – composers were little interested in timbre at this date – but for the more practical purpose of removing two sharps from the signature. It was commonly used in England during the late 18th and early 19th centuries – John Mahon in 1803 remarked that it was 'good for noisy music' – and certainly as late as 1826, since Willman lists it in his tutor of that year. Parts for it occur in J. C. Bach's *Orione,* Gluck's *Echo et Narcisse,* Cherubini's *Démophoon,* in Strauss's and Lanner's dance music, Liszt's *Mazeppa,* in Wagner's *Die Walküre* and *Tannhäuser,* and more recently its use by Mahler and Strauss is frequent. It is found, too, in Schoenberg's *Kammersymphonie.* Its tone is frank and warmer than that of the E flat; it is stated to have a rich harmonic content and to blend well with strings. It is, perhaps, the most interesting and individual of the higher-pitched clarinets.

West of the Rhine few exist. It is a question of tradition and economics. Clarinets are expensive to buy and difficult to tune. Why have two for occasional use, when one will suffice to play at both pitches? So English, French, and American players argue and content themselves with the E flat, transposing the parts for the instrument in D a semitone down.[3]

The C clarinet, the only non-transposing clarinet, is, like the D, a very old and popular member of the family. Many of the old 2-key clarinets were constructed in this pitch. In dictionaries and textbooks it is commonly stated to be obsolete. This is very far from the truth, again east of the Rhine. Here parts are not infrequently written for it, and are as a rule played upon the instrument for which they are intended. It is unknown in the orchestras of England and of France, and in countries not subject to German tradition, where the parts are played upon the B flat and are of course transposed up a tone. The C suffers by its proximity in pitch to the B flat and A. We are inclined to expect from it a tone not dissimilar in quality to these last, and are perhaps surprised to find it matter-of-fact, crisp, and frank, but lacking in mellowness and romance, invaluable for certain effects, but lacking in charm. Nor has it the individuality of the D. These slight defects, lack of charm and mellowness, with a tendency to hardness, no doubt account for it never having been adopted as the standard orchestral and solo clarinet. It is just devoid of the pleasing timbre of the lower-pitched instruments. When it is brilliant it is apt to be hard and incisive. In common with other clarinets of higher pitch it is difficult to make; for it demands small tone-holes and a smaller bore than that of the B flat and A. Pierced with large holes and fitted with a reed too wide for the bore, it can be hard and wild in tone, and frankly objectionable.[4]

To enumerate the composers who have used the C would be tedious and unnecessary. It must suffice to say that its use was common, only less common than that of the B flat and A, throughout the 18th and 19th centuries, extending to Brahms and Dvořák, and was continued rather than revived by Mahler and Richard Strauss. The latter makes particularly free use of it. To take only a few of his works. Two C clarinets will be found in *Die Frau ohne Schatten*, together with an E flat and a D, and one in *Friedenstag*, *Daphne*, and *Capriccio*, associated in each case with two clarinets in B flat and A and a bass clarinet. In the two last-named works a basset-horn is added as well. The parts are entirely independent, and are plainly written with a view to tone-colour. Is it legitimate in such cases to replace the C with the B flat? The artistic conscience of player or conductor must decide.

A semitone below lies the clarinet in B natural. Its part was written a

semitone above the key of the piece. Exactly when it came into use
would be difficult to determine. It was unknown to Roeser in 1764, but
is among the instruments listed by Laborde in 1780. It makes an
appearance in Mozart's *Così fan tutte* and in *Idomeneo*. It was evidently
used to some considerable extent in France; it is mentioned for instance
by Lefèvre in 1802, by Francoeur in 1812, who placed it among 'les
clarinettes les plus favorables', by Vanderhagen, and by Catrufo, *c.* 1836,
but it was already rare when Kastner wrote in 1836. In Germany it
would appear to have been less popular, since it is not listed by Gott-
fried Weber in 1829. There is no trace of it in England. In extreme
sharp keys its advantages were obvious, and no doubt the French
orchestral player availed himself of its resources fairly frequently.[5] No
surviving specimen of a clarinet made in this pitch is known to the
writer. They were undoubtedly made, however, since Brod, better
known perhaps for his oboes, supplied one to the Paris Opéra in 1831.[6]
Possibly the normal practice at this, and certainly at an earlier, date,
would have been to fit longer *pièces de rechange* to a C or shorter joints
to a B flat clarinet.[7]

One other clarinet remains to be noticed, the Clarinette d'Amour
(Ger: *Liebesklarinette*; It: *clarinetto d'amore*). There is no English
equivalent since this clarinet was seemingly all but unknown in Britain.[8]
It is a difficult instrument to place, but, since it is not definitely low-
pitched, it is considered here. It makes its first appearance just about,
or just after, the middle of the 18th century. Whether it was a development or a by-form of the 'grande clarinette in G', mentioned by Roeser,
Laborde, and others, would be difficult to substantiate. It may be that
the 'grande clarinette', as Laborde called it, was intended as an orchestral instrument, while the other was looked upon as a solo instrument.
It enjoyed special popularity in Flanders, Germany, Switzerland, and
Italy, and no doubt in France as well, since it is mentioned by French
writers. Most of the extant specimens, of which there are many, may be
dated between 1750 and 1820. It was pitched as a rule in G, less often
in A flat or F. It was made with a straight body. Since the compass was
not extended beyond written *e*, no contortions of the tube to bring the
tone-holes to the player's fingers were necessary. It was fitted at the top
with a short, slightly curved metal crook to carry the mouthpiece. At the
bottom it was provided with a *Liebesfuss*, a pear-shaped, incurved bell,
resembling that of the oboe d'amore and cor anglais. This and the
peculiarly narrow bore, with small tone-holes, were the distinctive
features of the instrument. The result was a peculiarly soft, sweet, and
plaintive tone, particularly rich in harmonics, veiled, but entirely lacking

in ictus, brilliance, and vigour, an ideal tone for sentimental warbling. The popularity of the instrument appears to have waned in Germany during the last decades of the 18th century. Here it was largely replaced by the basset-horn, with its luscious reedy tone, an instrument no less romantic, but richer in its resources. It is possible indeed that the basset-horn was developed from it, and that Mayrhofer's invention, which will be considered in the following chapter, consisted merely in replacing the bulbous bell with an extra length of tube.

Sachs cites the use of the clarinette d'amour in J. C. Bach's *Temistocle* of 1772.[9] Heckel of Biebrich has revived the manufacture of G clarinets with bells of ordinary design, but orchestral parts for them have yet to be written. Clarinets in G, Boehm system, of the normal shape but with a large wooden bell and a short, curved, crook feature in a recent Leblanc catalogue, and Orsi of Milan make simple-system G clarinets with some 16 keys for the Turkish market.

NOTES

[1] The truth of this is demonstrated by the recent recordings of the Molter *Concerti* (see above, p. 85) by Jost Michael; though in the opinion of no less an authority than Jack Brymer (himself noted for suavety of tone), it takes something of a specialist to get the best out of the D instrument.

[2] No. 916, R.M.E. 223.

[3] This was probably quite true in 1954. Since then, however, there seems to have been some revival in demand for D clarinets in the West. Today both Buffet and Leblanc list them as part of their very extensive ranges, and recently some are known to have been available in London.

[4] Here again we see a recent tendency in West European and American orchestras to restore the smaller clarinets to the position allotted to them by symphonic composers. The best makers now devote as much care to proper scaling and relative proportions in the C as in any other clarinet, and serious players give equal attention to appropriate mouthpieces and reeds.

[5] In French operatic scores round the turn of the century, the tonality of the clarinet is seldom indicated. It was left to the player's discretion to choose the instrument which suited him best.

[6] C. Pierre, *Les Facteurs d'instruments de musique*, Paris, 1893, p. 378. It had 13 keys and cost 150 francs.

[7] Such *pièces* adaptable to a C clarinet were supplied by Tuerlinckx for 14 florins. A C clarinet of the best quality with silver keys cost 30 florins.

[8] Only one specimen of British manufacture is known to the writer; it is of stained box by Cramer of London, *c.* 1820, and has 12 keys. It is preserved in the Glasgow Art Gallery and Museum, and is well shown in A. J. Hipkins, *Musical Instruments, Historic, Rare and Unique*, Edinburgh, 1888; 1921.

[9] Op. cit., p. 341.

CHAPTER 10

The Basset-horn and tenor clarinets
Fr. Cor de basset[1]. Ger. Bassethorn, Bassetthorn
It. Corno bassetto

THE NAME of this tenor clarinet, now pitched in F, with extension to written *c*, has caused some confusion and given rise to errors in dictionaries and reference books. To explain the name an inventor of the name of Horn of Passau has been created. Where the statement originated is not known, but it is to be found in Pontécoulant's *Organographie*, in Lavoix's *Histoire de l'instrumentation*, in C. R. Day's R.M.E. Catalogue, in T. Wotton's excellent *Dictionary of Foreign Musical Terms*, and as late as 1920 in U. Daubeny's *Orchestral Wind Instruments*; nor has it been deleted from successive reprints of Forsyth's *Orchestration*. Attention is drawn to this rather trivial matter not to depreciate these excellent writers, but that the ghost of the mythical Horn may be laid once for all.

The name is no doubt derived from the sickle-shaped appearance of the instrument as originally made, and may be paralleled in *cor anglais*, while 'basset' may be taken as a diminutive of *bass*. It is regrettable that a *di* is so often interposed between *corno* and *bassetto*. The correct nomenclature *corno bassetto* appears quite clearly in F. Antolini's *La retta maniera di scrivere per il clarinetto* of 1813. The English name has always been 'basset-horn', though Mahon in his tutor of 1803 calls the instrument the 'Clara Voce' or 'Corno Bassetta'. The final *a* in 'bassetta' may be charitably regarded as a printer's error.

There is little doubt that the basset-horn was the invention of A. and M. Mayrhofer of Passau. This would appear from a 7-key specimen in the Hamburg Museum (No. 159) which bears the inscription 'Ant: et Mich: Mayrhofer inven. & elabor. Passavii.'[2] (Plate 6 *a*). The date ascribed to the invention is *c.* 1770. The inventor or inventors were soon forgotten, for C. F. Cramer, writing in 1783,[3] tells us that the name of the inventor is unknown, though the instrument is believed to have originated in Passau.

At first, for the first ten or twenty years of its existence, the basset-horn was pitched more often in G than in F, and made in the form of a sickle or half-moon. This was to solve the difficult problem of bringing the finger-holes within reach of the fingers, of making the instrument convenient to hold, and of shortening a tube at least 40 inches in length. Another device for abbreviating the tube was provided in the *Büch*, *Kasten*, or *Kästchen*, an inseparable component of all early basset-horns. This was an oval block of wood in which the air-column passed up and down in three parallel lengths of bore before emerging through a brass bell attached to the bottom. The box was effectively sealed at top and bottom by corks and screwed-down plates of brass, far less commonly of wood or ivory. The features of Mayrhofer's invention were the extension of clarinet compass from written *e* to *c*, the bending of the tube, and the provision of the box. The credit for the extension of compass may be allowed him; but it is not improbable that the bending of the tube was suggested by the cor anglais and the 'box' by

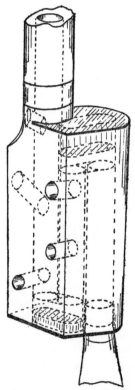

Fig. 19 The *Büch* or *Kasten* (semi-diagrammatic) as made by Grundmann, Dresden, Late 18th century.

the 17th-century *Racket, Ranket,* or *Cervelas,* the miniature bassoon in which the bore is turned upon itself nine times before emerging into the open. The problem of manufacture was no easy one. The insertion of melted lead allows a brass tube to be bent to any desired curve without risk of distortion of the bore or damage to the tube. This is plainly impossible in the case of a wooden tube. Such a tube cannot be steamed to shape without risk of serious damage to the accuracy of the bore. Other means were perforce adopted by the maker. An obvious solution of the problem was to excavate the bore in two halves in two pieces of plankwood, and then to glue and peg them together with brass or wooden pins. This was the method adopted by Papalini in his curiously contorted bass clarinet which will be considered later. The process, however, is laborious and detrimental to sonority. Another method, often adopted in the case of the bent cor anglais, was to make a series of deep and angular saw cuts into and through the bore to allow the removal of triangular pieces from the inside of the intended curve. This was an elaboration of a process familiar to every carpenter. The series of deep cuts allowed the tube to be bent to the desired shape and a thin strip of wood was sometimes glued to the inside of the bend to serve as a reinforcement. A covering of leather, added for security and as a precaution against leakage, afforded convenient scope for gilded tooling and decoration. To give a lighter and a more elegant appearance to the instrument the tube was often chamfered to a hexagonal or octagonal section. This would seem a weak method of construction, but so well was the work executed that many of these instruments survive to testify to the maker's skill. In passing it may be noted that the elder Triébert, the oboe-maker of Paris, used the same method for his early cor anglais some sixty or seventy years later. In some of his later models, where only the upper joint is bent, a still more elaborate method was employed. In these the curved portion is made of five or six short lengths of wooden tubing neatly dovetailed or tenoned together.[4] Mayrhofer's instrument was provided with the five keys of the contemporary clarinet, and with two basset keys giving, when closed, written *d* and *c.* For the extension of compass was at first diatonic. An open key to give low *f* when closed was sometimes added. This was not usual in the higher-pitched clarinets till some years later; it was in fact claimed as an innovation by I. Müller in the first decade of the following century. The basset-keys were manipulated by the thumb of the right hand. About 1782 Theodor Lotz is mentioned by Cramer as an improver of the instrument. The statement has been questioned, but there would seem to be no inherent difficulty in it. Lotz was an all-round musician in Count Esterhazy's orchestra, playing the contrabassoon, clarinet, and basset-horn, as well as other instruments. He is also stated rather later to have been an instrument-maker in Vienna. The nature of his improvement is guesswork. Was it the unbending of the tube? It is significant that an instrument by Joseph Rosmeisel of Graslitz, with the usual seven keys, dated 1782, in the Prague Museum (No. 12209), has two straight limbs set together at an angle of 90 degrees. This was the first step in the improvement of the instrument and exactly contemporaneous with Cramer's description. An instrument of similar design is illustrated in Sachs's Berlin Catalogue, col. 297. The Berlin collection possesses a basset-horn by Lotz himself (No. 2911) with the two limbs set at a more obtuse angle, and with eight keys. So his invention may again have consisted in resetting the angle and in the addition of an eighth key, that for low *f* already mentioned. The matter is, as has been said, pure guesswork and of small importance.

No instrument has been made in more contorted shapes, save possibly the bass clarinet, than the basset-horn. A rectangular model survives in the Baierisches Nationalmuseum, Munich (No. 139). Another interesting and curious type by Strobach of Carlsbad is thus described in Day's R.M.E. Catalogue, No. 272.

> 'This curious instrument is in shape almost unique. It is of box-wood with ivory mounts and mouthpiece. There are ten keys of plated metal, with square flaps, working upon knobs. The bore of the instrument is bent at an angle of about 120 degrees near its centre. The bell is globular and very much contracted at the mouth, and is turned back towards the player at right angles to the lower joint of the instrument . . . its total length is 3 feet 7 inches.'

This instrument, formerly in the Snoeck Collection, is now in Berlin (No. 2915). Another identical specimen is preserved at Hamburg (No. 1562), while a very similar model by Ignazio Miraz of Udine is in the writer's possession. In these three instruments, it should be noted, the *Kasten* is omitted and so the extra length of tubing has to be dealt with in the original manner described above. But the standard form which survived well into the first three or four decades of the 19th century, at any rate in Germany, consisted of two straight members set together at an obtuse angle of 120 degrees in a knee-joint of ivory, horn, or wood, the upper member carrying a straight or bent socket with mouthpiece, the lower the *Kasten* and oval bell. The weight of the instrument was carried on a sling and the oval bell fitted conveniently

—11 • •

between the player's legs or ankles. It is difficult to say when the knee-joint was dispensed with.

Possibly England gave the lead; for a specimen by Thomas Key of Charing Cross in the writer's collection is strikingly modern in design. Here the body-tube is entirely straight, united in the middle by the usual tenon and socket joint; a short bent brass crook carried the mouthpiece, the lower member terminates in a big wooden bell. There is no box. The use of boxwood for the tube, of ivory for the tips, and the general design of the brass keys mounted in knobs, suggests a date not much later than 1825. The rings fitted to the lower joint are a later addition. The basset-keys are located, as they should be, at the back of the instrument.

The modern form of the instrument differs little in appearance from the preceding. Boxwood has been abandoned in favour of thin-walled blackwood or cocus; rosewood has been used with excellent results, and maple is a favourite material with Heckel and some other German makers. Modern mechanism, whether Boehm[5] or Müller, is fitted, and the extension is now invariably chromatic. The German makers following old tradition usually place the basset keys at the back to be controlled by the right thumb; some French makers, however, prefer to fit them in front, giving the right little finger six touchpieces to control. This would seem a far less convenient arrangement and makes for heavy and complicated mechanism. The finger stretch is also considerable. The older French-made, Boehm-system basset-horns were usually provided with rings like those of the soprano clarinets, but modern examples by such firms as Selmer and Buffet have covered holes – admittedly easier to finger securely but thought by some players to stifle the tone somewhat. Today Leblanc makes a large-bore type of basset-horn on which cover-plates are essential. In Germany today both fingering systems are found, and both with or without rings in the usual places. The crook may be of wood or metal. Many of the older German makers used wood for this purpose, but modern practice favours metal. In this latter case a socket is fitted to take the mouthpiece, which is little bigger than that of the soprano clarinets, and the lower end is corked or lapped, to make an air-tight joint with the upper joint. In the instrument, just described, by Key the practice is reversed, the crook being fitted with a cap which fits over the top of the upper joint. Some recent basset-horns are provided with normal B flat clarinet mouthpieces (i.e. Selmer), others with externally identical mouthpieces with a slightly enlarged bore (Buffet). In Germany, however, the normal basset-horn mouthpiece is definitely larger than that of the soprano instrument and approximates to the external dimensions of an English B flat clarinet mouthpiece. The bell, too, is often made of metal and not infrequently carried up in front of the instrument. This practice, borrowed from the bass clarinet, is to be condemned in general and quite unreservedly when the lowest tone-hole is placed on the metal bend. The substitution of a short thick-walled wooden bell and the prolongation of the bore, if required, will effect a quite surprising improvement in tone, not limited to the lower notes, but discernible throughout the compass.[6] The basset-horn is now invariably made in F, a fourth below the B flat clarinet. The compass is four full octaves. The narrowness of the bore in proportion to the length (·635 inches or 16 mm. to 42 inches) gives great scope to the harmonics which speak with peculiar freedom.

It is essentially a soft-toned instrument, with less ictus and carrying power than might be expected from a hearing at close quarters. This is particularly observable in some recent recordings of chamber works in which two or three basset-horns are employed with clarinets. The tone of the *chalumeau* is fuller, more vibrant and ready than that of the orchestral clarinets; the *clarinet* register is at once sweeter and more diffuse, while the *extreme* notes are lacking in bite and brilliancy. Generally speaking the tone-quality, if luscious, tends to sombreness and melancholy. It reminded E. T. A. Hoffmann of red carnations.[7] It is in fact quite incapable of gaiety or brilliance. It has of course in common with all the clarinet family a quite phenomenal control of dynamics and great flexibility. It is summed up in a well-known phrase of Gevaert as possessing 'gravité onctueuse'. Unkind, perhaps, but not without some truth.

To turn to the musical history of the basset-horn. The large number of specimens which survive from the 18th century shows a rapid rise to popularity, especially in southern Germany, Bohemia, Hungary, and Austria. In the 1770s the Hauskapelle of Prinzessin Elisabeth in Freiburg could muster three basset-horns if required, Kirrstein playing Basset-horn *en premier* and clarinet, Czerny Basset-horn *en basse* or bassoon, and Matauschek bassoon and Basset-horn *en basse*.[8] The new instrument seems to have penetrated more slowly to northern Germany, or to have been slower in finding favour there. C. F. Cramer in the work of 1783, already cited, describes it as a completely new and unknown instrument. Credit for spreading its popularity far and wide was largely due to the two itinerant virtuosi Anton David (1730–96), a clarinettist, who is said to have learned the basset-horn in Hungary, and his pupil Vincent

Springer (1760– ?), a Bohemian. They were occasionally assisted by another Bohemian, Dworschack, who appears to have played the clarinet and bassoon as well. The trio visited London in 1789 and met with considerable success. It was the first time the basset-horn had been heard there. But Paris had enjoyed the experience fifteen years before, when in April 1774 a M. Valentin had distinguished himself 'sur le corno-bassetto ou contra-clarinette'.[9] The instrument, however, would seem not to have attracted more than passing attention in France. It was in Germany, Austria, and Bohemia that the basset-horn found its true spiritual home. Its luscious, somewhat melancholy, tone made a special appeal to the romantic, sentimental spirit of the time and of the people. The demand for the instrument was met by more than fifty makers; of these all but three or four plied their craft east of the Rhine. And that the demand was considerable is shown by the number of specimens still surviving in museums and private collections. The rich decoration and elaborate mounting of many of these suggest that they were intended for wealthy dilettanti.

When and where the basset-horn first came to the notice of Mozart we do not know. He began writing for it in 1781, and it was possibly the Stadler brothers who introduced it to him. Improvements of the instrument have been attributed to them, in particular the basset-keys for *e flat* and *c sharp*, which at first were missing. Whether this is more than a dictionary statement there is no evidence to show. Beginning with the Serenade in B flat, K.361, Mozart included it in at least twenty of his recorded works. Outstanding examples of its use are to be found in *La Clemenza di Tito, Die Zauberflöte*, in the *Adagio*, K. 411, where two clarinets are associated with three basset-horns, and in his last work, the *Requiem*. These will be well known to readers. Less well-known but no less striking examples are to be found in the six *Notturni*,[10] in three of which three basset-horns have obbligato parts, and in the Rondo for soprano 'Al desio, di chi t'adora', K. 577. Here the singer is accompanied by strings and two concertante basset-horns. Attention may be drawn to two interesting fragments, 102 bars of an *allegro* from a Quintet in F major for violin, viola, clarinet, cello, and basset-horn, K. 580b, and to 199 bars of the opening movement of a concerto, K. 584b, for basset-horn in G. This dates from December 1789 and was later rewritten for the clarinet. It is in fact the first half or rather more of the opening *allegro* of the Clarinet Concerto, of October 1791. Why it was rewritten is not known; it is only one of the queries connected with this puzzling work.[11] Possibly the demands on Stadler's virtuosity were too great; or possibly the sombre tone of the solo instrument was considered by the composer less suited to the *allegro* and *rondo* than to the *adagio*. It may be noticed in passing that the basset-horn, like the trombone, had an almost ritual significance for Mozart. It appears frequently in his Masonic works. It need hardly be said that Mozart realised at once the possibilities of the new instrument and used them to the best advantage. He writes for it much as he writes for the clarinet, making rather more use of bold sweeping arpeggios and displaying its agility and flexibility to the full. The range employed covers three octaves and a third.

It might be thought that Mozart's use of the basset-horn in the orchestra would have been followed by other composers. Not so; a solitary, but effective, instance of its use comes to mind in the *Prometheus Ballet* of Beethoven, but after that its appearances are infrequent and sporadic. It again became a solo instrument, and many successors to David, Springer, and Dworschack were forthcoming. Some of the better known were C. Bärmann, J. G. H. Backofen, Iwan Müller, Tausch, father and son, K. F. Bauersachs, and Beerhalter. There were a host of others,[12] and sonatas and concertos by F. Danzi, Chr. Rummel, G. A. Schneider, and Bochsa, were frequently given. It does not seem to have attracted the attention of Weber or Spohr – Hermstedt does not appear to have favoured the basset-horn – but Mendelssohn wrote two delightful trios for it with clarinet and piano, inspired by the fine playing of Heinrich and Carl Bärmann, father and son. These *Konzertstücke*, op. 113 and 114, are effective melodious works in the composer's best vein and never fail to gain applause. The scarcity of basset-horns makes performance of them infrequent. If the basset-horn failed to maintain a footing in the orchestra, it was welcomed by the military who were looking for a deep-tone clarinet and had not as yet found a bass to satisfy their needs. That many were used by the Prussian and other German bands is indicated by the numerous specimens surviving from the workshops of Griessling and Schlott of Berlin and the Potsdam maker Kirst, and others. These were of the conventional bent type with *Kasten*, but not infrequently the extension was diatonic only. Russia, too, made extensive use of them, supplied no doubt by the German makers.

The last virtuoso of note was Aloysius Beerhalter (1800–52), a clarinettist in the Stuttgart orchestra, who had considerable success in London in 1843. By this time the sixty-year popularity of the instrument in Germany had waned, and by 1855 the basset-horn was dead. In November of this year Brahms, writing to Clara Schumann, could say,

'The aria by Mozart was sung by Frau Guhrau with orchestra. To my great joy she was accompanied by two basset-horns which had been obtained with great difficulty. I do not think any instrument blends more perfectly with the human voice.'

This had been the opinion of Mozart some seventy years before.

If the basset-horn did not attract more than passing attention in France, it had a phase of popularity in England. After the visit of David and Springer in 1789, who had given 'most finished performances on novel instruments to this country', interest was temporarily revived by a concerto played upon it at a Salomon concert in April 1791. The name of the player is not given. In 1801 two 'corni di bassetto' (the *di* has already crept in) were available at Covent Garden for the performance of Mozart's *Requiem*. They were in the hands of Munro and Leffler junior. They figured, too, in the private band of George III and must have enjoyed some measure of popularity, since a quantity of *divertimenti* for them with other wind instruments is included in the Royal Music collection. In an inventory of the King's instruments taken at Windsor *c*. 1820 the presence of an 'old Corna Basetto' is noted. A scale of fingering for the instrument is given in John Mahon's clarinet tutor of 1803 accompanied by a rough delineation a 7-key sickle-shaped model. As already noticed, it was given the alternative name of *Clara Voce*.[13] Possibly Mahon, already known as a solo clarinettist, was the soloist in the Salomon concert of 1791. It was the performance of Willman, however, between 1820 and his death in 1840 which gave the basset-horn some measure of popularity. Willman was a sensitive artist, who excelled in accompaniment. 'Non, più di fiori' was not less a favourite with London audiences than with provincial, and no festival was considered complete without an obbligato by Willman on clarinet or basset-horn. And the player was considered the equal of the singer, even were she Catalani, Malibran, or Sontag, and was often praised more lavishly. Willman's role was continued by Lazarus, whose basset-horn has already been noticed. But by the turn of the half-century the instrument was all but forgotten, and it was not always easy to find players for the occasional performances of Mozart's *Serenade* or the *Konzertstücke* of Mendelssohn. The basset-horn parts in the *Requiem* and in the operas were only too often transferred to the clarinet. Correspondence in the *English Mechanic* of 1876 shows that the basset-horn was very rare at this date, but that Maycock, a player second only to Lazarus in popular esteem, still used it for solos in Balfe's *Bohemian Girl*.

The manufacture of basset-horns was revived by Mahillon of Brussels in the 1880s, and the instrument now figures in the catalogues of many German instrument-makers. In Germany and England two artists did much to foster a revival. Robert Stark taught it in the music school at Würzburg and, in addition to some original compositions, made many arrangements for it. Molbe included it in several chamber works.[14] In England Francisco Gomez, well known as a clarinettist and bass clarinettist, reintroduced 'Non, più di fiori' to audiences at Promenade Concerts after a long lapse. It may now be said that many opera houses and orchestras include basset-horns in their stock of instruments, and that there is now less excuse than there was for replacing them with clarinets in works wherein their use is intended. In 1909 Richard Strauss reinforced his remarkable clarinet chorus in *Elektra* with two basset-horns. The instrument appears again in *Die Frau ohne Schatten*, in *Der Rosenkavalier*, and in his later works *Daphne*, op. 82 (1938), and *Capriccio*, op. 85, of 1942. His example was followed in England by Holbrooke and Van Dieren, in the U.S.A. more recently by Frederick Converse and Roger Sessions, and in Holland by Marius Flothuis and Rudolph Escher.

Whether the basset-horn will ever be more than an occasional visitor in the orchestra is open to doubt. Although in theory it is immediately playable by any clarinettist, in practice it is a difficult instrument to handle,[15] and players with a reputation to consider tend to fight shy of it. There are few specialist players available, and these only in the big musical centres, so composers are not encouraged to include the instrument in their scores. It is to be regretted, however, that an instrument of such range and of such an individual tone-colour should be lost to the orchestra, and that every woodwind solo of a tender plaintive character should be automatically assigned to the cor anglais. A voice of tenor pitch, to link up the soprano and bass clarinets, and to reinforce the upper register of the latter, is clearly desirable and, if not provided by the basset-horn, might well be furnished by the *tenor* and *alto* clarinets.

These may now be considered. They are pitched in F or E flat, a fourth and fifth below the B flat clarinet. Their compass being unextended, they sound *A* and *G* as their lowest notes. In England the former is known as the *tenor*, while the latter, by an anomaly, is called the *alto*. Abroad there is no such distinction, and the instruments are known as *clarinette alto*, *Alt-Klarinette*, and *clarinetto contralto*. In outward form they resemble somewhat truncated basset-horns. The bells are usually of metal and upturned, but a downward-pointing wooden bell is preferable. Buffet-Crampon of Paris made many tenors of this design. The French makers, who seem to prefer the lower-pitched instrument in E flat, have recently given considerable attention to it, providing two speaker-keys, which may be simple or automatically controlled. Tonally the tenor is indistinguishable from the basset-horn, but the alto, with its wider bore and bigger reed, has a voice of considerable distinction and character. This instrument, easier to manipulate than the basset-horn, tonally more distinguished than the saxophone, might plainly be of great service to the orchestra, as Berlioz for one suggested more than a century ago. As it is, the alto clarinet has had a long and honourable career in military music and still maintains its place in many continental bands. But not in England, where its useful service was unwisely terminated not long since in favour of the saxophone with consequent impoverishment of variety and tone-colour.

The history of the alto and tenor clarinets is obscure. They may have been developments of the clarinet in G, *la grande clarinette*, which finds a place in Roeser, Laborde, and Francoeur; or of the clarinette d'amour, with a normal in place of a piriform bell to give a franker and more open tone. Again, they may be simply variants, truncated versions, of the basset-horn. There is every reason to think that the latter, with a history reaching back to 1770, was first in the field, and that the alto and tenor were not independent growths. In the midst of obscurity one fact emerges, that the credit for the 'invention' of the alto was taken by Iwan Müller. In 1808 he was in Berlin and Vienna performing upon an 18-key basset-horn by Grenser of Dresden. Possibly he found the thumb-keys an obstacle to rapid execution; certainly in his tutor, published *c.* 1825, his *clarinette-alto* is shown without them. Curt Sachs in his *Handbuch der Musikinstrumentenkunde* states that in 1808 Grenser began the manufacture of straight-bodied basset-horns without the supplementary keys, and thus claims the priority of the 'invention' for Germany.

In the matter of notation it may be observed that the basset-horn and tenor and alto clarinets are invariably written for in the G clef. Occasionally in Mozart (*Tito* and the *Adagio*, K. 411) the F clef is used for the bottom notes to economise in leger lines, the part being written an octave too low for the convenience of the player. In the case of the basset-horn the key-signature will require one flat less and one sharp more than that of the music.

NOTES

[1] In 1774 it was called *Corno-basetto ou contra-clarinette*.

[2] A similar specimen is recorded at Nuremberg.

[3] *Magazin der Musik*, p. 179.

[4] It is curious that the cor anglais should have been built in this curved shape for so long. Although Brod showed the way with his straight-bodied instrument *c.* 1836, other makers, including Triébert, continued with the older pattern some twenty years longer. In Italy the curved form survived till the early 1900s.

[5] The first basset-horn with Boehm fingering noted by the writer is branded Pask, London – a maker active between 1842 and 1870 – and was formerly owned by Henry Lazarus. It is probably of French workmanship, since the Boehm clarinet was all but unknown at this period in England, and the keywork is of typically French design. It may be dated *c.* 1856. The body is shortened by providing the basset-keys with a separate tube, parallel to the main body-joint and joined to it with long metal pins: the bores are united at the bottom with a U bend of metal. A similar model of neater design was made by E.-J. Albert of Brussels in the early 1900s. The instrument is shown in Plate 3.

[6] The experience of the writer in this matter has been strikingly and quite independently confirmed by a well-known professional player.

[7] *Kreisleriana*, 5.

[8] L. Schiedermair, 'Die Oper an den bädischen Höfen', I.M.G., Sammelband XIV (1912), pp. 3 *et seq.* Two of the basset-horns were played by Bohemians, it will be noticed.

[9] *Mercure de France*, April 1774, p. 165.

[10] In the other two a basset-horn joins two clarinets in the accompaniment. The *Canzonetta*, K. 549, is accompanied by a trio of basset-horns.

[11] George Dazely (*The Music Review*, ix, p. 169) repudiates the possibility of a simple transposition of a *complete* work written for the basset-horn in G. He argues, not without plausibility, that the Concerto was originally written for a clarinet in A with a compass extended to low C. This explains much obvious patching in the accepted version. Until 1967 there was no known contemporary, or nearly contemporary, evidence concerning these amendments, but in that year Ernst Hess, in a lecture to the Central Institute for Mozart Research in Salzburg, drew attention to a review of the printed score which had appeared in the *Leipziger Musikalische Zeitung* of March 1802. Here the reviewer said: 'Finally, the critic feels obliged to say that Mozart wrote this Concerto for a clarinet encompassing low C.' There follow a number of music examples culled from the score, and then the observation, 'However, since clarinets encompassing low C must at present be counted among the rarer instruments, thanks are due to the editors for these transpositions and alterations, though they have not improved the Concerto. Perhaps it would have been just as well to have published it in the original version, and to have inserted these transpositions in smaller notes.'

Prior to Hess's researches, Dr Milan Kostohryz of the Prague Conservatoire found himself sufficiently convinced in the matter to warrant the construction of a special extended lower joint with basset-keys to low C for his A clarinet; and in 1951 his pupil, Josef Janous, played what was probably the original version of the Concerto for the first time. In 1956 Jiri Kratchovil of the Prague Academy of Fine Arts, whose studies have done much to elucidate the true state of affairs, played a reconstruction of the Mozart Clarinet Quintet. Following him, the name 'basset-clarinet' is now generally accepted to denote the extended instrument in A or B flat, and a considerable number of the younger professional clarinettists are obtaining instruments either complete to special order, or with modified lower joints.

[12] Smart gives an amusing description of an itinerant basset-horn player, Francois Schalk, 'artiste en musique de Prague', whom he met at Spohr's house in Cassel in 1825. H. B. and C. L. E. Cox, *Leaves from the Journals of Sir George Smart*, London, 1907, pp. 209–13.

[13] This name has not been encountered elsewhere. Early basset-horns of English make are very rare. One or two by T. Key are known, and a solitary specimen by Cramer of London is preserved in the Victoria and Albert Museum. An early sickle-shaped model (incomplete when examined recently) may be seen in the University Museum, Oxford. It is precisely similar to that shown in Mahon's tutor.

[14] So, too, Poldowski in an unpublished octet for 2 flutes, oboe, oboe d'amore, basset-horn, and bass clarinet.

[15] The length of the lower member makes it a difficult instrument to tune, and the basset-keys do not recommend it to the occasional player.

CHAPTER II

The Bass Clarinet
Fr. Clarinette basse. Ger. bass Klarinette
It. Clarinetto basso, Clarone

THE DOCUMENTED HISTORY of the bass clarinet may be said to begin
with an announcement in the Paris newspaper *L'Avant-Coureur*, of
11 May 1772. The passage may be quoted in full from Constant Pierre's
Les Facteurs d'instruments de musique, pp. 103–4, since no specimen of
the instrument described is known to survive. It runs:

> 'Le sieur G[illes] Lot, facteur d'instruments à vent, demeurant
> dans la cour des moines de l'abbaye Saint-Germain, vis-à-vis de la
> fontaine, vient de faire paraître un instrument de musique d'une
> nouvelle invention, sous le nom de *basse-tube* (basso tuba) ou basse
> de clarinette. On n'a point encore vu d'instruments d'une étendue
> aussi considérable. Il est susceptible de trois octaves et demie pleine;
> il descend aussi bas que le basson et monte aussi haut que la
> flûte. Cet instrument, qui est d'une forme tout à fait particulière,
> contient plusieurs clés pour l'usage des semi-tons, toutes très
> artistement arrangées et d'un mécanisme fort ingénieux. Les sons
> qu'il produit sont très agréables et si parfaitement sonores, qu'ils
> imitent de fort près, dans les tons bas, ceux d'un orgue dans l'action
> des pédales. Cet instrument étant joué par un habile artiste, ne
> sçaurait manquer de produire un très bon effet et d'avoir l'approba-
> tion du public, soit qu'il soit entendu seul ou dans l'orchestre.'

If the documented history begins in 1772, the undocumented may
well begin rather earlier with a primitive instrument by an unknown
maker, constructed of plankwood covered with leather. Two well-
preserved specimens survive in the collections at Berlin (2810) and
Brussels (939). The first, formerly in the Snoeck collection (910), has
apparently only one key, while the second, formerly owned by Adolphe
Sax, has three, and is described at some length by V.-C. Mahillon
(*Catalogue*, vol. 2, p. 219). Both are in essentials identical in design.
The body, an inch in thickness, is considerably wider at the bottom
than at the top; it resembles in shape a narrow triangle with blunted

apex. A long crook of graceful and surprisingly modern appearance is
fitted at the top, an upturned widely-flared bell at the bottom. Both are
of brass. A third specimen, less well preserved, may be seen in the
Museo Storico Civico at Lugano, which differs little from the others,
but has a downward-pointing bell. The bore, approximately 18 mm. in
diameter, is contrived at the back, the longer side, of the instrument.
The left thumb-hole opens directly into it, while the seven finger-holes,
grouped within convenient reach of the fingers on the upper surface,
are bored obliquely through the full and increasing width of the wood
to reach the bore at the back at much more widely-spaced intervals.
The maker no doubt borrowed the idea from the wing-joint of the
bassoon, relying on slanting holes of small diameter and on impedance,
to gain depth of pitch and to economise thereby in the length of the
body. The result is far from happy according to Mahillon, who found
the tone of the Brussels specimen, pitched in A (or a flat B flat ?),[1]
lacking in timbre and vigour. In this specimen the three keys are
mounted in saddles; two of them are for the first finger and thumb of
the left hand; the third, for low *E*, is mounted on the left side, and
manipulated by the little finger of the same hand. The instrument was
plainly intended to overblow and to have a clarinet register. Not so the
Berlin specimen in which the solitary key is designed to give the
bottom note only. It is unfortunately impossible to date these interesting
instruments, since the maker and even the country of origin are
unknown.[2] To judge by the paucity of keys they may well be not later
than 1750; and quite possibly the Berlin specimen may be considerably
earlier. It may indeed be a true *basse de chalumeau* for which Graupner
wrote more than once.

It may be inferred from the passage quoted from *L'Avant-Coureur*
that the *basse-tube* was intended for solo or orchestral use. The next
model to be mentioned, the *Klarinetten-Bass* of Heinrich Grenser, the
noted Dresden maker, had probably a military purpose, to replace the
bassoon in military bands with its greater sonority. The revolutionary
period 1790–1815 gave a powerful fillip to military music and witnessed
the growth and development of innumerable military bands throughout
Europe. A bass clarinet for military purposes must necessarily be
portable. So with Grenser's bass begins a series of bass clarinets doubled
upon themselves in the manner of bassoons. The compactness of this
design has always fascinated makers, and is possibly not yet entirely
extinct. It sets the manufacturer, however, severe mechanical problems,
which have never been quite satisfactorily solved. And further, if the
clarinet is to replace the bassoon with greater robustness of tone, it must

have the same or approximately the same compass. So with the *Klarinetten-Bass* begins a not inconsiderable series of bass clarinets with extended compass. Little is known of its design and construction. One specimen only survives. It is preserved in the Gross-Herzogliches Museum, Darmstadt, and is described in Day's R.M.E. Catalogue (No. 266) as having nine keys. Gerber's *Lexikon der Tonkünstler* (1812–14) adds a few more details. It descended to B natural below the bass stave, had a compass of four octaves, and withal a pleasant and powerful tone. It could easily be played by any clarinettist or basset-hornist.

The next date of importance is 1807, when Desfontenelles of Lisieux devised an instrument of strikingly modern appearance. Again only one specimen is known, that in the Paris Conservatoire Museum (No. 1136). The straight body, bent wooden crook, and bell brought well up in front suggest a saxophone at first glance. And a predecessor of the saxophone it was at first considered to be by Sax's detractors, until closer examination and trial proved that it overblew not in octaves, but in twelfths, and was essentially a clarinet.[3] A striking feature is the equipment of 13 keys with which it is provided, a remarkable anticipation of Iwan Müller's invention. It was no doubt this formidable array of keys that militated against its wider adoption. The keys are mounted in saddles and between pillars. This is the first use of pillars on the clarinet which has been noticed.

If Desfontenelles gave a foretaste of modern design, Nicola Papalini returned to the unorthodox and primitive. This maker, active in Chiaravalle Milanese near Pavia, *c.* 1810, provided an ingenious, if grotesque, solution to the problem of shortening the tube, and of bringing the tone-holes within reach of the fingers. The bore of his instrument, pitched in C, is curved in serpentine fashion and some of the holes, normally fitted with keys, are stopped by the underpart of the hand or finger. There are in all 16 tone-holes, of which five are closed with keys. The bell is turned towards the player's right, and a double-coiled crook, cleverly carved from wood, brings the mouthpiece conveniently to the lips. The undulating bore is excavated in two blocks of pearwood, which are glued together and secured by iron or wooden pegs along the scalloped edges. The instrument is not covered in leather. The general design may be studied in Plate 7. The compass is, as with so many early basses, extended to *c*. It is certainly a portable model, but tone and timbre have been sacrificed to compactness: a clever specimen of wood-carving rather than a musical instrument. Five specimens at least survive in public collections, viz. Brussels 940,

Paris 550 (ex Sax), Heyer 1538 (ex Kraus), New York (2545), Boston 119 (ex Galpin).

Exactly contemporary with the invention of Desfontenelles was that of Dumas of Sommières, described as 'ancien chef de l'orfèvrerie de l'Empereur'. He was a clarinettist as well and in 1807 presented his bass clarinet for trial to the Conservatoire. It was warmly praised by Méhul, Cherubini, Catel, and others, and in 1810 was recommended to the Garde Impériale. But the artists of this *corps d'élite*, accustomed to the 6 keys of the ordinary clarinet, were alarmed by the 13 keys of the new invention and showed no disposition to re-learn their instrument. Such is the account given by Pontécoulant. It differs in some details from the succinct summary given in *Archives des découvertes*,[4] where the instrument is named the *Basse guerrière* and is stated to have been adopted by the Garde, and to have been approved by Grétry, Lesueur, Martini, Gebauer, and others. Unfortunately no details of the instrument are given, but the number of keys and the date are suggestive. It would be tempting to infer that Dumas, to keep his secret, entrusted his invention to a provincial maker, and to identify the creation of Dumas with that of Desfontenelles. Of this, however, there is no evidence whatever. The disappointed inventor, to continue Pontécoulant's romantic story, kept the instrument to himself and would never entrust it to an artist. Finally in 1832, when dying in hospital, he made over his precious bass to the well-known player Dacosta.[5] What happened to it later is surmise, but it is significant that just about this time, 1832, Dacosta was co-operating with Auguste Buffet in the production of a bass, and gave a recital upon it at the Salle Saint-Jean de l'Hôtel-de-Ville. The effortless execution of the artist and the beauty of the tone were much appreciated, not less by the audience than by the critics. It may be gathered from the brief account given in the *Revue Musicale*[6] that the body of the instrument was straight,[7] and that the crook which carried the mouthpiece was curved towards the player, no small advantages in the opinion of the writer Fétis. It was for this instrument, according to Lavoix, that the famous solo in Meyerbeer's *Les Huguenots* was written. Pillaut, on the other hand, states that Buteux was the first to play it on a bass by X. Lefèvre. Buffet's instrument had a compass of three octaves and a third without downward extension. The use of weak reeds was recommended.

To go back some twenty years. In 1812 appeared another bassoon-shaped model, the *Basse-orgue* of Sautermeister of Lyons. This city was, as we have seen, second only to Paris as a centre of instrument-making. All that is known of the instrument is that it had a perfectly cylindrical bore, resembled a bassoon in outward appearance, had a compass of rather more than three octaves, and that the 'pavillon [bell] peut se remplacer par un globe et même par un tube percé de part en part'.[8] It may be noted that a bass of very similar appearance, extended to low *c*, was brought out by his fellow citizen L. Muller, in 1846, the Mullerphone.[9]

Another bent-up model was introduced in 1828 by Gottlieb Streitwolf (1779–1837) of Göttingen, a clever maker who had worked for Hermstedt. It was made of boxwood and was extended to low *c* or to *b flat*. It was pitched at first in C, and later in B flat, and equipped with 17, 18, or 19 keys. Some of the tone-holes were bored obliquely and were uncovered. According to the careful account of it in the *Revue Musicale*,[10] the tone was similar in quality to that of the basset-horn, but fuller and richer. The instrument, obtainable from Schott of Mainz, was priced, with a method, at 225 francs. W. Altenburg in *Die Klarinette* speaks highly of its tone and intonation. To judge by the paucity of surviving specimens Streitwolf's invention enjoyed less success than it merited, less perhaps than the *Glicibarifono*, the 'premiata invenzione' of Catterino Catterini of Padua.[11] This ingenious instrument is made from a single block of boxwood of oval section, some 23 inches in length. Two parallel bores are pierced in it in the manner of the butt-joint of a bassoon. A long brass crook carries the mouthpiece, while the other end of the bore terminates in a widely-flared upstanding bell of wood. Twenty-four cleverly contrived brass keys, mounted in saddles, cover correctly located tone-holes of adequate size. These, with a biggish bore of modern dimensions, give a tone of no mean vigour and quality. The specimen examined by the writer is pitched in C and extended downwards chromatically to *c*. The specimen in the Brussels collection (No. 941) bears the stamp of P. Maino, Milan.[12] Catterini's instrument attracted the attention of Klosé in Paris, who communicated the details of it to Kastner.[13] The instrument obtained considerable success when heard at the Teatro Communale at Modena in February 1838. As has been said, the compactness of the bent-up model has always attracted players and makers, and very similar models by Stengel of Baireuth, Beck of Weimar,[14] Berthold of Speyer, and other German and Austrian makers, may be noticed in museums. They all have one serious defect, the great difficulty of drying-out the bore both during and after use.

More might have been heard of the Dacosta-Buffet model and of the *Glicibarifono* had not both been put completely in the shade by Adolphe Sax's bass clarinet. Sax, it will be remembered, was not only an inventor and a craftsman of unusual ability, but also a clarinettist of distinction.

It was to the clarinet that he first applied his brains and mechanical skill. The specification of his new bass clarinet is dated 19 June 1838. The features of it are the straight body, the accurately-placed tone-holes each covered by a padded cup, the properly proportioned bore, and, most important of all, the additional speaker near the mouthpiece. Serpentine contortions and narrow, obliquely bored tone-holes were gone for ever. Every hole was brought by mechanism comfortably under the fingers. Desfontenelles had provided a straight body some thirty years before; Catterini had just enlarged the bore and re-located and covered the tone-holes with padded cups. The more credit to them. There is not the smallest reason to suppose that Sax had seen either instrument. The new bass was provided with the usual metal crook and *downward*-pointing bell. The compass was increased at the top by the second speaker-key which permitted the highest notes to be sounded with ease and ended normally with low *E* sounding *D*. A metal reflector, as readers of Berlioz will remember, could be fitted to direct the lowest notes in any desired direction. Or, if required, a curved bell could be fitted, extending the downward range to low *C*. The four additional holes were located on the long neck of the bell. A modification was available for military use, having a shortened body and elongated bell brought well up in front. This was known as *Clarinette basse recourbée a pavillon de cuivre*.

The new instrument won immediate success in Brussels where it attracted the attention of Habeneck, and inspired him to the pungent remark that compared with it the ancient bass was a monstrosity. Its success in Paris was at first delayed by the opposition of the clarinettist Buteux and of interested makers, but was assured when it was adopted by E. Duprez and used by him in the famous solo in Act V of *Les Huguenots*, where the range employed is from written *e* to *g'''*, and in *Le Prophète*.[15]

The ink on Meyerbeer's score was hardly dry when a far more florid and extended obbligato for the bass appeared in England. This was in a setting of verses of Psalm 70 for 'a counter-tenor-Lady's voice, with the bass-clarionet concertant', composed in February 1836 by the Chevalier Neukomm, the pupil of Haydn, for Mrs Alfred Shaw, a famous contralto, and Willman. The clarinet part ranges from written *c* in the bass stave to *d* above the treble. The instrument was pitched in C and was described in contemporary accounts as a 'bass clarone', an obvious pleonasm, since *clarone* has always been a common Italian term for the bass clarinet. Three years before, in 1833, George Wood, a clever London maker, had introduced a bass of his own invention. No specimen of it is known to the writer, nor can details of its construction be gleaned from its chart of fingering beyond the fact that it was furnished with 18 keys. Since it was extended to written *b flat*, and pitched in C, it may be inferred that it was intended for military as well as orchestral use. In the band it would presumably have supplanted the bassoon.

J. H. Maycock (1818–1907) appears to have given more than passing attention to the bass clarinet as well as to the basset-horn. Balfe wrote some telling obbligati for him. M. Wuille, too, a Belgian clarinettist of some distinction, gave several recitals in the 1850s in which he displayed the capabilities of the bass. But there was long a tendency in England, as probably in many other countries, to regard the bass clarinet as a doubling instrument, safely relegated to any clarinettist not of the first rank. It need hardly be said that the position has long been materially altered. The increasing demands of composers – Wagner began writing for it in 1848 – have made specialist bass clarinettists a necessity, and the modern player is now regarded as an artist of the first importance.

It cannot be said, however, that even today sufficient attention is given to it by composers. Its value as a melodic instrument is too often overlooked. It is much more than an auxiliary to the bassoon; a soft general-utility pedal reed to support the woodwind chorus. This was the role frequently assigned to it by Wagner, although Meyerbeer and later Liszt in his *Dante Symphony* had shown its capabilities as a solo instrument.[16] Tonally no wind instrument excels it in harmonic richness. The *chalumeau*, which with its slower vibrations is much hollower and reedier than that of the soprano clarinets, may be modulated to any desired degree. It can be virile and majestic or sink to a pervading whisper. In the hands of an experienced player it is never flabby. The middle register, full and sweet and reminiscent of string-tone, may be utilised to advantage to reinforce and nourish, with its rich harmonic content, the weaker notes of the higher-pitched instruments. It is invaluable in imparting richness and body to the military band. Gilmore had one in his band in 1878, Sousa had two; the bigger continental organisations employ it in pairs, even in threes and fours. In chamber music, too, its value is beginning to be realised. York Bowen has shown its qualities in combination with a string quartet, op. 93, and among others to favour it are: Janácêk in his wind Sextet, Mládí; Marius Flothuis in his wind Quintet, op. 13; Poldowski in her wind Octet; and Kenneth Harding in his (1951) Quartet for clarinets in which it forms the base to three B flats.

With the gradual adoption of Sax's straight-bodied model with covered holes, the history of the development of the bass clarinet is all but finished. The bass of 1950 differs singularly little from that of 1838. The mechanism has been tidied up and modernised,[17] the crook has been given a more graceful curve, and the upturned bell gives more sonority to the bottom notes. The mechanism of the Boehm clarinet was soon applied to it. A model long popular in English orchestras and bands, and made by the Brussels makers Albert and Mahillon, had the mechanism of the 13-key clarinet in which the Boehm fingering for *b flat* in the *chalumeau* replaced the clumsier fingering of Müller. In its latest form, as made by E.-J. Albert, much length is saved by the use of a long double-coiled crook, while the bell and part of the bottom joint are brought well up in front. This neat and compact model found many friends not only in England, but in the Rhineland. But, speaking generally, Sax's model has never been liked in Germany. The bore was considered too large, the tone too hollow and too vigorous for orchestral use. German makers have always preferred a thinner, slighter model provided with a smaller bore and played with a smaller reed and mouthpiece. The more elaborate forms of Oehler mechanism are commonly fitted to it, and it may have as many as 27 keys. The weight of German (and more recently, French) instruments is often taken upon a foot-peg. In many of them, too, more efficient sound radiation is obtained by placing an open hole just above the bell.

One of the basic difficulties of bass-clarinet technique is the use of the second speaker placed upon the crook. It is usually necessary to change from the first to the second speaker at *e″* in the *clarinet* register. To do this neatly requires no little practice, hence many modern instruments of both German and French design are fitted with automatic speakers. The player fingers the instrument in the usual way and the change of speaker is effected for him mechanically, without thought or effort on his part. The mechanism is complicated and vulnerable, however, and not a few prominent orchestral players prefer the older method, distrusting the reliability of the new. German basses are often provided with special mechanism for a purer middle *b flat*, in addition to automatics.

The older basses were pitched, like the orchestral clarinets, in A, B flat, and C. The bass in C has long been extinct; that in A is dying a lingering death. It is employed by Bantock in *Fifine at the Fair*[18] (1912), by Schoenberg in his *Kammersymphonie*, by Strauss in *Daphne*, and by Ravel. Parts for it are now played upon the B flat instrument, an extension to low *e flat* being usual in all but military instruments. German basses commonly have an additional semitone to *d*. This note, it may be mentioned, occurs in Othmar Schoeck's *Sonata*, op. 41, of 1931.[19] The upward range is that of the other clarinets; Sax indeed played up to e'''' in the presence of Meyerbeer. Not that there is the smallest point in taking the bass up into the *extreme* register when soprano clarinets are available for the purpose. The body of the instrument is generally made of African blackwood, less often of cocus, a wood long favoured in England. Boxwood, too, was a favourite long after its use for the instruments of higher pitch had been abandoned. No doubt its lightness was a recommendation. German makers have experimented with the softer woods such as rosewood and maple. The latter is much favoured by Heckel. Metal, too, has been employed by Sax in the 1850s and later by Losschmidt of Olomouc, who in 1867 produced a bassoon-shaped model of some originality.[20] In 1931 M. Houvenaghel, technical adviser to Messrs Leblanc of Paris, and creator of a bass[21] and contrabass of strikingly novel design, declared himself in favour of metal for all clarinets of deeper tone (see Plate 8).

In the matter of notation practice varies. One method is to write the part in the G clef as for a soprano clarinet, treating it, as Widor remarks, like a 16-foot stop on the organ. This was Meyerbeer's constant, and Wagner's early, practice, and is still quite common in English and French scores. Widor finds it illogical that a bass clarinet playing in unison with a bassoon should not be playing in the F clef. Gordon Jacob disagrees with him, arguing that the G clef is more convenient to the player. Another method is to write the part entirely in the bass clef, only using the treble to economise in leger lines. This is common German practice.

NOTES

[1] R.M.E. Cat. 261, where the instrument is well illustrated. The illustration is reproduced in Plate 7.

[2] The Berlin specimen bears the initials v.f. Mahillon considered these instruments to be of German origin and possibly the first *ébauches* of H. Grenser's bass. This would seem to be unlikely.

[3] The error made in his former work, *La Facture instrumentale*, p. 50, was later admitted by C. Pierre, *Les Facteurs*, p. 402. See also J. Kool, *Das Saxophon*, Leipzig, 1931, pp. 184–5, and V.-C. Mahillon, *Catalogue du Musée instrumental du conservatoire*, Vol. IV, p.357.

[4] Tom. iii, 1811, p.222.

[5] Isaac Franco Dacosta, born Bordeaux 1778; died there 1866.

[6] 5 June 1834.

[7] Buffet also made a bent-up model. See the catalogue of the Stearns collection, No. 635.

[8] C.Pierre, op. cit. p.344.

[9] Ibid. p. 345.

[10] Tom. 8/9, 1830, p. 329.

[11] Catterini is described as 'bolognese' in A. Gandini's *Cronistoria dei teatri di Modena*, 1873. The instrument, kindly lent for examination by Mr Philip Bate, is stamped 'Catterino Catterini in Padova'. It is illustrated in Plate 7.

[12] Possibly a later model, since the keys are more neatly mounted. It is in B flat.

[13] See *Traité général, Supplément*, Paris, 1844, where it is stated to be pitched in B flat.

[14] Heyer-Leipzig, No. 1540.

[15] *La France Musicale*, 7 January 1844. Duprez's instrument is No. 1137 in the Museum of the Paris Conservatoire. As quoted by Berlioz in his *Traité*, the ascending arpeggio ends on g'', an octave lower. No doubt the composer found the extreme notes of less value than the lower.

[16] Since this was first written the situation has changed markedly. Apart from the solo passages written for it in the showy scoring for large stage bands and jazz combinations of all sizes, serious composers are today making increasing use of the bass clarinet, as witness, for example, the repertoire quoted by Kroll and Riehm in *The Clarinet* (English translation, London, 1968). The late Ian Whyte once told the present writer [P.B.] that of all the devices he knew of to fill out inadequate orchestral resources, the provision of a free bass clarinet part (and one for viola) was perhaps the best.

[17] The process was begun soon after 1838, when padded cups on rods replaced the original longitudinally mounted, simple-lever, keys of Sax.

[18] This work is notable for a formidable cadenza for the clarinet, no less than 43 bars in length.

[19] The latest catalogues of continental makers, both French and German, quote bass clarinets extended to low C as standard models, and these are proving more and more popular.

[20] No. 2459, Crosby Brown Coll., N.Y.

[21] A smaller edition of the contrabass described in the following chapter.

CHAPTER 12

The Contrabass Clarinet
Fr. Clarinette-contrebasse, Clarinette pedale
Ger. Kontrabass-klarinette
It. Clarinetto contabasso, Contraclarone

THIS INSTRUMENT has been made in several pitches, in F or E flat, an octave below the basset-horn and alto clarinet, or in C or B flat, an octave below the bass clarinet. The higher-pitched instruments, whether fitted with basset-keys or not, are sometimes known as 'contrabasset-horns'. The true contrabass, however, is an instrument of 16-foot tone and requires at least 8 feet of length, or of 9 or 10 if the compass is extended beyond the normal written E.

To consider first the contrabasset-horn. The first attempt in this field was made by G. Streitwolf who brought out his new instrument in September 1829, a year after his bass clarinet. It was built like a bassoon and equipped with 19 keys, including, it would seem, the thumb-keys proper to the basset-horn. It was pitched in F and E flat. The new invention, though warmly praised by Spohr and Fétis, does not appear to have had much success. The price of it was extremely low, 300 francs in boxwood, 250 in maple. This was followed some twelve or fifteen years later[1] by Sax's *Clarinette-contrebasse*, pitched in E flat, an octave below the alto clarinet. It was intended for military use, was made throughout of brass, and in its compact appearance resembled the *Glicibarifono*. It differed, however, from the latter in having a longer crook coiled up and down, and the bell turned outward. Some forty years elapsed before the next attempt. This was a contra-tenor in F made by E. Albert of Brussels to the order of Gustave Ponce-let and intended for his clarinet ensemble at the Brussels Conserva-toire. Its exact date has not been fixed, but it must plainly antedate C. Pierre's *La Facture instrumentale* of 1890 in which it is mentioned.[2] It was provided with 15 keys, from which it may be inferred that the compass was not extended. A similar instrument was made by Evette and Schaeffer. The short series of contrabasset-horns and contra-tenors may be closed with a reference to two later models. The first was created by the well-known Paris firm of Selmer at the suggestion of the American Bandmasters' Association. It is made of wood or of metal at choice and pitched in E flat. It is stated to be 4 feet 2½ inches in length, to which the crook and bell would add another 2 feet; it weighs 8½ pounds when made of wood. It is credited with unusual agility. The second was announced by Ernst Schmidt, the well-known maker of Mannheim, in the 1930s. It was stated to be pitched in G and to descend to written *D*.

The series of true contrabasses begins with the *Contre-basse guerrière* of the goldsmith Dumas. Little is known of it beyond the fact that it was invented in 1808. Its name sufficiently indicates its purpose, but whether the military adopted the new invention more readily than his bass is not known. The next invention, the *Bathyphon*, enjoyed a certain measure of success in military bands. It was devised in 1839 by W. F. Wieprecht, the well-known director of Prussian military bands and opponent of Sax, and made by E. Skorra of Berlin and C. Kruspe of Leipzig. It consisted of two parallel tubes of maple, or less commonly of brass, one carrying a metal crook of modern appearance, the other an upward-directed metal bell. The tubes were united at the bottom by a short wooden butt-joint. It was pitched in C and had the compass of the ordinary clarinet. Every tone-hole was governed by a key, lavish use being made of rods, an early application of this mechanism. A big bore gave ample volume, and mathematically located tone-holes ensured good intonation. In view of these qualities it might well have had a longer life. It is fully described by V.-C. Mahillon, who thought highly of it, in Volume I of his *Brussels Catalogue*, pp. 216–20. A year or two later followed Sax's *Clarinette-bourdon*. Details of its construction are wanting, but it is described by Kastner in his *Supplément* of 1844 as pitched in B flat, an octave below the bass clarinet. Few can have been made, since Sax himself did not possess a specimen in his collection, which was sold in 1877.

More than forty years were to pass before attempts in this field were renewed. In 1889, just in time for the Paris Exhibition of that year, Fontaine-Besson of Paris produced his famous contrabass, known in England as the *Pedal-clarinet*. There were apparently two models, a military model with the compass of the soprano clarinet, and an orchestral model with downward extension to *b natural*, sounding *A*. It consisted of two short and one long tubes of light wood, the tubes joined by metal U's, a crook, and a bold upturned bell. The bore was mainly cylindrical, but the short tube carrying the crook was definitely conical. This defect of design had, as might be expected, a disastrous effect upon intonation. The mechanism, moreover, though cleverly conceived, was somewhat flimsy in construction. Great efforts were made to push the invention, especially in London, where M. Bretonneau of the Paris Opéra gave a recital to more than 1,200 persons in December 1891. The audience included Sir George Grove, Lord Chelmsford (an amateur clarinettist), Col. Shaw-Hellier (of Kneller Hall), Dr Turpin, and Arditi, Randegger, Hipkins, Curwen, Blaikley, and the well-known clarinettists Lazarus and Maycock. It was pointed out by the makers that composers were forced to write in a restricted manner for the double bassoon. Beethoven and Mendelssohn, it was said, wrote nothing of consequence for it, Wagner was shy of it, while Massenet had to replace it with the bass sarrusophone in *Esclarmonde*. Saint-Saëns had a similar experience in *Samson*, but on hearing Besson's newly invented clarinet wrote, 'Your pedal-clarinet is my dream realised.' This elaborate puffing, of which only a fraction is given, was preceded by a denigration of Wieprecht's *Bathyphon* and of Sax's *Clarinette-bourdon*. It was observed that the former could only play in the simpler keys. It is difficult to see how the pedal-clarinet could have done much more, since that, too, was based upon the simple thirteen-key system. This might have recommended it to a few English players accustomed to not more than 14 or 15 keys, but less to the French professional who looked on the 17 keys of the Boehm as a bare minimum. Nevertheless, Fontaine-Besson deserves all praise for his attempt, and for drawing the attention of composers to a new voice.

The new instrument does not appear to have had much success, though a few were sold to English military bands. An informative description of the instrument will be found in C. Pierre's *La Facture*, pp. 77–82, where it is not too accurately illustrated. Specimens may be studied in the Horniman Museum, London, in the Metropolitan Museum, New York, and in the private collections of Messrs Boosey & Hawkes, Philip Bate, and others. Close on the heels of Besson followed the contrabass of Evette and Schaffer, who obtained a brevet on 29 December 1891. This was a much simpler design, consisting of a long wooden or metal body with a much shorter member coming well down behind to carry a short crook. A metal U-bend connected the two joints. The bell, carried up in front, was of more modest dimensions than that of the pedal-clarinet; two members only, it will be noticed, against the three of Fontaine-Besson. The total length was given as about $2\frac{1}{2}$ metres, and the bore was stated to be 42 millimetres. A third speaker-key was proposed. No details of mechanism are given in the drawing which accompanies the specification.

Several other contrabasses have been made. We have no details of the invention of Richard Kohl, of the Thomas Orchestra (1898), which was warmly praised by Strauss, Mottl, and Nikisch, and which *Musical Opinion*, of September 1898, credited with a length of sixteen feet! Heckel has produced an all-metal model of great simplicity, in which the slender body is only some six feet in length. The remaining three feet are accounted for by the crook and the bell. The latter, a striking feature with its slowly increasing flare, is carried up well in front of the instrument.[3] The mechanism, largely mounted on rods, is that of the simple clarinet. The mouthpiece is of metal. The inventor, a firm believer, as has been said, in maple for the deeper-toned clarinets and even for *oboi d'amore* and *cors anglais*, here prefers metal less on account of its lightness than for its immutability. Wood is always alive, he explains in a letter to the writer, and in an instrument which demands extended and complicated keywork the least shrinking or swelling of the material would be fatal to the alignment and free action of the mechanism. A contrabass by G. Hüller of Schöneck, made for military use in the later 1930s, is of similar design. The body of thin-walled blackwood, fitted with the mechanism of the 13-key clarinet, has a bore of 29 mm. It is very comfortable to finger, and requires no more exertion in playing than the bass clarinet. The latest modern catalogues of Selmer and Buffet offer contrabass clarinets 'sur demand'.

A total departure from such conventional design is provided by the contrabass in the *système intégral* designed by M. Houvenaghel for Messrs Leblanc of Paris. The creator of this novel design is a firm advocate of metal for bass clarinets, and so the instrument is wholly metal, the mouthpiece excepted. In bare essentials it consists of two slender parallel tubes of approximately equal height joined at the bottom by a U-bend. One carries a long crook bent well behind it in a natural position for the player's lips, the other is surmounted by a small, slightly flared bell. The instrument, pitched of course in B flat, has a downward extension to written C. Boehm mechanism is fitted which, in view of the extension, leads to not a few mechanical complications.[4] It is necessary, as almost always with instruments of this design, to carry the action across from tube to tube. Such problems, however, have no terrors for M. Houvenaghel. He has so contrived his instrument that it may easily be taken apart and packed into an alto saxophone case. This contrabass descends to B flat in the 32-foot octave and has, it is claimed, the phenomenal range of 5 octaves. The same inventor has produced at least one subcontrabass, an octave lower than the instrument described, and built to the same design: a tour-de-force, perhaps, and no more, since it is difficult to imagine any player endowed with sufficient power of lung to keep it supplied with air.

While the contrabass clarinet has found a place in many continental military and factory bands, its appearances in the orchestra have been transient and infrequent. First heard in d'Indy's *Fervaal* (1897), it has subsequently figured in Weingartner's *Orestes* (1902), in Schoenberg's *Fünf Orchesterstücke* (1912), and in R. Strauss's *Josephslegende* (1914). That this vigorous and robust new voice should be confined to the military band seems regrettable. It is quite unnecessary to join M. Fontaine-Besson in depreciating the double bassoon, but it is undeniable that in some respects the contrabass clarinet has the advantage, possibly in readiness of speech and agility, certainly in compass, expressiveness, and control of dynamics. It would add a most valuable octave or twelfth to the low register of the bass clarinet and enrich the woodwind bass of the orchestra with a new, striking, and much needed tone-colour.

NOTES

[1] It is illustrated in Kastner's *Manuel général*, Paris, 1848, Plate 26 and must have been made before 1844, as it is alluded to in Kastner's *Supplément* of this year.

[2] pp. 258, 260.

[3] This description appears to apply to the earlier model of this instrument, not that shown in Plate 8 which figures in the Heckel catalogue of *c.* 1935. In *Der Fagott*, 1931, Heckel illustrated the older model and this is shown also by Kroll and Riehm op. cit., p. 64, although the preface to this book is dated 'Winter 1944'. In the later model the relatively vast bell of the original is replaced by one much smaller and furnished with an open hole in the bend, thus securing equivalent efficiency as an acoustic radiator. See above p. 146, [P.B.].

[4] The little fingers are especially hard worked, having to control 10 keys, five on the right, five on the left, between them.

CHAPTER 13

Combination clarinets
Fr. Clarinette multiphonique
Ger. Kombinationsklarinette
Klarinette mit Mutation
Ital. Clarinetto a doppia tonalità
Radical reforms

IN THE FIRST EDITION of this book the author [F.G.R.] expressed a distinctly unfavourable opinion of bi-tonal clarinets – 'attempts to solve the really insoluble problem of combining two clarinets of different pitches in one' he called them – and it must be admitted that this view seems to be held by professional clarinettists in general. The present writer [P.B.] has never heard of a living orchestral player who uses one, though he has encountered several who prefer to play all orchestral parts on the B flat instrument equipped with the additional low E flat key. This of course implies great confidence in the ability to transpose at sight, and disregards the slight, though definite, difference in tone-colour between the A and B flat clarinets. How marked the difference is depends to some extent on the player, but also on the sensitivity of the listener, and among musicians there are many stories told of composers who either could detect infallibly, or had no idea, which instrument was playing a given passage in one of their own compositions.[1]

To revert; it seems that in spite of professional disregard, the idea of a combination clarinet has a perennial fascination and as soon as the pièces de rechange were abandoned, attempts in this direction were initiated by makers. Such endeavours did great credit to their ingenuity – less, it has been said, to their practical commonsense – but a look at some of the results leads us into some fascinating byways of clarinet lore.

Probably the first effort in this direction was that made in 1808 by Simiot of Lyons, who produced a C clarinet which, by means of no less than ten extendable joints distributed over the length of the tube, could be converted to B flat. It is interesting to note that this most skilful maker apparently reverted to the pièce de rechange system some twenty years later when he made the very fine instrument already referred to on p. 91. (See also Plate 4 *c*.) In succession we have reports of further experiments by Sundelin of Berlin, in the 1830s, and by Stövecken of Rheine in 1841. Carl Bärmann also devised a combination clarinet, which, owing to its many keys, proved on his own admission to be impossibly heavy in the hand. Hermstedt too – the pioneer of metal mouthpieces – had a clarinet with metal slides between the joints and a screw device uniting the mouthpiece and barrel. In 1847 F. Trié-bert of Paris went even further than Simiot, and devised a C clarinet which by means of slides could be retuned to B flat and to A. In Italy too, the combination problem was tackled, and in 1880 one Rossi is reported as having made such an instrument.

All the above were what we may perhaps call 'telescope' clarinets, and it seems likely that, owing to the comparatively small extensions possible with reasonable security, their intonation was far from pure in one or other of the attempted tonalities. An altogether different principle has been the basis of most of the more promising bi-tonal clarinets, and this we shall discuss next.

Some time prior to 1862, when the actual instrument appeared, L.-A. Buffet of Paris conceived the idea of furnishing a single clarinet tube with all the holes necessary for playing in B flat or A, either group being 'blanked off' at will by the rotation of a perforated metal liner to the bore (brevet 53494). This inner tube was attached to the bell. Ordinary 'Boehm' keywork was so planned that every touchpiece, bar one, operated a key with two cups and pads associated with the corresponding holes for either tonality. The exception was the E natural, the lowest key on the instrument. Here the hole belonging to the B flat series was formed in the outer tube, while that of the A series was placed in the neck of the bell. The two cups were sprung 'open' in the usual way for this key, but they were mounted on independent axles and the 'A' one had a tail-lug which overlapped the other. Thus, when the bell and lining-tube were turned to the A position the touchpiece of the key operated both cups together; but when the liner was in the B flat position the lowest cup of all was disconnected and automatically stood open, so compensating for the redundant length of bell in that tonality.[2] The fact that some of the upper holes came dangerously near to overlapping caused Buffet to modify the usual placings of some of them, and it may be that this also dictated his choice of metal rather than wood for the outer tube as well as for the inner, thus courting the criticism of those who objected to metal clarinets in general, viz. dead-ness of tone and lack of response. Later users of the metal-liner principle seem to have been able to employ wood or ebonite for the outer body quite successfully, though this hardly eliminates the objection on tonal grounds. A much more valid criticism is that it is difficult to fine-tune side-holes in metal tubes since fraising is virtually ruled out. At all events, this clarinet failed to commend itself, either because of the metal body or perhaps because of the weight of the mechanism; the reliability of the latter could hardly be called in question. Constant Pierre, to whom we owe the only first-hand description, says that only one or two actual examples were completed, one of which was in his hands when he wrote his comments.[3] The present writer [P.B.] has been privileged to examine detailed photographs of a specimen now in the Dayton C. Miller Collection, from which the above account is derived. The instrument, though clearly attributable to Buffet, does not appear to bear his mark. Perhaps the experimental nature of the few produced did not justify the making of a special stamp, or it may be that corrosion has obscured any mark that there may once have been.

According to Oskar Kroll, quoting Sachs, the above instrument was imitated in Austria,[4] but Kroll's statement that James Clinton took up Buffet's idea and obtained patents for it in 1891 requires some amendment.[5] While admittedly using perforated inner tubes, as did a number of flute-makers about the same time, Clinton's scheme was considerably more advanced, as we shall see shortly. Following Buffet's principle directly, the well-known Milan firm of Maino and Orsi also at one time produced a *clarinetto a doppia tonalità*, of which several examples survive, though their keywork appears to have been somewhat different.

There are in fact several British patents associated with the name of James Clinton, of which the two most important both relate to combination clarinets. In 1891 Clinton obtained coverage for a scheme based on the moveable-liner principle in a rather novel way. Here the inner tube was divided into two parts, one attached permanently to the barrel, the other fixed to the bell. The outer shell carrying the keywork was divided into upper and lower joints as in any normal clarinet of the period. By means of two screwed pins, one passing through the outer wall of each joint and engaging with a helical slot in the associated piece of lining-tube, a twist to the barrel in one direction, and to the bell the opposite way, caused an extension to the bore at either end. To prevent the two joints from accidentally getting out of alignment the middle tenon was provided with a feather and the socket with a corresponding groove. The two halves of the lining-tube carried duplicate sets of holes for the pitches of B flat and A, but the description as registered says nothing of any proposed modification of the finger-holes to accommodate the wider spacing of the deeper tonality. Presumably this would have been provided for had the instrument ever come into actual production. In a later design which was commercially produced this requirement was more or less satisfactorily met.

In 1898 H. E. Winter and the Clinton Combination Clarinet Co. patented another form of moveable-liner clarinet, and this is the instrument that for a time became generally known as the 'Clinton Patent'.[6] Externally it appeared to be a nearly normal Boehm-system instrument, except that it carried a very short bell. The different parts were united by ordinary tenon- and socket-joints which could be pulled out sufficiently to give the overall length of an A clarinet, but actual separation was prevented by pins and external catches. Attached to the barrel was the metal liner which only extended as far as the right-hand finger-holes. Again, duplicate sets of holes for B flat and A were cut in this, and either series could be brought under the openings in the outer shell by turning the barrel while pulling it out. This movement was permitted by the catch device connecting the barrel to the upper joint, and several forms of it were envisaged in the patent specification. To complete the scheme all the holes in the outer body were made much larger than normal so that either series in the liner could appear through them without obstruction. To assure proper coverage a padded plate was provided for the R. ring-finger. At one time great commercial hopes were entertained for this clarinet, and a company under the chairmanship of Sir Arthur Sullivan was formed to exploit it. Introductory recitals were given in 1896 at the Royal College of Music by well-known players, including Gomez, but, alas, once again the profession as a whole failed to respond. It is said that, *pace* the distinguished professionals who supported it, the intonation of the 'Clinton Patent' was not always above reproach, and the present writer has had a report, at one remove as it were, through the son of a man who attended one of the demonstrations. He said: 'the instrument was woefully out of tune in B flat; and in A it was much the same'. Be that as it may, the 'Clinton Patent', in spite of favourable comments written as late as 1908,[7] proved another disappointment – and still the quest for a satisfactory bi-tonal clarinet went on.

Undoubtedly the most ingenious version of the moveable-liner principle yet worked out is that patented in 1914 by N. Alberti of Chicago, and which is applicable to any woodwind having a mainly cylindrical bore. In this arrangement the holes in the outer tube of wood or ebonite take the form of oblong slots with cover-plates and pads of appropriate form. The liner is perforated with a series of helical slots which cross those in the outer shell so that the operative note-holes are actually the 'windows' which appear where the two sets of slots coincide. Guided by a pin working in a very coarse screw-thread the liner both turns and moves longways, thus altering the overall length of the tube. At the same time, by cutting the helical slots at progressively increasing pitch-angles the note-holes are made to move, not only as a group relatively to the whole tube, but towards or away from each other while maintaining their proper proportionate spacing. This mechanism of course calls for extreme nicety in design and layout, not to say in the making. The writer has not so far seen any clarinet constructed on this plan, but several flutes and piccolos have been so made and appear to work well.

All the instruments we have discussed in this chapter so far (and there may be others similar, of which the writer is unaware) have depended on telescopic joints and/or moveable perforated liners to the bore, and to both devices either practical or theoretical objections can be raised. There are, however, other approaches to the problem which have been tried.

It is part of the empirical knowledge shared by most instrument-makers that a finished clarinet will blow flatter than the same instrument before the side-holes are put in, and it seems that appreciation of this fact may have given rise to C. Binda's extraordinary clarinet which was patented in 1884 (Fig. 20). This was produced by E. Albert with his usual meticulous skill, but the paucity of surviving specimens bears witness to its lack of success. Probably, in common with most transposable clarinets, its overall intonation failed to satisfy critical ears, though its strange appearance may also have had some effect.

Fundamentally Binda's was a simple 13-keyed clarinet, but at ten places between finger-holes and keys the tube was pierced with large additional holes, each furnished with a projecting metal cylinder. The cylinders were fitted with moveable plungers, and these were connected by rods to bars running the length of the body. Moving the bars withdrew or pushed in all the plungers together, thus lowering or raising the pitch. In his patent specification Binda said nothing of a principle behind his invention other than that the pistons and cylinders 'alter the distance between fingering holes' – manifestly untrue in a mechanical sense, but possibly an acceptable explanation in terms of the acoustical knowledge of his time – and the instrument *did* to some extent work. The true explanation of the lower sounding of a finished clarinet compared with an identical plain tube is given by the modern theory of tone-holes which shows that the phenomenon is connected with the

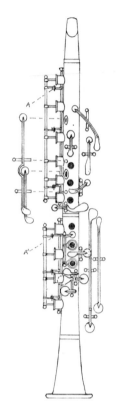

Fig 20 Schematic drawing of the Binda clarinet, adapted from the original patent.

In the specimen examined by the writer there is considerable crowding of the keys, and on the upper joint the heads of the *f'* and 'trill'-keys are very close to the side-tubes. For this reason they are shown offset to the left and their relationships indicated by dotted lines. Other keys not fully seen in the frontal view are offset to the right.

Note that the first of the side-tubes is inserted at a point that would be on the barrel of a conventional instrument. The hinged links A, A', etc., were intended to limit the excursion of the plungers and to ensure equality of motion among them.

quasi-regular spacing and dimensions of cavities in the bore formed by a row of *closed* tone-holes.[8] Binda's row of cylinders and plungers had a similar effect, and A. H. Benade has pointed out that, guided by modern theory, it should not be impossible to make a Binda clarinet quite acceptably in tune, mechanical monstrosity though it might be.

In summing up his views on combination clarinets F.G.R. wrote: 'Quite as satisfactory results, if fine tuning is not a prime desideratum, may be obtained by hanging a thin wire down the bore to lower the pitch'; and this brings us to yet another bi-tonal device. A wire or a piece of string hung down the bore is a hack player's 'dodge' which was not uncommon, particularly in the North, before the universal acceptance of 'Flat Pitch' in Britain and the U.S.A. The present writer has heard old clarinettists, equipped only with high-pitch instruments, get round the problem of an occasional low-pitch engagement by these means, and it must be admitted that some have shown great skill in correcting the resultant intonation troubles. In this case, of course, the necessary drop was less than a semitone, and it is perhaps doubtful if a B flat instrument so treated could be safely used in A. Nevertheless, in 1896 C. E. Vaughan patented a pitch-adjusting device which consisted of a rod slightly coned at the lower end and of adjustable length. This was retained in the bore of the clarinet by a sort of spring 'spider' at the top and the foot. It was claimed that this could be used either for tuning or for altering the pitch of the instrument, and we may assume that the arrangement was based on the fact that for a given length of tube a reduction in cross-sectional area will give some lowering of pitch, though not so much as is commonly supposed (see above, p. 43). This appears to have been Vaughan's idea, since he also patented a system of sprung-in metal liners for the same purpose.

Recent research has confirmed that the pitch-lowering properties of a smooth wire nipped in the mouthpiece socket and suspended down the bore depend simply on the reduction of cross-sectional area of the air-column, and the reason for the disturbance of intonation is that in these conditions the cavity of the mouthpiece remains too big for the bore (see above, p. 5), producing an effect equivalent to lengthening disproportionately the section above the first note-hole – putting on too long a barrel in fact.[9] The effect of a string – sometimes known as the 'A String' – is not quite the same, for here there is some actual slowing-up of the compression waves passing along the tube. Like the smooth wire, the string does to some extent reduce the cross-section of the air-column, but more importantly, because it is in fact a bundle of extremely fine fibres, it very greatly increases the surface area of the confining walls. This, in turn, multiplies the viscous friction effects etc. which are always present where a vibrating air-mass meets the bounding surface of a pipe.[10]

We have already seen (ch. 5) that the behaviour of a clarinet – the tonal spectra typical of its different registers etc. – depends largely on the configuration of the bore, and it has also been noted that while makers of repute adhere to their individual formulae, which do show small differences in detail, all produce instruments which in their overall sound conform within close limits to what the educated ear has learnt to identify as 'clarinet'. Such devices as Vaughan's which radically interfere with the proportions as originally worked out by the maker seem bound, therefore, to have deleterious effects.

There remain to be discussed some combination clarinets in which there is no interference with the bore in changing from the B flat to the

A condition, and all is effected by external mechanism. In 1889 the Hamburg clarinettist T. Lässig patented a rather clumsy-looking instrument which was made for him by the Berthold Brothers of Speyer. Parallel tubes of B flat and A dimensions were bored in a single joint of wood, and the mouthpiece could be connected to either at will by means of a sort of tubular switch (Fig. 21). At the foot both bores communicated with one bell, and a single set of keywork with duplicate cover-plates controlled corresponding holes in either tube. The idea of parallel bores in a single body was, of course, by no means new; double flageolets had been so constructed for centuries – long indeed before Samuel Pepys's famous visit to 'Drumbleby the pipe maker'[11] – but this is believed to be the first application of it to the European clarinet.[12] The Lässig instrument seems to have had no more popular success than any other of its *genus*, but its salient feature was later revived, as we shall see, for a rather different purpose. Certainly it was a true example of F.G.R's 'two clarinets of different pitches in one'.[13]

A most promising bi-tonal instrument against which no criticism could be levelled on the score of either metal in the bore or variable

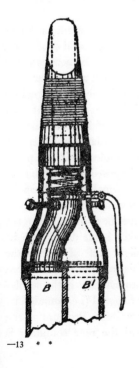

Fig 21   Section of Lässig's 'switch' as patented in 1889.
B and B' indicate the twin bores in the body of the instrument.

—13   * *

dimensions was designed in 1900 by the Bologna clarinettist Giuseppe Leonesi and made for him the following year by Rampone of Milan. Here a tube of full A clarinet length was provided with duplicate sets of holes, one for each tonality (except for the speaker and the two topmost trill-holes which remained single). Twin keys mounted on tubular sleeves governed corresponding holes in the two series, and these pairs were in turn controlled by single touchpieces through the action of overlying lugs similar to those employed by Boehm in his 1832 flute. Beneath the key-tails were three strips of metal, sliding longways in grooves cut in the surface of the body. Each strip carried a number of tiny wedges so placed that, depending on the position of the strip, they held closed the keys belonging to one or other tonality. All the strips were linked together and moved by a touchpiece located near the thumb-hole.[14]

The present writer has been fortunate in having his attention drawn to this instrument by the inventor's granddaughter, who now possesses the only example made, as well as the original working drawings. It is reported that the Leonesi mechanism was found technically satisfactory and not over-delicate, but the high cost of producing it told against any general adoption. One wonders what such a piece of miniature engineering would cost to produce today.

And still they come. If some of the above-mentioned instruments have seemed too complicated to be reliable in ordinary orchestral conditions, what are we to think of one of the latest combination clarinets patented by the late Dr Loos of Vienna in 1927, and exhibited at the Frankfurt Musical Exhibition of that year? The principle involved is ingenious indeed. Broadly it may be said that the tone-holes are divided into two series and placed in two staggered rows, one providing the diatonic scale of the instrument in A, the other the intermediate semitones. All holes are covered, and the covers of the semitone-holes are in two parts, a padded ring and a further padded cup superimposed on it. Both cups and rings are lightly sprung 'open', but are normally held down by tails on the whole-tone covers immediately above and on the semitone touchpieces which lie between. These have superior springs. When the instrument is in the A condition a semitone-key holds down both its cup and the underlying ring; but when a slight shift of part of the mechanism establishes the B flat condition, this restraint is transferred to the ring only, and the cup then opens automatically if the whole-tone cover above is depressed. Thus the note fingered (i.e. sounded by the next open hole *below*) is sharpened by a semitone. Pressure on the semitone-touch will now release the *ring* and the note sounding is sharpened by a further semitone. It will be appreciated that this general arrangement is repeated eight times to complete the scale of a clarinet, and that numerous inter-connections are required to provide a logical system of fingering.

Finally we must just glance at certain clarinets which seem to embody radical reforms of the traditional instrument, far though this has already advanced. The idea that all woodwinds should conform to a common fingering-system has long attracted makers and players alike, as, for example, Schaffner (see above, p. 106) with his clarinet, flute, and oboe all on common lines. This would of course require the clarinet to overblow at the octave like the others, and, as we have seen, this is foreign to its acoustical nature. Nevertheless instruments that *seem* to do so have been constructed – or rather clarinets have been designed in which the *fingering* repeats at the octave while the actual overblowing occurs at the twelfth as usual. Needless to say, the mechanism involved has proved extremely complicated. Oskar Kroll quotes the name of T. Valand in this connection, and in 1932 G. Carnock and A. Konrád of Prague were granted a German patent (No. 567405) for such a clarinet.[15]

In the closing years of the 19th century certain European composers, in their restless search for a more flexible and expressive musical resource than they found in the generally accepted chromatic scale, began to concern themselves with what have been called – not too happily perhaps – microtone scales, that is, scales divided into more than twelve degrees to the octave.[16] If such music were not to be confined to the voice or to the unfretted strings (for at that period electronic tone-generators were of course unknown), it was obvious that some radical rethinking had to be done in respect of conventional orchestral instruments. One of the most significant experimentors in this field was Alois Hába, who, born in Moravia in 1893, had by 1923 made sufficient impression to be placed in charge of a class in quarter-tone music in the Prague Conservatoire. Later, official recognition was withdrawn from this class and it was finally dissolved in 1948 – possibly for political reasons. Hába's work in quarter and one-sixth tone-scales led to the construction of a quarter-tone piano, a harmonium tuned in sixths of a tone, a quarter-tone trumpet devised by Haekel of Dresden, and a corresponding clarinet by Kohlert of Graslitz. This latter instrument was designed by a Berlin clarinettist, Dr R. H. Stein, and differed from a normal instrument only in the existence of supplementary keys for the interpolated notes. Obviously such a clarinet would call for very special study and much practice. In 1923, however, Schüller of Markneukirchen produced a quarter-tone clarinet based on a normal fingering-system. The general construction was similar to that devised by Lässig (see above, p. 161) with parallel tubes of dimensions to sound a quarter-tone apart, terminating in a single bell, and with duplicated keywork controlled by a single set of touchpieces. By means of a rotary valve similar to that of an orchestral horn (though of bigger bore) situated in the throat of the instrument the mouthpiece could be connected to either tube almost instantaneously. Thus to play a quarter-tone sequence the clarinettist had to add to his normal technique only the mastery of a single additional lever. This is not to say that much practice would not be required to attain fluency. In recent years little seems to have been heard of such instruments.

NOTES

[1] Disregarding the question of tone-colour, there are many occasions in the standard orchestral repertoire where a change of instrument, even for a few bars, may greatly ease the clarinettist's difficulties if he can transpose well. Moreover, not all composers are well versed in the technical problems of individual instruments. The reader is referred to a most illuminating short article, 'The use of the A and B Clarinets', published in *Symphony* for April 1952 by Augustin Duques, for many years First Clarinet in the N.B.C. Symphony Orchestra. Here he will find an analysis of several standard orchestral clarinet parts from this point of view, as well as some amusing anecdotes much to the point. See also H. Sarlit in *Woodwind Magazine*, January 1952. A different view is expressed.

[2] This feature is not included in the original brevet, but appears on the only surviving example known to the writer.

[3] Pierre, *La Facture instrumentale*, Paris, 1890, pp. 170 *et seq.*

[4] Curt Sachs, *Reallexikon*, reprint New York, 1964, p. 222.

[5] Kroll and Riehm, op. cit., p. 38.

[6] Not to be confused with the so-called 'Clinton-Boehm' devised by *George* Clinton. The 'Clinton Combination Clarinet Company' appears to have been a private association, since no account of its formation or winding-up is to be found in the Public Records Office at the time of writing. The dates concerned are curious. Demonstrations of the instrument took place at the Royal College of Music in 1896; James Clinton died in 1897; and the British patent for the instrument was granted to the Company and one H. E. Winter in 1898. Clinton's own instrument is said to have been made for him by J. B. Albert.

[7] Kathleen Schlesinger, in her *Modern Orchestral Instruments*, London, 1910, writes of the 'Clinton Patent' as if it was at that time a well-recognised and successful instrument, and on p. 30 has a good engraving of it. The present writer has only examined a single specimen.

[8] Arthur H. Benade, *Horns, Strings, and Harmony*, New York, 1960, p. 218.

In letters to the writer (1969), Dr Benade also makes the following points, which are quoted with his permission: 'It *is* true that putting a row of holes along the bore increases its effective size, but there is also a reduction in the actual speed of sound in the tube.' And again: 'There is another way to lower the pitch of a clarinet, and that is to put in a supply of extra closed side holes (like tone holes). Closed tone holes on the bore reduce the average elasticity of the air in the column and so reduce the speed of sound. The fractional change in sound speed is given quite well by

$$\Delta c/c \simeq (V_h/2x)$$

where V_h is the volume of the closed tone hole and x is the interhole spacing. On a clarinet this speed change amounts to several per cent, and plays an important part in the overall tuning of the instrument.'

Putting the matter in a slightly different form, 'A tube of cross-section S has its effective area increased ΔS by putting closed tone holes on it.'

The above equation can then be written as:

$$\Delta S/S = V_h/2x.$$

But, 'in practice one has to take into account changes in the speed of sound and also changes produced by cross-sectional alterations. The first keeps the same *sign* wherever it is located in the active bore. The second may sharpen or flatten, depending on its position relative to the nodes and loops. The former is concerned with absolute pitch and the latter with tone colour and the relation of the various registers.'

[9] Ibid. Results of an investigation personally communicated to the writer, 1969. Benade points out that the effect of bore diameter on pitch is often exaggerated in accepted accounts. For example, the experiments conducted by Mahillon (*Instruments à Vent*, pp. 158–63) proved exactly reproducible under the conditions in which he made them, but the results are exaggerated because the different tubes investigated were all energised by the same mouthpiece without adjustment of the tone-chamber diameter to correspond.

[10] Kinsler and Frey, *Introduction to Acoustics*, New York 1950.

Benade has also kindly furnished the following 'short-form' explanation of the function of the 'A String'. 'Putting a wire or rod into a clarinet lowers the pitch chiefly via the mouthpiece cavity effect. The use of a suitably chosen cord made of fine fibres however can usefully lower the pitch of an instrument by lowering the speed of sound in the bore. Conduction of heat into and out of the bounding surfaces of the pipe effectively reduces the elasticity of the air. Viscous friction at the surface constricts the size of the oscillating portion of the air in the tube so that at any instant each tiny disc shaped cross-sectional element of air in the bore stores more kinetic energy in proportion to the (already reduced) potential energy belonging to the same element. Because of this the speed of sound is reduced and the instrument plays flatter. We see that the dynamics of the situation are immensely more complicated than the mere assumption that 'friction slows down the waves'.

[11] Samuel Pepys, *Diary*, 'Jan. 20th. 1668'.

[12] Various idioglot instruments employing paired tubes, and by

ethnologists often generically termed *clarinets*, are of extremely ancient origin. They are typified today by the Arabic *zummâra*.

[13] Certain 'double clarinets' to be seen in the Berlin and Brussels Collections are not combination instruments but true 'Siamese Twins'. They have paired small mouthpieces, separate bores, and independent sets of piano-type keywork. Their object appears to have been to permit playing in simple harmony as with the double flageolets of Bainbridge, Simpson, *et al*. It is not impossible for a specially gifted – or extrovert – player to manage two or even three normal single-reed mouthpieces at once – but such achievements would seem to have their place rather on the variety stage than in the concert room.

[14] The Leonesi clarinet has been cited as a combination instrument in which there is no interference with bore dimensions in changing from the B flat to the A condition, and *vice versa*. This is true in a strictly mechanical sense, but from an acoustical point of view there are two other matters to be considered. First, the provision of two alternative sets of holes, one or other of which is at any instant *externally* closed off, will have a pitch-lowering effect (see note 8 above) which must be allowed for in the basic design of the instrument. Second, in the two conditions, the position and group spacing of the operational and the closed-off sets of holes will differ in their relation to each other and to the ends of the tube. Thus, although in either tonality the instrument may yield acceptable 'clarinet' tone in all registers, detailed mathematical analyses of the two states might well differ.

[15] Among more or less radical reformers of the clarinet, Kroll, op. cit., p. 45, lists the names of Shohe Tanaka of Japan; Allen Loomis of Toledo, Ohio; J. W. McAvoy of Bangor, North Wales; Max Zacherl of Landshut, Bavaria; and Fritz Stein of Saarbrücken. It seems therefore that although there are today several basic fingering-systems, and a multiplicity of variants on these, from which to choose, some clarinettists still remain unsatisfied. One has even heard of an attempt to bring the keys of the clarinet under the control of a small piano-type keyboard, as in Moritz's 'Klaviaturkontra-faggott'.

[16] Surely the term is best reserved for those much finer subdivisions which are so distinctive a feature of certain Eastern musical systems.

A List of Music

ABBREVIATIONS

B. & B.	Bote & Bock	fl.	flute
By. & H.	Boosey & Hawkes	ob.	oboe
Brit. & Cont.	British and Continental	cl.	clarinet
Br. & H.	Breitkopf & Härtel	bhn.	basset-horn
H.M.	Hudební Matice	bcl.	bass clarinet
M.P.	Music Press	ca.	cor anglais
O.L.	Oiseau Lyre	bn.	bassoon
O.U.P.	Oxford University Press	cbn.	double bassoon
S.D.	Stichting Donemus	hn.	horn
Sk.M.	Skandenavisk Musikforlag	trpt.	trumpet
S.M.	Southern Music Publishing Co.	vn.	violin
U.E.	Universal Edition	va.	viola
P.R.	Piano reduction	vc.	cello
		cb.	double bass
		hp.	harp

BIBLIOGRAPHIES

Foster, L. W. *A Directory of Clarinet Music*. Author, Pittsfield, Mass., 1940.

Tuthill, B. C. 'The Clarinet in Chamber Music', Cobbett's *Cyclopedic Survey of Chamber Music*, 1929.

—— 'Bibliography of Clarinet Sonataş, Quintets, etc.', *Woodwind Magazine*, Vol. 2, No. 4, etc., 1949—.

Kroll, O. In *The Clarinet* (English translation). London, 1968, pp. 141–75.

TUTORS

The Clarinet Instructor . . . by a capital performer . . . to which is added several Duo's . . . and a Quintetto for Horns, Clarinets and a Bassoon. *Longman & Broderip*, c. 1780.

Compleat Instructions for the Clarinet. *S. A. & P. Thompson*, c. 1785.

New and Complete Instructions for the Clarionet. *Preston*, c. 1790.

New and Compleat Instructions for the Clarionet. *Bland & Weller*, c. 1790.

Vanderhagen, A. Méthode nouvelle et raisonnée pour la Clarinette. *Boyer & Lemenu*, Paris, 1785. (The first serious tutor, reviewed in the *Mercure de France*, April 1785.)

—— 2nd edition. *Pleyel*, c. 1830.

Blasius, M.-F. Méthode de Clarinette. *Michel*, Paris, *c.* 1795.
—— Nouvelle Méthode de Clarinette. *Porthaux*, Paris, *c.* 1800.
Lefèvre, J.-X. Méthode de clarinette . . . adoptée par le Conservatoire. Paris, 1802. (Approved by Gossec and a committee of 10 professors. Tablature for 6-key clarinet.)
—— Méthode de clarinette . . . augmentée du mécanisme de l'instrument perfectionné par I. Müller. Par Buteux. *Troupenas*, *c.* 1830.
Backofen, J. G. H. Anweisung zur Klarinette, nebst einer kurzen Abhandlung über das Basset-Horn. *Breitkopf & Härtel*, 1803. (For 5-key clarinet.)
—— 2nd edition. 1824. (For 13-key clarinet and 15-key basset-horn.)
Mahon, John. A new and complete Preceptor for the Clarinet . . . to which is added the gamut for the Clara Voce or Corno Bassetto. *Goulding*, 1803. (Tablatures for 5-key clarinet and 7-key basset-horn.)
Froelich, J. F. Vollständige theoretisch-practische Musik-Schule. *Bonn*, 1810, 1811. (Part 2, pp. 7–34, contains instructions for 5-key clarinet and for preparation of reeds.)
Müller, Iwan. Méthode pour la nouvelle Clarinette et Clarinette-Alto. *Gambaro*, *c.* 1825.
—— Anweisung zu der neuen Clarinette. *Hofmeister*, *c.* 1825.
Willman, T. L. A Complete Instruction Book for the Clarinet. *Goulding*, 1826–27. (Tablature for 13-key instrument.)
Berr, F. Traité complet de la clarinette à quatorze clefs. *Duverger*, 1836.
—— English edition. Revised and fingered by G. Clinton. *Boosey*, 1909.
Fahrbach, J. Neueste Wiener Klarinetten-Schule. *Diabelli*, 1840. (Tablature for a 19-key instrument without rings. The clarinets of Ziegler, Uhlmann, and Koch, all of Vienna, are recommended.)
Klosé, H.-E. Méthode pour servir à l'enseignement de la clarinette à anneaux mobiles. *Meissonnier*, 1843.
—— English edition. *Lafleur*, 1874.
—— English edition, ed. C. Draper. *Hawkes*, 1906.
Blatt, F. T. Méthode complète de clarinette. *Schonenberger*, *c.* 1845. (The original German edition is stated to have been published in 1828.)
Romero y Andía, A. Método completo de clarinete . . . segunda edición. *Romero*, *c.* 1860. (For 13-key and Boehm systems. The first edition is stated to have appeared in 1845. A later edition with exercises for the author's own clarinet was published in 1868 according to Lavoix. The *Ejercicios practicos* were published separately with a tablature *c.* 1900.)
Bärmann, C. Vollständige Clarinett-Schule. 5 parts. *André*, 1864–75.
—— Modern edition, adapted for the Boehm Clarinet by H. Bettoney. *Cundy-Bettoney*, 1910.
Bender, Hermann. Practischer Lehrgang für das Clarinettspiel. Op. 26. 3 parts. *Litolff*, 1879.
Lazarus, H. New and modern method for the Albert and Boehm system Clarinet. *Lafleur*, 1881.
Busoni, Ferdinando. Scuola di perfezionamento per il clarinetto. *Cranz*, 1883. (The author recommends the embouchure with reed against the upper lip.)
Stark, R. Die hohe Schule des Clarinett-Spiels. *Schmidt*, *c.* 1900.

Magnani, A. Méthode complète de Clarinette. 3 parts. *Evette & Schaeffer, c.* 1900. (Part 3 contains a collection of duets arranged from Mozart and many original compositions and arrangements by the author.)

Modern Tutors

Langenus, G. Modern Clarinet Playing. *Fischer,* 1913. (Intended for players changing from the Albert to the Boehm system.)

—— Complete method for the Boehm Clarinet. 3 parts. *Fischer.* (Part 3: *Virtuoso Studies and Duos.*)

Gay, E. Méthode progressive et complète pour l'étude de la clarinette du début à la virtuosité. *Andrieu,* 1932.

Thurston, F. J., and Frank, A. The Clarinet. A comprehensive tutor. *Boosey & Hawkes,* 1939. (Includes a valuable series of orchestral studies.)

Lefèvre, J.-X. Metodo. Riordinato e rinovato A. Giampieri. 3 parts. *Ricordi,* 1939.

Klosé, H.-E. Méthode complète de clarinette. Nouvelle édition en 5 parties. *Leduc,* 1942. (Unusually complete tutor. The many modern studies by the well-known clarinettists P. Jeanjean and A. Périer make this virtually a new work. Many excerpts from orchestral works are included.)

Krtička, S. Škola pro normální a francouzský Klarinet. *L: Hnyk, Králové,* 1945. (By the professor at the Prague Conservatoire. Fingerings provided for both Müller and Boehm instruments up to *d''''*. Copious extracts from Czech composers and 3 cadenzas for the Mozart Concerto are included.)

Rozanov, S. Shkola dlya Klarneta. *Gosmuziz,* 1940. (Tablature for instrument of German type. Fingerings are given up to *d''''* sharp.)

Jettel, R. Klarinettenschule . . . bis zur höchsten Virtuosen Vollendung. 3 parts. *Doblinger,* 1949, 1950. (For Oehler-type clarinet.)

Willaman, R. The Clarinet and clarinet playing. *Author, New York.* (see also under Appendix II).

Music for the Clarinet
STUDIES

Orchestral Studies

Heyneck, E. Orchester-Studien. 10 parts. *Merseburger.*

Hinze, Fr. Orchester-Studien. 2 parts. *Br. & H.*

Giampieri, A. Studi d'orchestra per clarinetto e clarinetto basso. 2 parts. *Ricordi.*

Savage, T. Difficult Passages. 3 parts. *By. & H.*

Wagner, R. Orchesterstudien aus seinen Bühnen u. Konzertwerken. Ed. F. Hinze. *Br. & H.*

Strauss, R. Orchesterstudien aus . . . symphonischen Werken, ed. P. Bartholomey. *U.E.,* 1910.

Strauss, R. Orchesterstudien aus . . . Bühnenwerken, ed. C. Essberger. 6 parts. *Fürstner,* 1912.

Technical Studies

Cavallini, E. 30 capricci. *Ricordi.*
D'Elia, A. Dodici grandi studi. *Ricordi.*
Gabucci, A. 28 Grandi studi. *Carisch.*
—— 10 études modernes. *Evette.*
—— 12 studi brillanti. *Carisch.*
—— 50 duetti. *Carisch.*
Jeanjean, P. Vade-mecum du clarinettiste. *Leduc.*
—— Études progressives et mélodiques. *Leduc.*
—— 18 études de perfectionnement.
—— 16 études modernes.
Langenus, G. Clarinet Cadenzas. *The Author, New York.*
Marasco, G. 10 studi di perfezionamento. *Ricordi.*
Périer, A. 331 exercices journaliers. *Leduc.*
—— 30 études. 2 parts. *Leduc.*
Sarlit, H. 25 études de virtuosité extraites des oeuvres de Chopin et
  Schumann. *Leduc.*
Thurston, F. J. Passage Studies. 3 parts. *By. & H.*
Uhl, W. 48 Etüden. 2 parts. *Schott.*
Stark, R. Ganzton-Technik. Op. 56. *Schmidt.*

CONCERTOS

Arnold, Malcolm. With string orchestra. P.R. *Lengnick,* 1951.
Bautista, Julián. Fantasia Española. 1946.
Berezovsky, N. T. Op. 28. P.R. *By. & H.,* 1941.
Bonsel, A. *S.D.,* 1950.
Bozza, E. With chamber orchestra. P.R. *Leduc,* 1952.
Busoni, F. B. Concertino. P.R. O. Taubmann. *Br. & H.,* 1920.
Cimarosa, D. Concerto . . . arr. by A. Benjamin from Piano Sonatas.
  P.R. *By. & H.,* 1942.
Copland, A. P.R. *By. & H.,* 1952.
Debussy, C. Première Rhapsodie. P.R. *Durand,* 1910, 1911.
Dresden, S. Symphonietta. *S.D.*
Finzi, G. P.R. *By. & H.,* 1951.
Handel, G. F. Concerto. Arr. J. Barbirolli from works of Handel.
  O.U.P., 1952.
Hindemith, P. P.R. *Schott,* 1950.
Horowitz, J. Concertante, with string orch. *Chester,* 1952.
Jongen, J. Concertino. Op. 132. *Gervan,* 1947.
Koppel, H. D. Op. 35. *S.M.*
Kubín, R. P.R. *Kudelík,* 1946.
Mann, J. G. H. Op. 90. *Ruhle & Wendling.*
Milhaud, D. *Elkan-Vogel,* 1942.
Molter, J. M. 4 Concerti (D-clarinet) with strings and cembalo. *c.* 1740.
  Br. & H., 1957.
Mozart, W. A. K.622. *André,* 1802, *Br. & H.* Other editions: (1) ed. and
  P.R. C. Bärmann. *André,* 1870. (2) ed. F. J. Thurston. P. R. E. Roth.

By. & H., 1946. (3) ed. F. J. Thurston. P.R. H. Geehl. *Brit. & Cont.*,
1948. (4) rev. L. Cahuzac. *Costallat*, 1939. (5) rev. U. Delécluse,
cadence de J. Ibert. *Leduc*, 1951. Cadenzas: (1) Busoni, F. B. *Br. & H.*,
1922. (2) Krtička, S. (in his *Skola*).

Nielsen, C. Op. 57. *Kistner*, 1931.

Pitt, P. Concertino. Op. 22. *Boosey*, 1898.

Pokorny, F. X. 2 Concerti. *c.* 1770. *Br. & H.*, 1957.

Rawsthorne, A. With string orch. *O.U.P.*, 1936.

Reissiger, C. G. Concertino. Op. 63. *Schmidt.*

Rietz, J. Op. 39. *Kistner.*

Rimsky-Korsakov, N. A. P.R. *Omega*, 1949.

—— P.R. L. Rudolph. *Russian-American.*

Rosetti, F. A. Concerto à Clarinette principalle. *Sieber, c.* 1780.

Seiber, M. Concertino. With string orch. P.R. *Schott*, 1952.

Spohr, L. 4 Concertos. No. 1, Op. 26; No. 2, Op. 57. P.R. F. Demnitz.
Peters, 1922, 1923. No. 3; No. 4. P.R. C. Rundnagel. *Br. & H.*, 1885.

Stamitz, J. Ed. P. Gradenwitz. *Musicofot, Tel-Aviv.*

Strategier, H. Concertino. *S.D.*, 1950.

Strauss, R. Duet-Concertino for clarinet and bassoon. With string orch.
and hp. P.R. *Hawkes*, 1944.

Tartini, G. Concertino. Arr. from sonatas of G. Tartini by G. Jacob.
P.R. *Hawkes*, 1945.

Weber, C. M. Concertino. Op. 26. *By. & H.*, *etc.*

—— Concerto. Op. 73. rev. U. Delécluse. *Leduc*, 1951.

—— Concerto. Op. 74. rev. U. Delécluse, Cadence de J. Ibert. *Leduc*,
1951.

Concertos in manuscript

Hoddinott, A. With string orchestra. 1950.

Stanford, C. V. Op. 80. 1902.

SONATAS

Sonatas: clarinet and piano

Adajewski, E. Schultz-Sonate grecque. *Tischer & Jagenberg*, 1913.

Arnold, M. Sonatina. Op. 29. *Lengnick*, 1951.

Bax, A. *Murdoch*, 1935.

Bernstein, L. *Witmark*, 1943.

Brahms, J. 2 Sonatas. Op. 120, 1 and 2. *Simrock*, 1895, *By. & H.*

Bumcke, G. Op. 9. *Simon*, 1905.

Burgmüller, N. *Kistner*, 1865.

Dunhill, T. Phantasy Suite. Op. 91. *Hawkes*, 1941.

Gouvy, T. Op. 67. *Richault*, 1882, *Costallat.*

Heap, C. S. *Br. & H.*, 1880.

Hill, E. B. Op. 32. *Schirmer*, 1926–27.

Hindemith, P. *Schott*, 1940.

Honegger, A. Sonatine. *Rouart, Lerolle*, 1925.

Howells, Herbert. MS.

Ireland, J. Fantasy-Sonata. *By. & H.*, 1945.

Jenner, G. Op. 5. *Br. & H.*, 1900.
Jettel, R. *Hofmeister.*
Juon, P. Op. 82. *Schlesinger*, 1924.
Karg-Elert, S. Op. 139b. *Zimmermann*, 1924.
Koechlin, C. Sonata 1. *O.L.*, 1949.
—— Sonata 2.
Lefèvre, J.-X. 5me Sonate. *Richli*, 1949.
Mason, D. G. Op. 14. *Schirmer, Ditson*, 1920.
Mendelssohn, F. *Sprague-Coleman*, 1941.
Milhaud, D. Sonatine. *Durand*, 1927.
Mirandolle, L. Sonata. *Leduc.*
—— Sonatine. *Leduc*, 1940.
Moeschinger, A. Sonatina. Op. 65. *By. & H.*, 1947.
Prout, E. Op. 26. *Augener*, 1890.
Reger, M. Op. 49, 1 and 2. *U.E.*, 1903.
—— Op. 107. *B. & B.*, 1909.
Rheinberger, J. G. Op. 105a. *Kistner*, 1893.
Saint-Saëns, C. Op. 167. *Durand*, 1924.
Setaccioli, G. Op. 31. *Ricordi*, 1921.
Sowerby, L. *S.P.A.M.*, 1939.
Stanford, C. V. Op. 129. *Stainer & Bell*, 1918.
Szalowski, A. Sonatina. *Omega*, 1948.
Tovey, D. Op. 16. *Schott*, 1912.
Tuthill, B. C. Faantsy Sonata. Op. 3. *Fischer*, 1936.
Wanhal, J. *McGinnis & Marx*, 1948.
Weber, C. M. Grand Duo Concertant. Op. 47. *Lemoine, etc.*
—— Grand Duo Concertant. Op. 47. Ed. E. Roth. *By. & H.*
Weber, C. M. Grand Quintetto. Arr. cl. and pf. C. Bärmann. *Lienau.*
Weinberger, J. Sonatine. *Fischer*, 1940.

Transcriptions by E. Stiévenard
Bach, J. S. Trois sonates. *Evette.*
Handel, G. F. Deux sonates. *Evette.*

Sonatas: clarinet alone
Karg-Elert, S. Op. 110. *Zimmermann*, 1925.
Magnani, A. 3 sonates. *Evette.*

Sonata: clarinet and cello
Tate, Phyllis. *O.U.P.*, 1949.

Sonata: 2 clarinets
Poulenc, F. *Chester*, 1918.

Sonatas: basset-horn and piano
Danzi, F. Grande sonate. Op. 62. *André.*
—— Grande sonate. Op. 62. *Sieber.*

Sonata: bass clarinet and piano
Schoeck, O. Op. 41. *Br. & H.*, 1931.

SUITES AND OCCASIONAL PIECES

Suites and occasional pieces with piano
Akimenko, T. Petite Ballade. Op. 19. *Belaieff*, 1902.
Babin, V. Hillandale Waltzes. *By. & H.*, 1947.
Berg, A. Vier Stücke. Op. 5. *Schlesinger*, 1920.
Browne, P. A. Truro Maggot. *Hawkes*, 1944.
Busoni, F. B. Elégie. *Br. & H.*, 1921.
Cahuzac, L. Fantasie variée. *Hansen*, 1947.
Cavallini, E. Elégie. *Ricordi*.
Clifton, Chalmers. Intermezzo and Humoresque. *Le Roy*, 1926.
Debussy, C. Petite Pièce. *Durand*, 1910.
Ferguson, H. Four Short Pieces. *Hawkes*, 1937.
Finzi, G. Five Bagatelles. *Hawkes*, 1945.
Frugatta, G. Suite de 6 pezzi. *Ricordi*.
Gade, N. Fantasiestücke. Op. 43. *Br. & H.*, 1864, *Augener*.
Glière, R. Deux morceaux, Op. 35, nos. 6 and 7. *Jurgenson*.
Goedicke, A. F. Zwei Stücke. *U.E.*, 1947.
Gretchaninov, A. T. Suite miniature. Op. 145. *Leduc*, 1938.
Hahn, R. Sarabande et thème variée. *Heugel*, 1903.
Holbrooke, J. Andante and presto. Op. 6/2. *Hawkes*, 1908.
Holmès, A. Fantasie. *Evette*, 1900.
Hopkins, A. Fantasy. *Chester*, 1951.
Hugon, G. Scherzo. *Costallat*, 1951.
Hurlstone, W. Y. Four characteristic Pieces. *Novello*, 1909.
Jeanjean, P. Arabesques. *Andrieu*, 1926.
Laurischkus, M. Miniaturen. Op. 4. *Simon*, 1900.
—— Miniaturen. Op. 30. *Simrock*.
Lloyd, C. H. Suite in olden style. *Hawkes*, 1914.
Magnani, A. Mazurka-Caprice. *Evette*.
Murrill, H. Prelude, Cadenza, Fugue. *O.U.P.*, 1933.
Oubradous, F. Cadence et divertissement. *O.L.*
Pierné, G. Canzonetta. Op. 19. *Leduc*.
Poldowski. Pastorale (C cl.). *Chester*, 1927.
Pratt, A. Idylle printanière. *Hawkes*, 1913.
—— Souvenir d'Ispahan. *Hawkes*, 1913.
Rainier, Priaulx. Suite. *Schott*, 1945.
Raybould, C. The Wistful Shepherd. *O.U.P.*, 1939.
Rossini, G. Fantaisie. *Schott, c.* 1828.
Rungis, R. 7 pièces. *Lemoine*, 1937.
Samuel, H. Three Light Pieces. *Hawkes*, 1913.
Schumann, R. Phantasiestücke. Op. 73. *Augener*.
Seiber, M. Andantino Pastorale. *Schott*, 1950.
Spohr, L. Fantasia and Variations. Op. 81. *Schmidt*.
—— 3 Adagios. *Augener*.
Stanford, C. V. Three Intermezzi. Op. 13. *Novello*, 1880.
Taneiev, S. I. Arabesque. *Andrieu*.
Wagner, R. Adagio. Arr. E. Schmeisser. *Br. & H.*, 1926.
Walthew, R. Suite in F. *Boosey*, 1899.

—— Four meditations, 2 sets. *Boosey*, 1897, 1903.
—— Mosaic in ten pieces. *Boosey*, 1900.
Webber, Lloyd. Theme and Variations. *Francis, Day, Hunter*, 1952.
Weiner, L. Ballade. Op. 8. *Rózsavölgyi*, 1912.
Widor, C. M. Introduction et Rondo. Op. 72. *Menestrel*, 1898?
Wuille. Fantasie. Ed. S. Bellison. *Ricordi, New York*, 1951.

Transcriptions

Litolff, H. Scherzo (fr. Concerto Symphonique No. 4). Tr. N. Richard-
son. *By. & H.*
Schumann, R. Romances. Op. 94. (For oboe.) *Augener.*
Sinigaglia, L. 12 Variationen über ein Thema von F. Schubert. Op. 19.
(For oboe.) *Br. & H.*, 1898.

Bass clarinet and piano

Diethe, F. Romanze. *Merseburger.*
Klughardt, A. Romanze. *Schmidt.*
Orlamünder, J. G. Romanze. *Schmidt.*

Clarinet alone

Bentzon, J. Tema med variationer. *Hansen*, 1929.
Pfeiffer, H. Musik für A-Klarinette. *Lienau*, 1937.
Stravinsky, I. Trois pièces. *Chester*, 1919.

DUETS

Two clarinets

Bonfil, J.-S. 3 grands duos. *Decombe, c.* 1810.
Crusell, B. 3 duos d'une difficulté progressive. Op. 6. *Peters, c.* 1820.
Gambaro, J. B. 3 duos concertans, Op. 7. *Gambaro, c.* 1810.
Lefèvre, J.-X. 6 duos concertans, Op. 9, 10, 11. *Naderman*, 1810.
Mahon, J. 4 duets. *Clementi*, 1805.

———

Frank, A. Suite. *O.U.P.*, 1934.
Koechlin, C. Idylle. *Chant du Monde.*
Mirandolle, L. Trois duos. *Leduc.*
Nocentini, D. 14 duetti. *Carisch.*
Poulenc, F. Sonate pour 2 clarinettes. *Chester*, 1918.

Clarinet and violin

Busch, A. Hausmusik. Op. 26/1 and 2. *Br. & H.*, 1926.
Hindemith, P. Pièce. *Schott*, 1932.

Clarinet and flute

Szalowski, A. *Omega*, 1948.
Villa-Lobos, H. Chôros, No. 2. *Eschig*, 1927.

Clarinet and oboe

Høffding, F. Dialoger. *Sk. M.*, 1944.
Phillips, G. Suite. *Schott*, 1950.

Two basset-horns

Mozart, W. A. 12 Duette. K. 487. *Br. & H.*

Clarinet and bassoon

Beethoven, L. van. 3 Duos. Op. '147'. *Br. & H.* (An arrangement for
2 clarinets is contained in Langenus, G. *Virtuoso Studies.*)
Goepfert, C. A. VI duos faciles. *Hofmeister.*
Poulenc, F. Sonate. *Chester,* 1922.
Reuter, F. Spielmusik. *Kistner,* 1936.

TRIOS

A. Trios; with piano

Clarinet, violin and piano

Bartók, B. Contrasts. *By. & H.,* 1942.
Khachaturian, A. I. *Anglo-Soviet,* 1932.
Mason, D. G. Pastorale. Op. 8. *Mathot,* 1913.
Milhaud, D. Suite. *Senart,* 1937.
Stravinsky, I. Suite de l'Histoire du Soldat. *Chester,* 1920.
Walthew, R. *Boosey,* 1897.

Clarinet, viola and piano

Amberg, J. Fantasiestücke. Op. 12. *Hansen,* 1910.
Bruch, M. Acht Stücke. Op. 83. *Simrock,* 1910.
Mozart, W. A. K. 498. *Br. & H.*
Reinecke, C. Op. 264. *Simrock.*
Schumann, R. Märchenerzählungen. Op. 132. *Br. & H.*

Clarinet, cello and piano

Amberg, J. Op. 11. *Hansen,* 1912.
Beethoven, L. van. Op. 11. *Br. & H.*
—— Op. 38. (An arrangement by the composer of the Septet, Op. 20.)
  Br. & H.
Berger, W. Op. 94. *Kahnt,* 1905.
Brahms, J. Op. 114. *Simrock,* 1892.
Eberl, A. Op. 36. *Kühnel,* 1805?
Farrenc, L. Op. 44. *Leduc.*
Indy, V. d'. Op. 29. *Hamelle,* 1887.
Kahn, R. Op. 45. *Schlesinger.*
Lefèvre, J.-X. Sonates 2 and 3. Ed. E. Borrel. *Richli.*
Ries, F. Op. 28. *Simrock.*
Zemlinsky, A. Op. 3. *Simrock,* 1897.

Clarinet, flute and piano

Emmanuel, M. Trio-Sonate. *Durand.*
Saint-Saëns, C. Tarantelle. Op. 6. *Durand.*
Schmitt, F. Sonatine en trio. *Durand,* 1935.

Clarinet, basset-horn and piano

Mendelssohn, F. 2 Konzertstücke. Op. 113, 114. *Br. & H.*

Clarinet, bassoon and piano
Glinka, M. I. Trio pathétique. *Jurgenson*, 1827.

Clarinet, horn and piano
Reinecke, C. Op. 274. *Senff.*
Tovey, D. Op. 8. *Schott*, 1906.

B. Trios; without piano
Clarinet and strings
Busch, A. Deutsche Tänze. Op. 26/3. cl, va, vc. *Br. & H.*
Juon, P. Divertimento. Op. 34. cl, 2 va. *Schlesinger.*
Markevitch, I. Serenade. cl, vn, bn. *Schott*, 1931.

Clarinet and other wind instruments
Arnold, M. Divertimento. Op. 37. fl, ob, cl. *Paterson*, 1952.
Bentzon, J. Sonatine. fl, cl, bn. *S.M.*
De Haan, S. fl, cl, bn. *Schott*, 1951.
Flothuis, M. Nocturne. Op. 11. fl, ob, cl. *Chester*, 1952.
Handel, G. F. Ouverture. Ed. K. Haas. 2 cl, hn. *Schott*, 1952.
Karg-Elert, S. Op. 49. ob, cl, ca(hn). *Merseburger*, 1905.
Koechlin, C. fl, cl, bn. *Senart.*
Kummer, K. fl, cl, bn. *Schott.*
Mozart, W. A. 5 Divertimenti. K.A. 229. 2 cl, bn. *Br. & H.*
—— Divertimenti 1 and 2. *By. & H.*
Pijper, W. fl, cl, bn. *S.D.*
Stark, R. Sonata. Op. 55. 2 cl, bhn. *Schmidt*, 1897.
Wailly, P. de. Aubade. fl, ob, cl. *Br. & H.*
Walckiers, E. 3 Trios. fl, cl, bn. *Richault.*

Flute, clarinet, harp
Ingenhoven, J. *Senart.*

Oboe, clarinet, bassoon
Arrieu, C. *Amphion*, 1948.
Auric, G. *O.L.*, 1948.
Barraud, H. *O.L.*, 1938.
Bentzon, J. Racconto No. 3. *S.M.*
Bozza, E. Suite brève. *Leduc*, 1947.
Constant, M. *Chester*, 1949.
Ferroud, P. O. *Durand*, 1934.
Françaix, J. Divertissement. *Schott.*
Ibert, J. Cinq pièces. *O.L.*
Ikonomov, B. *O.L.*
Juon, P. Arabesken. Op. 73. *Lienau*, 1940.
Maintenon, J. Sonatine n. 4. *Costallat.*
Martelli, H. Op. 45. *Costallat*, 1947.
Migot, G. *Leduc*, 1946.
Milhaud, D. Suite d'après Corrette. *O.L.*, 1938.
Pierné, P. Bucolique variée. *Costallat*, 1947.

Ropartz, G. Entrata e Scherzetto. *Salabert*, 1947.
Sauguet, H. *O.L.*, 1948.
Schulhoff, E. Divertissement. *Schott*, 1928.
Szalowski, A. *Chester*, 1948.
Tomasi, G. Concert champêtre. *Lemoine*, 1938.
Villa-Lobos, H. *Eschig, Schott*.

Three clarinets
Mihalovici, M. Sonate. Op. 35. cl. in E flat, in A, and bass. *Salabert*.

Two Basset-horns and bassoon
Mozart, W. A. Kanonisches Adagio. K. 410. *Br. & H.*

Transcriptions
Bach, J. S. Three Fugues. Arr. for 2 clarinets and bassoon by F. J.
    Thurston. *By. & H.*, 1941.
Bach, J. S. Prélude et fugue. Tr. (for ob, cl, bn) F. Oubradous. *O.L.*, 1938.
Mozart, W. A. Cinq divertissements. K.A. 229. Tr. (for ob, cl, bn)
    F. Oubradous. *O.L.*, 1946.

QUARTETS

Quartets: with piano
Amberg, J. Suite. fl, ob, cl. *Hansen*, 1905.
Castéra, R. de. Concerto. fl, cl, vc. *Rouart*.
Hindemith, P. cl, vn, vc. *Schott*, 1938.
Honegger, A. Rapsodie. 2 fl, cl. *Senart*, 1923.
Messiaen, O. Quatuor pour la Fin du temps. cl, vn, vc. *Durand*, 1942.
Milhaud, D. Sonate. fl, ob, cl. *Durand*, 1923.
Rabl, W. Op. 1. vn, vc. *Simrock*, 1897.
Riisager, K. Sonate. fl, cl, vc. *Hansen*, 1931.
Saint-Saëns, C. Caprice. Op. 79. fl, ob, cl. *Durand*, 1887.
Schmitt, F. A Tour d'anches. Op. 97. ob, cl, bn. *Durand*, 1943.

Quartets: clarinet with violin, viola and cello
Bärmann, H. J. Op. 18. *Schott*, 1882.
Bochsa, C. Trois Quatuors concertans. *Monsigny, c.* 1805.
Crusell, B. Quatuors. Op. 2, 4, 7. *Peters, c.* 1820.
Hindemith, P. Variations. *Schott*.
Hummel, J. H. Quartet in E♭. MS. 1808.
Pichl, W. Three Quartettos. Op. 16. *Longman, c.* 1795.
Rawsthorne, A. *O.U.P.*, 1950.
Stamitz, C. 6 Quatuors. Op. 8. *Sieber, c.* 1780.
—— Op. 8/4. *Raabe*, 1919.
—— 2 Quartets. *McGinnis & Marx*.

Quartets: clarinet with other wind instruments
Blacher, B. Divertimento. Op. 38. fl, ob, cl, bn. *B. & B.*, 1951.
Bridge, Frank. Divertimenti. fl, ob, cl, bn. *By. & H.*, 1940.
—14   • •

Chwartz, L. Evening in the Turkestan Steppe. fl, ca(ob), cl, bn. *Hawkes*, 1937.

Domansky, A. Divertimento. 2 cl, hn, bn. *Schmidt*.

Haydn, F. Divertimento. 2 cl, 2 hn. *Hansen*, 1932.

Ibert, J. Deux mouvements. 2 fl, cl, bn. *Leduc*, 1923.

Mirandolle, L. fl, ob, cl, bn. *Leduc*.

Rossini, G. 6 Quartette. fl, cl, hn, bn. Ed. W. Zachert. *Schott*, 1935.

Walckiers, E. 3 Quatuors. Op. 7. fl, cl, hn, bn. *Costallat*.

Quartets: four clarinets

Harding, K. 3 (B flat) cl, bcl. MS. 1951.

Mirandolle, L. 2 cl, cl. alto, bcl. MS. 1937.

Stark, R. Serenade. 2 cl, bhn, bcl. *Schmidt*.

Waterson, J. Grand Quartet. *Mahillon*.

QUINTETS

Quintets: with piano

Abramsky, A. Concertino. fl, cl, hn, bn. *U.E.*, 1929.

Beethoven, L. van. Op. 16. ob, cl, hn, bn. *Br. & H.*

Duncan, E. fl, cl, hn, bn. *Rudall*.

Dunhill, T. F. Op. 3. cl, hn, vn, vc. *Rudall*, 1913.

Fibich, Z. Op. 42. cl, hn, vn, vc. *Urbánek*, 1894.

Gieseking, W. ob, cl, hn, bn. *By. & H., New York*.

Hauer, J. M. Op. 26. cl, vn, va, vc. *Lienau*.

Herzogenberg, H. v. Op. 43. ob, cl, hn, bn. *Peters*.

Hindemith, P. Drei Stücke. Op. 35. cl, trpt, vn, cb. *Schott*, 1925.

Huber, H. Op. 136. fl, cl, hn, bn. *Hug*, 1920.

Kahn, R. Op. 54. cl, vn, hn, vc. *B. & B.*, 1910.

Magnard, A. Op. 8. fl, ob, cl, bn. *Rouart*.

Mozart, W. A. K. 452. ob, cl, hn, bn. *Br. & H.*

Rimsky-Korsakov, N. A. fl, cl, hn, bn. *Belaieff*, 1911.

Rubinstein, A. fl, cl, hn, bn. *Schuberth*.

Spohr, L. Op. 52. fl, cl, hn, bn. *Peters*.

Weingartner, F. Op. 50. cl, vn, va, vc. *Br. & H.*

Quintets: clarinet with strings

Blatt, F. T. Theme and variations. *Simrock*.

Bliss, A. *Novello*, 1933.

Brahms, J. Op. 115. *Simrock*, 1892, *etc.*

Coleridge-Taylor, S. Op. 15. *Br. & H.*, 1906.

Fuchs, R. Op. 102. *Robitschek*, 1919.

Hindemith, P. Op. 30. (Score only.) *Schott*, 1922.

Holbrooke, J. Op. 27/1. *Novello, c.* 1914.

—— Op. 27/2. *Chester, c.* 1914.

Howells, H. Rhapsodic Quintet. Op. 31. *Stainer & Bell*, 1921.

Jacob, Gordon. *Novello*, 1946.

Krehl, S. Op. 19. *Simrock*, 1902.

Krein, A. A. Esquisses hébraïques, 1 and 2. Op. 12. *Jurgenson*, 1914.

Mozart, W. A. K. 581. *Br. & H.*, *By. & H.*
Raphael, G. Op. 4. *Simrock*, 1925.
Reger, M. Op. 146. *Peters*, 1916.
Romberg, A. J. Op. 57. cl, vn, 2 va, vc. *Peters*.
Spohr, L. Andante with variations. Op. 34. *Schmidt*.
—— Fantasie with variations. Op. 81. *Schmidt*.
Strässer, E. Op. 34. *Simrock*, 1920.
Täglichsbeck, T. Op. 44. *Heinrichshofen*, 1863.
Weber, C. M. Op. 34. *Costallat*.

In Manuscript
Somervell, A. Walthew, R. H.

Quintet: bass clarinet and strings
Bowen, York. Op. 93: in one movement. MS. 1932.

Quintets: clarinet with other wind instruments and strings
Bentzon, J. Variazioni interrotti. Op. 12. cl, bn, vn, va, vc. *Hansen*, 1928.
Casella, A. Serenata. cl, trpt, bn, vn, vc. *U.E.*, 1929.
Kaminski, H. cl, hn, vn, va, vc. *U.E.*, 1917.
Nielsen, C. Serenata-in vano. cl, hn, bn, vc, cb. *S.M.*
Prokofiev, S. Op. 39. ob, cl, vn, va, cb. *Gutheil*, 1923.

Quintets: clarinet with flute, oboe, horn, bassoon
Badings, H. Quintet 1. *S.D.*
Bakaleinikov, V. Introduction and Scherzo. *Belwin*.
Bentzon, J. Racconto No. 5. *S.M.*
Bozza, E. Variations sur un thème libre. *Leduc*, 1943.
Damase, J.-M. 17 Variations. *Leduc*.
Danzi, F. Op. 56/2. *Br. & H.*
Domansky, A. *Schmidt*.
Foerster, J. B. Op. 95. *H.M.*, 1927.
Françaix, J. *Schott*, 1951.
Grainger, P. Walking Tune. *Schott*, 1912.
Heim, M. *Schmidt*, 1903.
Hindemith, P. Kleine Kammermusik. Op. 24/2. *Schott*, 1922.
Ibert, J. Trois pièces brèves. *Leduc*, 1930.
Ingenhoven, J. *Wunderhorn-Verl*.
Juon, P. Op. 84. *Lienau*.
Klughardt, A. F. M. Op. 79. *Zimmermann*, 1901.
Laurischkus, M. Suite. Op. 23. *Simrock*, 1914.
Lendvai, E. Op. 23. *Simrock*, 1922.
Mederacke, K. Bohemian Suite. *Hofmeister*.
Milhaud, D. La Cheminée du Roi René. *Andraud*, 1939.
Moritz, E. *Zimmermann*.
Nielsen, C. Op. 43. *Hansen*, 1923.
Onslow, G. Op. 81. *Br. & H.*
Pierné, G. Pastorale. *Leduc*.
Pijper, W. *S.D.*

Reizenstein, F. *Hawkes*, 1937.
Ropartz, G. Deux pièces. *Durand*, 1926.
Schmid, H. K. Op. 28. *Schott*, 1921.
Schoenberg, A. Op. 26. *U.E.*, 1924.
Taffanel, C. P. *Leduc*.
Tomasi, H. *Lemoine*, 1952.
Weis, F. Serenade. *Hansen*, 1941.

Quintets: clarinet and other wind instruments
Berezovsky, N. T. Suite. Op. 11. fl, ob, cl, ca, bn. *Ed. Russe.*
Domansky, A. fl, 2 cl, hn, bn. *Schmidt.*
Flothuis, M. Op. 13. fl, ob, cl, bcl, bn. *S.D.*
Karg-Elert, S. Op. 30. ob, 2 cl, hn, bn. *Kahnt.*
Mozart, W. A. Adagio. K. 411. 2 cl, 3 bhn. *Br. & H.*

SEXTETS

Sextets: clarinet, string quartet and piano
Berezovsky, N. T. Theme and variations. Op. 7. *Ed. Russe.*
Copland, A. *By. & H.*, 1952.
Petyrek, F. *U.E.*, 1921.
Prokofiev, S. Overture on Yiddish Themes. Op. 34. *U.E.*, 1924.

Sextets: clarinet, flute, oboe, horn, bassoon and piano
Dresden, S. Derde Suite (1920). *S.D.*
—— Suite naar Rameau. *S.D.*
Foerster, J. B. *H.M.*, 1925.
Holbrooke, J. Op. 33a. *Chester.*
Poulenc, F. *Hansen*, 1945.
Reuchsel, A. *Lemoine*, 1909.
Roussel, A. Divertissement. Op. 6. *Rouart*, 1905.
Thuille, L. Op. 6. *Br. & H.*, 1889.
Onslow, G. Op. 30. fl, cl, hn, bn, pf, cb. *Br. & H.*

Sextets: without piano
Beethoven, L. van. Op. 71. 2 cl, 2 bn, 2 hn. *Br. & H.*
Boisdeffre, C. de. Op. 49. fl, ob, cl, bn, hn, cb. *Hamelle.*
Herrmann, E. Serenata. ob, cl, str. quartet. *Raabe.*
Janáček, L. Suite Mládí. fl, ob, cl, hn, bn, bcl. *H.M.*, 1925.
Jettel, R. fl, ob, 2 cl, bn, hn. *Doblinger.*
Reinecke, C. Op. 271. fl, ob, cl, 2 hn, bn. *Zimmermann*, 1904.
Stolzenberg, G. Op. 6. cl, 2 vn, va, vc, cb. *Br. & H.*
Wagner. Adagio. cl, str. quintet. *Br. & H.*, 1926.

SEPTETS

Septets: with piano
Hummel, J. N. Septet militaire. Op. 114. fl, cl, trpt, vn, va, vc. *Haslinger*, 1878.

Janáček, L. Concertino. 2 vn, va, cl (E flat and B flat), hn, bn. *H.M.*, 1949.
Kittl, J. B. Op. 25. fl, ob, cl, hn, bn, cb. *Kistner*, 1846.
Spohr, L. Op. 147. fl, cl, hn, bn, vn, vc. *Peters*, 1855, *Costallat*.

Septets: without piano
Beethoven, L. van. Op. 20. cl, hn, bn, vn, va, vc, cb. *Br. & H.*
Genzmer, H. fl, cl, hn, vn, va, vc, hp. *Schott.*
Hindemith, P. fl, ob, cl, bcl, bn, hn, trpt. *Schott*, 1949.
Indy, Vincent d'. Chanson et danses. Op. 50. fl, ob, 2 cl, hn, 2 bn. *Durand, c.* 1898.
Ravel, M. Introduction and Allegro. fl, cl, hp, str. quartet. *Durand, c.* 1906.
Röntgen, J. Serenade. Op. 14. fl, ob, cl, 2 bn, 2 hn. *Br. & H.*, 1878.
Villa-Lobos, H. Chôros, No. 7. fl, ob, cl, alto sax, bn, vn, vc. *Eschig*, 1928.

OCTETS

Octets: with piano
Juon, P. Op. 27. ob, cl, hn, bn, vn, va, vc. *Schlesinger.*
Ries, F. Op. 128. cl, hn, bn, vn, va, vc, cb. *Kistner.*
Rubinstein, A. Op. 9. fl, cl, hn, vn, va, vc, cb. *Peters.*
Weingartner, F. v. Op. 62. cl, hn, bn, str. quartet. *Chester.*

Octets: without piano
Beethoven, L. van. Op. 103. 2 ob, 2 cl, 2 hn, 2 bn. *Br. & H.*
—— Rondino. Op. '146'. 2 ob, 2 cl, 2 hn, 2 bn. *Br. & H.*
Dubois, T. Suites 1 and 2. 2 fl, ob, 2 cl, hn, 2 bn. *Heugel & Leduc.*
Ferguson, H. cl, bn, hn, 2 vn, va, vc, cb. *Hawkes*, 1934.
Gal, H. Divertimento. fl, ob, 2 cl, trpt, 2 hn, bn. *Leukart*, 1925.
Gouvy, L. T. Op. 71. fl, ob, 2 cl, 2 hn, 2 bn. *Kistner.*
Haydn, F. 2 ob, 2 cl, 2 hn, 2 bn. *Kahnt*, 1901.
Lachner, F. Op. 156. fl, ob, 2 cl, 2 hn, 2 bn. *Kistner.*
Mirandolle, L. cl, hn, bn, 2 vn, ca, vc, cb. MS. 1942–43.
Mozart, W. A. Serenades. K. 375, 388. 2 ob, 2 cl, 2 bn, 2 hn. *Br. & H.*, *André.*
Novaček, R. Sinfonietta. Op. 48. fl, ob, 2 cl, 2 bn, 2 hn. *Br. & H.*, 1905.
Poldowski. 2 fl, ob, ob. d'amore, ca, cl, bhn, bcl. MS.
Reicha, A. Op. 96. ob, cl, bn, hn, 2 vn, va, vc. *Janet.*
Reinecke, C. Op. 216. fl, ob, 2 cl, 2 bn, 2 hn. *Kistner.*
Schubert, F. Op. 166. *Costallat, By. & H.*
Spohr, L. Op. 32. cl, 2 hn, vn, 2 va, vc, cb. *Costallat.*
Stravinsky, I. fl, cl, 2 bn, 2 trpt, 2 tromb. *Ed. Russe*, 1924.
Wellesz, E. Op. 67. cl, bn, hn, str. *U.E.*

NONETS

Nonets: flute, oboe, clarinet, horn, bassoon and strings
Dubois, Th. *Heugel*, 1926.
Massenet, J. Introduction and variations. ?

Rheinberger, J. G. Op. 139. *Kistner*, 1885.
Samazeuilh, G. Divertissement and Musette. *Durand*, 1912.
Schoeck, O. Serenade. Op. 1. *Hug*, 1907.
Spohr, L. Op. 31. *Litolff, Costallat.*

Nonets: clarinets with other wind instruments

Goossens, E. Phantasy Nonet. Op. 40. fl, ob, 2 cl, 2 hn, 2 bn, trpt. *Curwen*, 1924.
Gounod, C. Petite Symphonie. fl, 2 ob, 2 cl, 2 hn, 2 bn. *Costallat*, 1904.
Gouvy, L. T. Petite Suite Gauloise. Op. 90. fl, 2 ob, 2 cl, 2 hn, 2 bn. *U.E.*
Kornauth, E. Kammermusik. Op. 31. fl, ob, cl, hn, str. *U.E.*, 1925.
Martín y Soler, V. 4 Divertimenti. 2 ob, 2 bhn, 2 hn, 2 bn, serpent. MS.

LARGER GROUPS

Dvořák, A. Serenade. Op. 44. 2 ob, 2 cl, 3 hn, 2 bn, vc, cb. *Simrock*, 1879.
Mozart, W. A. Serenade. K. 361. 2 ob, 2 cl, 2 bhn, 2 bn, 4 hn, cb (cbn). *Br. & H.*
Raff, J. Sinfonietta. 2 fl, 2 ob, 2 cl, 2 hn, 2 bn. Op. 188. *Siegel*, 1874.
Strauss, R. Serenade. Op. 7. 2 fl, 2 ob, 2 cl, 2 bn, 4 hn, cbn (tuba). *U.E.*, 1884.

Voice with clarinet

Bliss, A. Two Nursery Rhymes. *Chester*, 1921.
Cherubini, L. Ave Maria. *Diabelli.*
Dallapiccola, L. Due Liriche di Anacreonte. Soprano with 2 cl (E flat and A), va, pf. *Suvini Zerboni.*
Gaveaux, P. Polacca from Le Trompeur trompé. Ed. M. Flothuis. *Broekmans*, 1952.
Guglielmi, P. Gratias agimus. *Lonsdale, c.* 1865.
Jacob, Gordon. Three songs. Soprano voice and clarinet. *O.U.P.*, 1932.
Kaminski, H. Drei geistliche Lieder. *U.E.*
Lloyd, C. H. Annette. Song for baritone with cl. and pf. *Novello.*
Macfarren, G. A. Pack clouds away. *Chappell.*
—— The Widow Bird. *Chappell.*
Mozart, W. A. Parto. La Clemenza di Tito, no. 9. Arr. with pf. acc. O. W. Street. *Br. & H.*
—— Parto. La Clemenza di Tito, no. 9. Arr. W. Bergmann. *Schott*, 1950.
—— 6 Notturni for 2 sopranos and a bass. *Br. & H.*
  K. 346, 436, 439, 549, acc. 3 bhn. K. 437, 438, acc. 2 cl. and 1 bhn.
Neukomm, S. v. Psalm 70. For a Counter-tenor-Lady's voice, with Bass-Clarionet concertant. MS. 1836.
Petyrek, F. Der Wind. Acc. cl, vn, va, pf. *U.E.*
Schubert, F. Der Hirt auf dem Felsen. cl, pf. *Br. & H.*
—— Offertorium. Op. 46. *Br. & H.*
—— Romanze. Die Verschworenen, No. 2. Ed. M. Flothuis. *Broekmans.*

Seiber, M. Three Hungarian Songs. MS.

Spohr, L. Sechs deutsche Lieder. *Br. & H., Bärenreiter.*

Stravinsky, I. Berceuses du Chat. Suite pour une voix de femme et 3 clar. *Henn,* 1917.

Villa-Lobos, H. Poêma da Criança e sua Mamâ. 1923. fl, cl, vc. *Eschig,* 1929.

Bibliography

A. BOOKS

Altenburg, W. *Die Klarinette*. Heilbronn, 1904.

Antolini, F. *La retta maniera di scrivere per il clarinetto*. Milan, 1813.

Apel, W. *The Harvard Dictionary of Music*. Cambridge, Mass., 1945.

Backofen, J. C. H. *Anweisung zur Clarinette*. 1803.

Baines, A. C. *Woodwind Instruments and their History*. London, 1957.

Becker, H. *Studien zur Geschichte der Rohrblattinstrumente*. Hamburg, 1961.

—— 'Zur Geschichte der Klarinette im 18. Jahrh.', *Die Musikforschung*, VIII, 1955, pp. 271–92.

—— foreword to *Klar.-Duette aus der Fruhzeit des Instruments*. Wiesbaden, 1954.

—— foreword to 'Klar.-Konzerte des 18. Jahrh.', *Erbedeutscher Musik*, Vol. 41, Wiesbaden, 1957.

—— Section 'European Clarinets' in *Klarinette, Die Musik in Geschichte und Gegenwart*. Kassel/Basel/New York, Vol. 7, 1958.

Benade, A. H. *Horns, Strings, and Harmony*. New York, 1960.

Berlioz, H. *Traité de l'instrumentation*. Paris, 1844.

—— *Instrumentionslehre*. Erganzt u. revidiert von Richard Strauss. Leipzig, 1905.

Blaes, A. J. *Souvenirs de ma vie artistique*. Brussels, 1888.

Boese, H. *Die Klarinette als Soloinstrument in der Musik der Mannheimer Schule*. Dresden, 1940.

Bonnani, F. *Gabinetto armonico*. Rome, 1722; reissued as *The Showcase of Musical Instruments*, with new explanatory notes by Harrison and Rimmer. New York, 1964.

Brand, E. D. *Selmer Band Instrument Repairing Manual*. Elkhart, Ind.

Brenet, M. *Rameau, Gossec, et les Clarinettes*. Le Guide Musicale, Paris and Brussels, 1903.

Burbure, L. de. *Les Oeuvres des anciens musiciens belges*. Brussels, 1882.

Carse, A. *The History of Orchestration*. London, 1925; reprinted New York, 1964.

—— *Musical Wind Instruments*. London, 1939.

—— *The Orchestra in the 18th Century*. Cambridge, 1940.

—— *The Orchestra from Beethoven to Berlioz*. Cambridge, 1948.

Chatwin, R. B. 'Some Notes on the History of the Clarinet', *Musical Progress and Mail*, Vol. ix, 1–3, 1938.

—— 'Handel and the Clarinet', *G.S.J.*, Vol. III, 1950.

Clappé, A. A. *The Wind-Band and its Instruments*. London, 1912.

Cobbett, W. W. *Cyclopaedic Survey of Chamber Music*. Oxford, 1929.

Cucuel, G. *Études sur un orchestre au XVIII* siècle*. Paris, 1913.
—— 'La question des clarinettes dans l'instrumentation du XVIIIᵉ siècle', *Zeitschrift der Internat. Musikgesellschaft*, XII, 1910–11, pp. 280 *et seq.*
Daubeny, U. *Orchestral Wind Instruments*. London, 1920.
Diderot and d'Alembert. *Encyclopédie*. Paris, 1767, 1776.
Dittersdorf, K. D. von. *Lebensbeschreibung nach dem Erstdruck*. ed. E. B. Loets. Leipzig, 1940.
Donington, R. *The Instruments of Music*. London, 1949.
Doppelmayr, J. G. *Historische Nachricht von den Nürnbergischen Mathematicis und Künstlern*. Nuremberg, 1730.
Drury, M. 'Étude sur la clarinette', *Musique & Concours*, Nov. 1933–Nov. 1934.
Eisel, J. T. *Musikus Autodidaktos*. Erfurt, 1738.
Elsenaar, E. *De Clarinet*. Hilversum, 1927.
Engel, H. 'Dar Instrumentalkonzert' in *Kretzschmars Führer durch den Konzertsaal*. Vol. 3, Leipzig, 1932.
Ergo, E. *Dans les propylées de l'instrumentation*. Antwerp, 1908.
Euting, E. *Zur Geschichte der Blasinstrumente in 16. und 17. Jahrhundert*. Berlin, 1899.
Fétis, F.-J. *Biographie universelle des musiciens*. 2nd edn. 8 vols. Paris, 1868.
Forsyth, C. *Orchestration*. London, 1922; 2nd edn., 1935.
Francoeur, L.-J. *Diapason général des instruments à vent*. Paris, 1772.
—— *Traité général des voix et des instruments d'orchestre*. Revised by A. Choron. Paris, 1813.
Frolich, J. *Systematischer Unterricht in den vorzuglichsten Orchesterinstrumenten*. 1829.
Gabucci, A. *Origine e storia del Clarinetto*. Milan, 1937.
Galpin, F. W. *European Musical Instruments*. London, 1937.
—— *Old English Instruments of Music*. 3rd edn. London, 1932; edition revised by R. Thurston Dart, London, 1965.
Gerber, E. L. *Historisch–biographisches Lexicon*. Leipzig, 1790–92.
—— *Neues historisch–biographisches Lexikon der Tönkunstler*. Leipzig, 1812–14.
Gevaert, F. A. *Neue Instrumenten-Lehre*. Leipzig, 1887.
Gollmick, C. 'Ein Wort uber die Verbesserung der Klarinette', *A.M.Z.*, 1845.
Gradenwitz, P. 'The Beginnings of Clarinet Literature', *Music and Letters*, April 1947.
Grove, G. *Dictionary of Music and Musicians*. 5th edn., London, 1954.
Hanslick, E. *Geschichte des Concertwissenschaft in Wien*. Vienna, 1869–71.
—— *Concerte, Componisten und Virtuosen der letzten 15 jahre*. Berlin, 1886.
Hiller, J. A. *Wochentliche Nachrichten . . .*, 1769, 1777.
Kappey, J. A. *Military Music*. London, 1894.
Karstadt, G. Article 'Saxinstrumente' in M.G.G.
Kastner, G. *Traité général de l'instrumentation*. Paris, 1837, 1844.
—— *Manuel général de musique militaire*. Paris, 1848.

Kingdon-Ward, M. 'Mozart and the Clarinet', *Music and Letters*, April 1947.

Koch, H. C. *Musikalisches Lexikon*. Offenbach, 1802.

Kolneder, W. 'Die Klarinette bei Vivaldi', *Die Musikforschung*, 1951, pp. 185–91; and 1955, pp. 209–11.

Komorzynsky, E. von. *Mozarts Kunst der Instrumentation*. Stuttgart, 1906.

Kool, J. *Das Saxophon*. Leipzig, 1931.

Kroll, O. 'Das Chalumeau', *Zeitsch. für Musikwissenschaft*, May 1933.

—— 'Die Klarinette in der Gegenwart', *Die Musik-Woche*, 8 February 1936.

Kunitz, H. *Die Instrumentation*. Vol. IV, 'Klarinette'. Leipzig, 1957.

Laborde, J.-B. de. *Essai sur la musique*. Paris, 1780.

Langwill, L. G. *An Index of Musical Wind-Instrument Makers*. Edinburgh, 1960. 2nd edn. revised and enlarged, 1962.

Laurencie, L. de la. 'Rameau et les clarinettes', *Sammelbände der Internat. Musikgesellschaft*. 1913.

Lavoix, H. *Histoire de l'instrumentation*. Paris, 1878.

Lefèbvre, P., and Goffin, R. *La Technique du son dans les instruments à anche battante simple*. Paris, 1939.

Mahillon, V.-C. *Catalogue descriptif et analytique du Musée instrumental du conservatoire*. 5 vols., Brussels, 1893–1922.

—— *Elements d'acoustique*. Brussels, 1874.

Majer, J. F. B. C. *Museum musicum*. Nuremberg, 1732. (Facsimile, Kassel, 1954.)

—— *Neu-eröffneter Musik-Saal*. 2nd edn., Nuremberg, 1741.

Mang, W. *Das deutsche Vorurteil gegen die Böhmklarinette*. Lucerne, 1937.

Maramotti, R. *Il Clarinetto*. Bologna, 1941.

Marcuse, S. *Musical Instruments, A Comprehensive Dictionary*. New York, 1964.

Mattheson, J. *Das neu-eröffnete Orchester*. Hamburg, 1713.

Mendel-Reissmann. *Musikalisches Konversations-Lexikon*. Berlin, 1870–83.

Menke, W. *Das Vokalwerk G.Ph. Telemanns*. Kassel, 1942.

Mersenne, M. *Harmonie universelle*. Paris, 1636. (Various facsimile reprints.)

Miller, D. C. *The Science of Musical Sounds*. New York, 1922.

—— *Sound Waves*. New York, 1937.

Mimart, P. 'La Clarinette'. In Lavignac and de la Laurencie, *Encyclopédie de la Musique*. Paris, 1927.

Mixa, F. *Die Klarinette bei Mozart*. (*Phil. Diss.*) Vienna, 1929.

Müller, I. *Anweisung zu der neuen Clarinette und der Clarinette-Alto*. Leipzig, 1825.

Nederveen, C. J. *Acoustical Aspects of Woodwind Instruments*. Amsterdam, 1969.

Norlind, T. *Musikinstrumentenhistoria i ord och bild*. Stockholm, 1941.

Opperman, K. *Repertory of the Clarinet*. New York, 1960.

Paradis, H. *Fascicule du clarinettiste*. Paris, n.d.

Paumgartner, B. *Mozart*. Berlin, 1927.

—— 'Die Instrumentation Mozarts', *Das Orchester*. 1929.

Pierre, C. *Les Facteurs d'instruments de musique*. Paris, 1893.

—— *La Facture instrumentale à l'Exposition Universelle de 1889*. Paris, 1890.

Pincherle, M. *Antonio Vivaldi et la musique instrumentale*. Paris, 1948.

Pohl, C. F. *Haydn*. Vol. II. Leipzig, 1882.

Pontécouland, L.-G. le Doulcet de. *Organographie*. Paris, 1861.

Praetorius, M. *Syntagma musicum*. Wolfenbüttel, 1619. (Various facsimile reprints.) English translation by Harold Blumenfeld. New York, 1962.

Prestini, G. *Notizie intorno alla storia degli strumenti a fiato in legno*. Bologna, 1925.

Prod' homme, J. G. 'Notes d'archives concernant l'emploi des clarinettes en 1763', *Bulletin S.F. de M.* 1919.

Profeta, R. *Storia e letteratura degli strumenti musicali*. Florence, 1942.

Refield, J. *Music, a science and an art*. New York, 1928.

Reich, W. 'Bemerkungen zu Mozarts Klarinettenkonzert', *Zeitschrift für Musikwissenschaft*, XV, 1933, pp. 267 *et seq.*

Rendall, F. G. Article 'Clarinet' in Grove's *Dictionary of Music*. 5th edn., 1954.

—— 'The Saxophone before Sax', *Musical Times*, December 1932.

—— 'A Short Account of the Clarinet in England', *P.M.A.*, LXVIII, 1942.

Ricci, V. *L'Orchestrazione*. Milan, 1920.

Richardson, E. G. *Acoustics of Orchestral Instruments*. London, 1929.

Riemann, H. *Musiklexikon*. 1922, new edn., Mainz, Berlin, 1959.

Rockstro, R. S. *A Treatise on . . . the Flute*. London, 1890, 1928; reprint 1967 (Musica Rara, London).

Roeser, V. *Essai d'instruction à l'usage de ceux qui composent pour la clarinette et le cor*. Paris, 1764.

Sachs, C. *Handbuch der Musikinstrumentenkunde*. 2nd edn., Leipzig, 1930.

—— *Reallexikon der Musikinstrumente*. Berlin, 1913; reprint New York, 1964.

—— *The History of Musical Instruments*. New York, 1940.

Savo, G. *Cenni storici sull'origine del clarinetto*. Salerno, 1939.

Schiedermair, L. 'Die Oper an den bädischen Höfen', I.M.G., Sammel-bande XIV (1912), pp. 3 *et seq.*

Schilling, G. *Universal-Lexikon der Tonkunst*. Stuttgart, 1835–42.

Schlesinger, K. 'Basset Horn'; 'Bass Clarinet'; 'Clarinet'. *Encyclopaedia Brit.* 11th edn., 1910.

—— *Modern Orchestral Instruments*. London, 1910.

Schletterer, H. M. *Vereichnis der Were von L. Spohr*. Leipzig, 1881.

—— *Verrede zu Spohrs III Klar.-Konzert*.

Schlosser, J. *Kunsthistorisches Museum in Wien; Sammlung alter Musik-instrumente*. Vienna, 1920.

Schmidl, C. *Dizionario universale dei musicisti*. Milan, 1826–38.

Schneider, W. *Historisch-technische Beschreibung der musicalischen Instru-mente*. Leipzig, 1834.

Schreiber, O. *Orchester und Orchesterpraxis in Deutschland zwischen 1780 und 1850*. (Phil. Diss.) Berlin, 1938.

Schubart, D. *Ideen zu einer Ästhetik der Tonkunst*. Vienna, 1806.

Spohr, L. *Selbstbiographie*. Kassel, Göttingen, 1861.

Steet, O. 'The Clarinet and its Music', *P.M.A.*, XLII, 1915–16.

Stubbins, W. H. *The Art of Clarinetistry*. Ann Arbor, Michigan, 1965.

Tenschert, R. 'Fragment eines Klar.-Quintetts von W. A. Mozart', *Zeitschrift für Musikwissenschaft*, XIII, 1930–31, pp. 218 *et seq.*

Teuchert, E., and Haupt, E. W. *Musik-Instrumentenkunde in Wort und Bild*. Tl. 2, *Holzblasinstrumente*. Leipzig, 1911.

Tosoroni, A. *Trattato pratico di strumentazione*. Milan, 1851.

Walther, J. G. *Musicalisches Lexicon*. Leipzig, 1732. (Facsimile, Kassel, 1853.)

Weber, G. 'Einiges über Clarinett und Basetthorn', *Cäcilia*, Bd. XI, Heft 41, Mainz, 1829.

Weber, M. M. von. *Carl Maria von Weber*. Leipzig, 1864–66.

Welch, C. *History of the Boehm Flute*. 3 edns. London, 1883, 1892, 1896.

Whewell, M. 'Mozart's Bassethorn Trios', *Musical Times*, January 1962.

Willaman, R. *The Clarinet and Clarinet Playing*. New York, 1954.

Wright, R. *Dictionnaire des instruments de musique*. London, 1941.

B. PERIODICALS

Acoustical Society of America. Journal. Menasha, 1929—.

Allgemeine Musikalische Zeitung. Leipzig, 1798–1849, 1863–82.

The British Musician. 1887–1902.

Cäcilia. Mainz, 1824–48.

The Clarinet. New York, 1950—.

Galpin Society Journal. London, 1948—.

Harmonicon. 1823–33.

Music and Letters. 1920—.

Musical Association (from 1944 Royal Musical Association). Proceedings. 1875—.

Musical Opinion. 1877—.

Musical Times. 1844—.

Musical World. 1836–91.

Revue Musicale, afterwards *Revue et Gazette Musicale*. Paris, 1827–80.

Woodwind Magazine. New York, 1948—.

Zeitschrift für Instrumentenbau. Leipzig, 1880—.

C. ARTICLES ON THE ACOUSTICS OF THE CLARINET

Aschoff, V. 'Experimentelle Untersuchungen an einer Klarinette', *Akustische Zeitschrift*, October 1936.

Benade, A. H. (and Gans, D. J.). 'Sound Production in Wind Instruments' (Case Western Reserve University, Department of Physics). Part of Report on New York Academy of Science Conference on Sound Production, *Man*, 1966.

—— 'On Woodwind Instrument Bores', *J.A.S.A.*, Vol. 31, No. 2, 1959.

—— 'Acoustics of Various Clarinets', *National Clarinet Clinic*, University of Denver, Colorado, 1968.

—— 'On the Propagation of Sound Waves in a Cylindrical Conduit', *J.A.S.A.*, Vol. 44, No. 2, 1968.

—— 'On the Tone Color of Wind Instruments'. Article for *Band Wagon*, Selmer, May 1969.

Das, P. 'Theory of the Clarinet', *Indian Journal of Physics*, Vol. 6, part 1, 1931.

Ghosh, R. N. 'The Theory of the Clarinet', *J.A.S.A.*, Vol. 9, pp. 255–64, 1938.

Hague, B. 'The Tonal Spectra of Wind Instruments', *P.R.M.A.*, LXIII, 1946–47.

McGinnis, C. S., and Pepper, R. 'The Intonation of the Boehm Clarinet', *J.A.S.A.*, Vol. 16, pp. 188–93, 1945.

McGinnis, C. S., and Gallagher, C. 'The Mode of Vibration of a Clarinet Reed', *J.A.S.A.*, Vol. 12, pp. 529–31, 1941.

McGinnis, C. S., Hawkins, H., and Sher, N. 'An Experimental Study of the Tone Quality of the Boehm Clarinet', *J.A.S.A.*, Vol. 14, pp. 228–37, 1943.

Miller, D. C. 'The Influence of the Material of Wind Instruments on the Tone Quality', *Science*, Vol. 29, 1909.

Parker, S. E. 'Analyses of the Tones of Wooden or Metal Clarinets', *J.A.S.A.*, Vol. 19, pp. 415–19, 1947.

Redfield, J. 'Air Column Behavior in Orchestral Wind Instruments', *J.A.S.A.*, Vol. 6, pp. 34–6, 1934.

D. REEDS: MAKING AND RETOUCHING

Malot, J.-F. *L'Art de bien faire une anche de clarinette*. Avallon, 1820.

Hansen, R. *Wie werde ich Soloklarinettist? Wie verfertige ich meine Soloklarinettenblätter selber?* Leipzig, 1903.

Lefèbvre, P., and Goffin, R. *La Technique du son*. Paris, 1939.

Paradis, H. *Fascicule du clarinettiste*. Paris, n.d.

See also the methods of Froelich (1810–11), Blatt (1845), Bärmann (1864), Lazarus (1881), and *Woodwind Magazine*, New York (1948—).

List of Makers

A choice has been made from several hundred names to aid the collector. Care has been taken to include only actual makers. *Place-names*, it may be noted, are seldom found on wind instruments before the second half of the 18th century.

Dates: Wherever ascertainable the years of the birth and death of the maker are given. In other cases dates of a maker's activity have been sought in directories. Occasionally when directories are not available only an approximate date can be supplied; in fixing it, the style and appearance of the instrument have been taken into account.

Centres of Manufacture: London has always been the principal centre of *English* woodwind manufacture. A few clarinets were made by T. Morrall of Birmingham *c.* 1900 and a few by the oboe-maker J. Sharpe of Pudsey. Joseph Higham of Manchester (1842—) would appear to be the only notable provincial maker.

Two or three *Irish* makers are known – John and Matthew Dollard, Ellard, and Robinson, all of Dublin. All worked in the first half of the 19th century.

From 1800 on *France* has produced enormous numbers of musical instruments in all categories. Woodwind instruments have always taken pride of place, and are accounted one of the glories of French industry. Paris is and has always been the chief centre with Lyons up to 1850 or so a very good second. Other centres of manufacture for the Paris market are Mantes, La Couture-Boussey, Ivry-la-Bataille, and Ezy. At La Couture wood instrument-making has been a specialised industry for more than 200 years. In the first quarter of the 19th century two or three makers were established at St Omer in the Pas-de-Calais, a district which has produced many of France's most famous clarinettists.

German woodwind-makers have shown little tendency to group themselves unless it be at Markneukirchen where several large manufacturers have long been established. This is the La Couture of Germany. But in general German firms are smaller than French and more widely dispersed. Important firms exist or have existed at Baireuth, Berlin, Biebrich, Cologne, Dresden, Fulda, Göttingen, Hamburg, Kassel, Leipzig, Mannheim, Munich, Potsdam, Schöneck, and Speyer. The Göttingen makers Eisenbrant, Boie, and Streitwolf were particularly bold in their conceptions.

Italy's largest centres of manufacture have ever been Milan and Turin. But here, too, the makers are pleasantly dispersed and Bologna,

Chiaravalle, Florence, Naples, Rome, Siena, and Verona have all made their contribution.

Apart from the important manufactory of the Tuerlinckx at Malines and a few early makers at Ghent the *Belgian* industry has found its home at Brussels. Here was Mahillon's very extensive factory and here the elder Sax, *c.* 1815, and E. Albert, in 1846, set up their more modest establishments. Albert's sons, it may be noted, all had separate businesses.

Vienna has always been the centre of *Austrian* woodwind manufacture. There would appear to have been few makers of note before 1800. In the next half-century Griesbacher, Merklein, Koch, Ziegler, the Uhlmanns, Schemmel, and Sulz were makers of international repute. Graslitz has long been the La Couture or Markneukirchen of *Czechoslovakia*. Here are several large factories, the most notable, perhaps, that of the long-established firm of Kohlert. Among the earlier Prague makers may be mentioned Doleisch, Horák, and Messani. Bratislava (Pressburg) and Olomouc (Olmütz) have also had their makers.

The *United States* has long been curiously dependent on imported instruments. Among American makers may be cited the Cundy-Bettoney Co. and W. S. Haynes of Boston, King of Cleveland, and Conn of Elkhart, Ind. In this city too are established the Selmer Company and Linton, the oboe- and bassoon-maker.

Makers 1700 to 1775	*After 1775*
Denner, J. C. (1655–1707), Nuremberg	Adler, O., Markneukirchen, 1885–
Denner, J. (–1735), Nuremberg	Adler, F. G., Paris, 1810–54
Joseph, T. W., Triftern	Albert, Eugène (1816–90), Brussels, 1846–90
Klenig, *c.* 1700	Albert, Jacques, Brussels. Son of E. Albert
Liebav, *c.* 1700	Albert, Jean-Baptiste (d. 1918), Brussels. Son of E. Albert
Boekhout, T.	
Kelmer, G. N.	
Kenigsperger, J. W.	Albert, E.-J. Brussels. Son of E. Albert
Kraus, C.	
Lindner	Albert *fils*, Jacques (Lucien), Brussels. Modern
Lot, G., Paris	
Mayrhofer, Anton and Michael, Passau, *c.* 1770	Amlingue, M., Paris, 1782–1830
Oberlender, G. W.	Bachmann, G. C. (1804–42), Brussels
Rottenburgh, J. H. G., Brussels	Baumann, Paris, *c.* 1790–1830
Rottenburgh, G. A., Brussels	Bercioux, E., Paris, *fl.* 1900
	Berlingozzi, L., Siena, *c.* 1825
Scherer, I.	Berthold, G., Speyer, 1850–
Schlegel, C., Basle	Besson, F., Paris, 19th century
Walch, Johann Stephan	Besson & Co., London, 1862–
W[alch], I. S.	Bié, P. Successor to F. Lefèvre. Paris, 1855–86
Willems, I. B., Brussels	
Woberl, J.	Bilton, R., London, 1826–56

Bimboni, G., Florence, c. 1850

Bischoff, C., Darmstadt, c. 1810–25

Boie, F., Göttingen, first quarter of 19th century

Boosey, London, c. 1850–1930

Boosey & Hawkes, London, 1930–

Bosa, Naples, mid-19th century

Braun, Mannheim, c. 1850

Brelet, Lyons, c. 1820–60

Bruggemann, Leyden, c. 1850

Buffet *jeune*, L.-A. (d. 1885), Paris, 1831–67

Buffet-Crampon. Founded by Buffet-Auger; successive proprietors: Buffet-Crampon; Tournier and Goumas; P. Goumas; Evette and Schaeffer. Paris, 1825–

Bühner and Keller, Strassburg, 1780–1835

Cabart. Successor to Thibouville-Cabart. Ezy. Modern

Cahusac, T., London, c. 1755–98

Cahusac, T. & W. M., London, 1799–c. 1825

Chapelain, F., Paris. Modern

Collier, T., London, c. 1770

Conn, C. G., Elkhart, Ind., 1875–

Couesnon. Successor to Guichard, Gautrot, and Triébert. Paris. Modern

Cundy-Bettoney, Boston, Mass. Modern

Cuvillier, *père et fils*, St Omer, c. 1800–50

Distin, London, 1850. Acquired by Boosey, 1868

Dölling, C. F., Potsdam, 1820–50

Dolnet & Lefèvre, Mantes, Paris. Modern

Eisenbrant, Göttingen, late 18th century–early 19th century

Euler, P., Frankfurt, 1818–40

Fieldhouse, Jesse, London, c. 1855–70

Floth, J. F. (d. 1807). Pupil of J. F. Grundmann. Dresden

Gason, Brussels, c. 1875

Gautrot (see also Couesnon). Paris, 1845–82

Gehring, Adorf, late 18th century

Geisler, C. G., Amsterdam, c. 1820–1884

Gentellet, Paris, 1819–54

Gerock, C., London, 1805–20

Gerock & Wolf, London, c. 1830

Glier, E. R., Markneukirchen, 1884–

Golde, C., Dresden, mid-19th century

Goulding, G. Later Goulding, d'Almaine, Potter. London, 1784–1825

Goumas (see under Buffet-Crampon)

Grenser, A. (1720–1805). Pupil of Pörschmann, Leipzig. Dresden

Grenser, H. (1764–1813), Dresden

Griesbacher, Vienna, c. 1800

Griessling & Schlott, Berlin, c. 1805–35

Grundmann, J. F. (1727–1800). Pupil of Pörschmann.

Guerre, Paris, 1825–50

Guichard (see also Couesnon). Paris, 1827–45

Gyssens, F. J. From L.-A. Buffet. Paris, 1845–60

Halary, J.-H.-A., Paris, 1777–c. 1840

Harrach, M., Vienna, c. 1850

Haseneier, H. J., Coblenz, 1849–64

Hawkes. Amalgamated with Boosey, 1930. London, 1858

Heckel, Biebrich a/Rh, 1831–
Hess, W., Munich, c. 1870
Higham, J., Manchester, 1842–
Hofinger, F., Brussels. Modern
Horák, W., Prague, early 19th century
Hüller, G., Schöneck. Modern
Kayser, H., Hamburg, c. 1835
Key, T. Acquired by Rudall, Rose, c. 1855. London, 1800–55
Kirst, F. G. A., Potsdam, 1777–1802
Knochenhauer, A., Berlin, c. 1840
Koch, S. (1772–1828). Vienna, early 19th century
Kohlert, V., Graslitz, 1840–
Koktan, F., Vienna. Modern
Kruspe, C., Leipzig, 1829–
Kruspe, E., Erfurt, 19th century
Laube, La Couture, Paris, c. 1878–
Leblanc, G., Paris. Modern
Lefèvre, F. Succeeded by P. Bié, 1855; André Thibouville, 1886. Paris, 1812–45
Losschmidt, Olmütz, mid-19th century
Louis & Co., London. Modern
Magazzari, E., Bologna, early 19th century
Mahillon. Founded by Charles Mahillon (1813–39), continued by V.-C. Mahillon. Brussels, 1836–
Mahillon, C. London
Maino, P., Milan, 1830–80
Maino & Orsi, Milan, 1880–
Majorano, Naples, mid-19th century
Maldura, A., Milan, c. 1870–80
Marigaux, G. (see also Strasser). Paris. Modern

Martel frères, Paris. Modern
Martin, La Couture and Paris. Modern
Merklein, J., Vienna, early 19th century
Milhouse, Newark, 1760–89; London, 1789–1838
Millereau, F., Paris, 1861–
Mollenhauer, J., Fulda, 1822–
Mollenhauer, G., Kassel, 1864–
Monzani, T. (1762–1839). Later Monzani & Hill. London, early 19th century
Muller, L., Lyons, 1820–60
Neidhardt, O., Schöneck. Modern
Oehler, O. (d. 1940), Berlin. Modern
Orsi, Romeo (see under Maino & Orsi)
Ottensteiner, G., Munich, c. 1854
Papalini, N., Chiaravalle, c. 1810
Pask, J., London, 1840–72
Pentenrieder, Munich, 1837–49
Penzel-Mueller, New York. Modern
Piana, P., Milan
Piatet. Pupil of Simiot. Lyons, 1840–60
Pinder, H., Dresden, fl. 1900
Ponfoort, J., Ghent, fl. 1850
Porthaux, D., Paris, c. 1780–1820
Pupeschi, P., Florence, c. 1890–
Quilter, S., London, 1875–1925
Raingo, N. M. (1746–1823), Mons
Raingo, J. B. (1754–1834), Mons
Raingo, C. P. (1786-1839), Mons
Rampone & Cazzani, Milan. Modern

Robert, A.,   Paris, 1895–
Rudall & Rose,   London,
  1821–50
Rudall, Rose, Carte & Co.,
  London, 1851–71
Rudall, Carte & Co.,   London,
  1872–
Sautermeister, F.,   Lyons,
  early 19th century
Sax, Adolphe (1814–94),
  Paris, 1842–c. 1880
Sax, Charles (1791–1865),
  Brussels
Schemmel,   Vienna, mid-19th
  century
Schmidt, E.,   Mannheim.
  Modern
Schuster, G., Markneukirchen,
  c. 1820
Seidel, J.,   Mainz, c. 1825
Selboe, J. C.,   Copenhagen,
  c. 1840
Selmer, H. & A.,   Paris.
  Modern
Simiot, J.-F.,   Lyons, c. 1800–
  30
Simiot & Brelet,   Lyons,
  c. 1840–70
Skorra, E.,   Berlin, c. 1825–65
Stengel, J. S.,   Baireuth,
  c. 1825–55
Strasser, Marigaux, Lemaire,
  Paris. Modern
Streitwolf, J. H. G. (1779–1837),
  Göttingen
Strobach,   Carlsbad, early 19th
  century
Sulz,   Vienna, c. 1850

Tabard, F.,   Lyons, 1820–48
Thibouville, André. Successor
  to Bié.   Paris, 1886
Thibouville-Cabart, J.-B.
  Thibouville was subsequently
  omitted.   Paris and Ezy,
  1869
Thibouville-Lamy, Jérôme,
  Paris and London, 1867–
Tournier & Goumas (see also
  Buffet-Crampon).   Paris,
  1855–59
Triébert G. (1740–1848)
Triébert, F. (1813–78),   Paris
Tuerlinckx, J. A. A. and C. J. J.,
  Malines, c. 1775–1850
Uhlmann, J., L., and T.,
  Vienna, 19th century
Vinatieri & Castlas,   Turin,
  early 19th century
Vinatieri, C.,   Turin,
  mid-19th century
Ward, Cornelius,   London,
  1836–67
Warschewski,   Stockholm.
  Modern
Wood, George,   London,
  c. 1805–22
Wood & Son, James,   London,
  c. 1820–32
Wood, George. Late James
  Wood & Son.   London,
  c. 1830–37
Wood & Ivy,   London, 1837–47
Wünnenberg, Eberh.,   Cologne,
  1844–
Ziegler & Son, J.,   Vienna,
  early and mid-19th century

Index of Instruments

Condensed Subject Index

Index of Names

(Names in the Preface and Appendix are not included. Individuals specifically mentioned as players are entered in italics. Composers, writers, and celebrities are identified by surname only, except where common usage is otherwise. Where identification is certain, initials have been added, though these do not always appear in the main text.)

Printed in Great Britain by The Garden City Press Limited
Letchworth, Hertfordshire, SG6 1JS